A Saint For
The Summer

By MARJORY McGINN

(A novel by the author of
Things Can Only Get Feta)

Pelagos Press

A Saint For The Summer

Published by Pelagos Press, 2018
ISBN: 978-1999995713.

A CIP catalogue of this is available from the British Library.

This book is a work of fiction, Names, characters, businesses, places and events are either the product of the author's imagination or are used fictitiously. Any resemblance to actual persons, living or dead, events of locales is entirely coincidental.

Front cover illustration by Tony Hannaford (www.anthonyhannaford.co.uk)

Editing, formatting and author photograph by Jim Bruce (www.ebooklover.co.uk)

Dedication

In memory of my parents, John and Mary

About the author

Marjory McGinn is a Scottish-born author and journalist, brought up in Australia and now based in England. Her journalism has appeared in leading newspapers in Australia and Britain, including *The Sydney Morning Herald, The Sun-Herald, The Daily Mail, The Times* and Scotland's *The Herald*.

A youthful work/travel year in Athens inspired a lifelong fascination for Greece. In 2010, together with her husband Jim and their Jack Russell dog, Wallace, she set off from Britain on an adventure to the southern Peloponnese that lasted four years and was the basis for her three travel memoirs and two novels, available on Amazon. This is her first novel.

Marjory also writes a blog with a Greek theme on the website www.bigfatgreekodyssey.com. Follow her on Twitter www.twitter.com/@fatgreekodyssey and Facebook www.facebook.com/ThingsCanOnlyGetFeta

Other books by the author

Things Can Only Get Feta
Homer's Where The Heart Is
A Scorpion In The Lemon Tree
How Greek Is Your Love?

Author's note

Some of the narrative in this book is based on real events relating to the Second World War in southern Greece, particularly the little-known Battle of Kalamata and the evacuation, capture and escape of British and allied troops in April 1941, which has been described as the 'Greek Dunkirk'. Although the two main villages in the book were inspired by real villages in the Mani, their names have been changed and the characters are fictitious.

Greek language note: Masculine names in Greek that end in 'os', 'as' or 'is' will drop the final 's' in the vocative case (when addressing someone directly). The name Dimitris, for example, will change when you say, "Dimitri, are you there?"

Map of the area

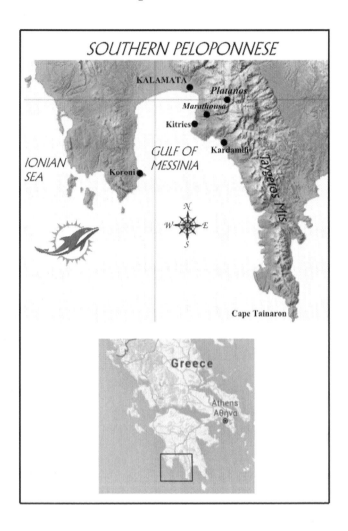

Contents

Calamity Bay

Way down south in Calamity Bay,
Sat 10,000 men who were trying to get away.
The Navy came and took away the ill,
While the rest of us crept back up the hill.

– Part of a poem by British signalman Fred Bundy, who
was captured by the Germans at Kalamata in April 1941

1

Marathousa

On the journey to the hillside village of Marathousa, I had an entourage of twelve Greek saints. It was a notable crew and a promising start to an expedition that was otherwise underscored with doubt, not least from the knowledge that Greece, in that late summer of 2012, was sliding into the vortex of economic crisis.

Fiscal folly was probably a minor scourge to this celestial group I was travelling with. They were in the taxi I hailed at Kalamata Airport, under the watchful gaze of the nervous driver. He was chewing gum and fingering his mobile phone at sporadic intervals. It was clamped, when not in use, between his legs. The saints were arranged across the dashboard of the taxi in images the size of postcards encased in cheap plastic frames. How they were attached exactly was unclear, unless by some ecclesiastical sleight of hand. Occasionally, when the taxi hit a pothole, the frames jiggled and then resumed their beatific calm.

After I settled myself in the taxi, it didn't take long to discover the reason for this holy line-up. I chose the front seat because the back had no workable seatbelts and I had been forewarned by those more familiar with Greece about the maverick stunts of its drivers. The front seat felt like it had no springs, as if it had been salvaged from some old wreck, and the seat belt sagged when it was attached. It was also a very hot day – about 90 degrees – and the driver told me the air-con wasn't working properly.

"Air conditioning is having a crisis too," the driver guffawed. "You lucky, Miss, you did not come in August. *Po, po, po!*" I took the last bit to be an expression with more pizzazz than real meaning. "August is hell! Too hot, too many people, and every day the traffic is craaazy."

I had never been to Greece in August and now I was sure I would never want to. September was frantic enough, and the traffic was barmy as well. The route from the airport to the city was a busy single carriageway, with drivers jockeying for dominance, overtaking on a whim, sometimes forcing other cars onto the dirt edges of the road, bordered on the right by tall ranks of wild bamboo. Along the verges, gypsy families were walking with kids in tow, trailing puffs of dust from their bare feet, and bone-thin dogs. The presence of nearby gypsy camps was explained gustily by the driver with plenty of hand gestures, sometimes two at once, meaning the steering wheel was unmanned for seconds. I found myself imploring the saints a lot, and my forehead was beginning to bead with sweat. The driver noticed my obsession with the dashboard.

"My beautiful icons. You like, eh?" he said, kissing the fingertips of his right hand. And then he rattled off their names. I caught a Yiorgos, Andreas, Nektarios, Mihalis … on it went. No women in the group. I didn't bother to ask. Why provoke him when we still had miles of this road to travel apparently.

"Why so many saints in the car?" I asked, as if I didn't have an inkling already.

"Not so many! Twelve out of hundreds. They keep me safe. If they are here, no accidents, no trouble. In the crisis, no money for car insurance," he said, holding up his right hand and rubbing his index finger and thumb together. While he was doing this, he suddenly swerved the car with his left hand to avoid a dead dog on the road and then straightened up again without missing a beat. He nodded vibrantly towards the line of saints.

"This is what I have for the Greek car insurance now," he said, laughing loudly. His black eyes, with small fleshy pillows for eyelids, crinkled at the edges.

I imagined this was the wind-up he offered all his passengers as an icebreaker on this devil of a highway. But I laughed as well, until further along the road, he had to brake hard when a car pulled out of a dirt track without looking. The seat belt that had seemed useless gripped at my chest and I felt relieved. The saints jostled a lot. The driver let out several rounds of the word *'gamoto!'* which sounded curiously like some kind of Japanese motor scooter but which I later discovered meant 'fuck it!'

Finally, we arrived at the city centre, a bubbling expanse of apartment blocks hunched together along narrow streets. Cafés were plentiful and filled with lively punters. On the surface, at least, there was little sense of crisis. On the roads it was a different story. There were countless intersections through the city and a nervous urge for drivers to gun engines and run red lights, including the taxi driver, with a few more *'gamotos!'* thrown in. The only other thing that caught my attention were the industrial-sized bins on street corners overflowing with refuse, being picked over by scabrous cats. The council workers were on strike, the driver told me, protesting against a recent round of austerity measures that marked out this economic crisis.

"Greece under the boot of the European dictatorship now. Always the strikes now. Always trouble. Welcome to our country, to Kalamata, eh?"

He fell silent for a while, then the mobile rang between his legs. He plucked it out, barked down it for 30 seconds and dropped it back into position.

"Kids, eh? That was my son, Iraklis. Cannot do anything without first ask the father. Calls me all day for this and that. Twenty-five. No baby, eh?"

"No, indeed he's not," I said, wondering why the son bothered when he only ever got 30 seconds of paternal wrath.

We sped on through the city. I was starting to feel weary after a dawn flight from Edinburgh to London, then another from London to Kalamata. I was unimpressed by my Greek arrival so far, until we stopped at traffic lights on a T-junction joining Navarino Street. In front of us, a wide gulf was spread out between the Mani peninsula on the left and the Messinian peninsula on the other side, two of the three prongs that hang down from the southern Peloponnese like pulled roots. With small coves along the coast and, high above, the tall peaks of the Mani's Taygetos mountains, the scene resembled one of those famed highland paintings of Scotland, with lochs and hills wrapped in strange pearly light. It was beautiful. After the chaos of the city, the view ahead of me shimmered with promise, so much so that I hoped I would be proved wrong about the wisdom of this Greek mission.

The lights changed and the driver gunned the tin can and roared left, leaving a cloud of burning rubber behind us. Navarino Street stretched along the southern edge of the city, parallel to a long strip of beach, the sea bubbling with swimmers at its edge. Further on were small coastal villages that hinted at secret coves. We reached a fork in the road with one branch continuing along the coast, the other was the main road down through the Mani that would zigzag along the lower reaches of the Taygetos mountains for part of the way, though we were apparently not going that far. The higher we climbed, however, past olive and orange groves, the more breathtaking the view of the gulf. I felt we were entering a different kind of Greece, but not without the occasional unsettling image, like the round safety mirrors on switchback roads that were smashed and useless.

"Cowboys, shoot out mirrors," said the driver. "Maniots, all cowboys." Then he roared with laughter.

Cowboys or not, I felt myself relax for the first time since I'd left Scotland.

"You here on holiday?"

I shook my head. "I'm here to see my father. He lives in the hillside village where we're going. He's not been well."

"Oh! I hope he gets better soon."

"Thanks. We'll see."

"So, you going to look after him, like a good Greek daughter?" he said, his pillow eyes flickering towards me.

I said nothing.

"So how long you stay?"

"No longer than I have to," I said.

I kept my eyes on the passing scenery. I couldn't see the expression on his face, but I could sense it. My comment was something a Greek daughter probably wouldn't say. But I wasn't a Greek daughter. I was barely any kind of daughter. And Angus was hardly the perfect father, if the truth be told, and someone I'd hardly seen in the past 10 years and had irregular communication with, apart from birthday and Christmas cards.

A letter had arrived from Greece a few weeks earlier, however, asking me to come over to help him as he had a health problem. He would explain in more detail when I got there. I guessed he'd asked me because I was the only one in the family available. My sister Shona had kids to look after, and my mother had recently remarried, so that ruled her out.

"Think of it as a late summer holiday," Shona had urged me. "I mean, I wish I could go myself."

"No you don't."

"But it's Greece. It will be fabulous, apart from Dad being unwell."

I wasn't sure about having a holiday in Greece. I had only been here once before, not long after Angus first arrived. I didn't remember much about that visit but it wasn't Greece in crisis at least. It was a simpler time but I recalled not liking the food much, or the beach, or the sunburn on my pale Celtic skin. And it was only spring. I wasn't built for hot climates. Maybe that was the main reason I didn't care for the place and had never bothered to return. The other reason was more complicated, not something I wanted to analyse on the way up a steep mountainside with a saint-toting taxi driver whose son might ring again at any second, necessitating another perilous one-handed manoeuvre.

"What's wrong with your father?" asked the driver.

"Something to do with his heart, I think."

The driver nodded sagely and lapsed into his own thoughts as we drove ever higher into the hills. It was a fraction cooler up here and I wound down the window. The turn-off to the village had a near-obscured sign and the road was narrow, cut into the side of a steep hill. It swung round a sharp bend, where the view opened up again, with thick swathes of olive orchards right down to the coast. It was easy to see how Kalamata was the olive oil capital of Greece. The city was now visible, spread out along the head of the gulf. The apartment blocks from this distance looked squat and cubist, sparkling in the intense sunshine.

By the time we reached the centre of Marathousa, I knew we had come too far, according to the sketchy instructions Angus had given me. We were in front of a square that sat in the crook of a low hillside, where much of the village was built in tiers above. On the left of the square was a large white church with an imposing bell tower. At the back was a taverna with tables placed outside under a tall tree, and on the right a café. Small groups of people dressed in black were huddled around the café's outdoor tables, talking quietly. The church bell was tolling, a heavy single note that carried easily in the warm air.

"Must be a funeral today, Miss. Sounds like a service."

Twelve saints – and now a funeral! But I had more mundane things to worry about.

"We've come too far," I said. "We have to turn and go back. We've passed the house."

The driver manoeuvred the car slowly and we set off back the way we'd come, past a graveyard, another small church and more olive groves and, here and there, a modern villa half-hidden behind the trees. From this approach, rather than the other, we could finally see the sign for Villa Anemos, nothing more than a ragged bit of wood nailed to an olive tree by the roadside. The word 'villa' offered some rural humour perhaps because the property, at the end of a long pathway, was an old stone house with a scuffed blue door and a roof that from a distance looked like a badly assembled jigsaw made from ancient pantiles.

"This it?" asked the driver, his eyes strafing the front of the property with an unguarded, critical look.

"I guess so."

I sat for a moment, staring at the house. I had the sudden urge to just drive on, but then the front door opened slowly and a man, dressed in what looked like a long black robe, stood in the shadowy doorway, looking out, his long hair tied back at the nape of his neck. He held up his hand in a kind of greeting and retreated inside, leaving the door ajar.

The driver turned his big eyes towards me and scratched his chin. "Looks like *papas*, Greek priest, Miss."

That's exactly what I thought. Like one of the old guys on the dashboard display.

"I get your things. I hope we are not too late," he said, swinging himself out the driver's side and unlocking the boot to fetch my suitcase.

Too late? But I knew what he meant. A funeral bell. A priest at the house. I hadn't spoken to Angus for a couple of days. I'd called him on the mobile number he'd given me but he'd already warned me he wasn't good with mobiles, or emails either, which is why we heard from him intermittently by ordinary mail.

I paid the driver and told him to leave my case at the front gate. I'd manage from there. He shook my hand vibrantly.

"Good luck, Miss. But do you need me to stay? See that everything is okay here?"

I was touched by his thoughtfulness. "No, whatever happens, I'll be fine. Thank you," I said, trying to sound calm, but I was far from that.

He drove away slowly, watching the house for a while, then sped off, the wheels throwing up dirt from the side of the road. I took my case and walked slowly down the long path, almost wishing I was anywhere but Greece.

2

Villa Anemos

The front door opened again and the man in black reappeared, holding something in his hand. He seemed agitated, and started talking. It took me a few moments to work out he wasn't speaking Greek, as I expected, but perfect English. Funny kind of Greek priest.

"Gone already? I wanted to give the driver a tip," he said, with a shrug.

I stared at him with a rising sense of shock — and then relief.

"Angus? …. Is that you?" I said in a small voice, like a plucked string.

"Well who the bloody hell do you think it is? I've a few euros here for the driver but he's bolted."

"You were in the house a long time."

"Couldn't find my wallet. Oh, well, I bet you gave him a generous tip. Probably didn't deserve it. He drove like a lunatic, I suppose, overtaking, talking on his mobile, yes?" he said.

I nodded. "The taxi driver and I both thought you were a Greek priest. You're certainly dressed like one," I said, checking the outfit again, although from close up I could see it was an amalgam of black layers: a T-shirt, a long kind of waistcoat and baggy trousers.

He stared at me wide-eyed and then chortled, throwing his head back as if he hadn't had a good laugh for a while.

"I don't think anyone here would ever think of me as a Greek priest. Okay, it's the hair perhaps," he said, grabbing the ponytail briefly between his fingers.

"Could be," I said. The hair made him look more ageing rock star than Greek priest, though it was thick and healthy as it had always been, with just a smattering of grey.

"You don't like it?"

"No, it's fine," I said, with forced lightness. "I didn't expect it, that's all."

"I lost interest in getting it cut all the time. This is easier... Och, let's not blether on about hairdos, Bronte. Come on in. You'll be tired after the flight," he said, picking up my suitcase and leading me inside.

I followed him into a darkened room that smelt of coffee, herbs and something else I couldn't place. He set the case down and gave me a hug. It was sudden and strong, as if to cover a feeling of awkwardness at meeting up after such a long absence. I caught the unidentified aroma once more, only this time it smelt like incense, which chimed strangely with my first impression of Angus. He stepped back and stared at me.

"You're looking great, Bronte, if a wee bit peely-wally though." I smiled at his Scottish reference to my pale complexion.

"Thanks, Angus."

I had called him Angus since he left the family home 10 years earlier. It was not just an act of defiance on my part but because in a sense he had become a stranger, someone outside of our lives. To his credit, he never complained about the moniker, or the rebuff.

"I heard the church bell. Who's the funeral for?" I asked.

"An old guy in the village. He was 95. I planned to go to the service but it was later than expected. And you were due, so I decided to wait in for you. I'll wander over to the *kafeneio* later, where Yiorgos's family will be gathered, and offer my condolences."

I gave his casual black outfit another appraisal and wondered if this was normal funeral attire here, or just Angus's take on formal clothing. He picked up my suitcase as if to take it somewhere, then put it down again. He seemed a bit nervous and he coughed, a sandpapery smoker's cough.

"Still smoking?"

"Sometimes."

"Won't do your heart any good."

He frowned and didn't answer. Despite the levity a few minutes earlier, I had a sudden sense of how this mission would play out, with certain antagonism. I was going to spend my weeks with a father I didn't really know, who had probably gone slightly feral. A Greek mountain man.

"Anyway, sit yourself down and relax. I'll get you a cold drink. You look hot. I keep most of the shutters closed in the heat but I'll open them later to get the afternoon breeze. Are you hungry? I've got some bread, feta cheese and olives."

"I could eat a bit, I suppose, if you are."

I wasn't really hungry but I hoped that eating would give us both something else to concentrate on, apart from each other.

"Would you like a beer?"

I nodded.

"Come and sit at the table and I'll put the fan on for you. I never bother much, but you won't like this heat. I know how the hot weather gets to you, pet."

The comment jarred on me, as if the past 10 years had never happened and I was nothing but a kid again, my parameters well-known. And the Scottish endearment 'pet' was something I would have to bat off into the undergrowth. But I was too tired for acrimony.

He flicked a switch on a pedestal fan and a strong current of cool air moved around the room, dispersing the slightly fetid aroma of the old house.

This part of the property was one long room, with a kitchen and dining table at one end, and the sitting room at the other, with a wood-burning stove. The room had a high pitched ceiling lined with long strips of bamboo, with thick, smoke-blackened crossbeams below. Cool in summer perhaps but probably cold and draughty in winter. Double doors, shuttered against the afternoon sun, led from the kitchen onto what I imagined was a balcony. In the corner, a spiral staircase led to a lower floor.

In the sitting room, an old tartan rug – a nod to Scotland no doubt – covered the sofa. A coffee table was strewn with books and papers. There were heavy wooden bookcases, and on the walls hung prints with a Greek theme and several wooden icons of saints. The place had a shabby chic quality, more like a bachelor pad, and I had the impression that nothing much had been done to it for a few years. The inside could have done with a fresh coat of white paint.

Angus put some cans of beer on the dining table and ferried over small plates of food. There were cubes of feta, black olives glimmering in an oily coating, and slices of cucumber and tomato.

"The olives are mine from the trees below. I didn't prepare them though, a neighbour does that. Och, life's too short to pickle an olive!"

I smiled. It was a Greek take perhaps on Gloria Steinem's famous quip that 'life's too short to stuff a mushroom'. I couldn't have agreed more, but it crossed my mind what Angus did with his time. I tried an olive. It was a bit salty and tart and I tried to bury the taste with a piece of bread that he'd cut from a rustic-looking loaf. The crust was rugged, earthy-tasting, and I feared for my dental work. I winced.

He laughed. "*Kali orexi*, as they say here. Good appetite. But I can see you're not enjoying the bread much. Never mind, you'll get used to it. I buy it from the village bakery. Proper bread cooked in a wood-fired oven. Lasts for days." I didn't doubt it. This was a loaf that would survive a nuclear disaster.

He drank his beer but ate little, apart from the bread, and I sensed that his even white teeth, one of his better features, hadn't suffered at least from his Greek lifestyle or the volcanic loaves. He stopped chewing for a moment, a hunk of bread in his hand.

"Thanks for coming here at short notice, pet. I know it can't be easy for you. We haven't exactly been close these past 10 years."

I frowned. It was a poor choice of words. The only reason 'we' hadn't been close was because that's what Angus had wanted. I had seen him three times in the past decade: once when I came to Greece with Shona, after he moved here, and twice in Scotland. It was obvious he hated going back there now. He said he couldn't abide the cold and damp, the smirring rain and glum faces. But the main reason was that there was nothing there for him any more.

I picked at the cheese and salad and drank some beer. It made me feel more relaxed. I watched him while he drank from his can. He looked a lot older, of course, and different, with the shoulder-length hair tied back, but good for a man of 71. He was lined about the eyes but deeply suntanned and fit-looking, despite the health problems and a bit of weight round his middle.

"What's wrong with your heart exactly?"

"I'm not sure yet. I get breathless when I'm out walking. You can see how hilly it is round here. Once I had some chest pains. The landlord is a doctor. I called him and he told me to go to A&E at Kalamata Hospital. They gave me one of those bike stress tests and everything looked normal. I was told all the usual things: no booze, no cigarettes. The landlord said the tests they do here aren't conclusive. You can get false negatives, or some such thing, and that I may have narrowed arteries. He said I need to see a cardiologist to arrange more tests, or else I'll end up having a heart attack."

"Why haven't you then?"

"Had a heart attack?" he asked, with a sardonic smile, as if I'd just made a kind of Freudian slip.

I shook my head. "You know what I meant. Why haven't you seen a cardiologist?"

He sighed and ripped off another piece of bread, chewing it quickly and washing it down with beer.

"It's a faff here, medical stuff. The Greek health system is going down the pan in the crisis. There are only a couple of cardio guys for this region and a long wait to see them. Even if I could see one straight away by paying privately I'd have to go to Athens for the tests. They don't have heart scanners in Kalamata. But I don't want to bore you with my health problems right now."

"That's why I'm here, isn't it?"

He shifted on the hard wooden chair and toyed with his ponytail. I regretted the rancour that kept surfacing, despite my best intentions. I could see now how much I had bottled up over the years without realising it. Being face to face with Angus in this remote location was harder than I'd imagined.

"Look, pet. There's plenty of time to talk about my old ticker and what I need to do about it …"

"But in your letter you made it sound like you were on a bit of a knife-edge with your health."

"Did I?" he said, looking dubious.

"Well, yes. Like I said before, that's why I'm here, right?"

"Okay. Clearly I'm not at death's door just yet and there's time enough to talk about the whole thing," he said, with a conciliatory smile. He sipped his beer.

We lapsed into silence. Maybe it was just fatigue but I was starting to feel confused about why the hell I was here. Angus had always been very independent, and fairly tough. A man doesn't decide to walk out on his marriage and his old life to resettle in a foreign country unless he has some inner resolve. So surely he didn't need me to fly out from Scotland just to hold his hand at the doctor's? He could have dealt with this himself or with one of the expat friends he was bound to have by now. Or perhaps the nonchalance was just a cover for his anxiety.

"Anyway, you can ask the doctor about it all when he comes here tomorrow to collect the rent. He speaks very good English."

Angus went over to the kitchen and opened a white cardboard box set on one of the work benches. He took out two large slices of a sticky-looking confection he described as honey cake and brought them over on small plates. They looked cloyingly sweet, but I cut off a sliver to please him.

"Thekla, the woman who runs the bakery, makes sweets as well. Honey cake is her best, though on the contrary she's quite a nippy character ... you'll see." I doubted I'd have the time to develop an acquaintance with a woman who could knock out your gnashers and ignite your blood sugar in one hit.

He polished off his honey slice in no time and I could see how his waistline had expanded and his arteries had log-jammed.

"How long have you been renting this place?"

"Five months. It's a good house but a bit cold in the winter, I imagine. The landlord offered to fix the place up a bit but I can't be bothered with all the faff and, really, it needs a total renovation, not just cosmetic stuff. But it suits me and it's cheap. And I like this village. It has a different vibe to the coastal settlements."

"Why did you never buy anything here before the crisis? Small houses must have been cheap even then, and you had your redundancy money."

"I was having too nice a time to worry about real estate and I didn't know how long I'd stay. Now it's too late. Only a fool with deep pockets would buy a property in Greece."

"What's your landlord like?"

He gave me a long, searching look. "I can see why you're a journalist, pet. You like asking questions. But then you always did. You were like this as a kid, always asking stuff. Your grandmother used to say you asked so many questions, you'd spear the arse out of a donkey. Remember?" he said, with a big belly laugh.

I chuckled as well. "I do, yes." I didn't know if it was a Scottish expression or just my maternal grandmother's own eccentric saying, of which she had many. Catriona was from the Isle of Mull and despite having had a remote existence she had a spirited slant on life and a great sense of humour.

"Okay, forgive the inquisition. Just curious," I said. I figured I was talking out of nerves or tiredness.

"Well, yeah. It must be a bit bewildering for you."

I nodded.

"The landlord's a decent guy. He's got the big villa next door, for weekends. Nice pool too. Always telling me to use it. I have a key to the door into the back garden and I cast an eye over the place for him when he's not there. But swimming in the landlord's pool seems a bit naff to me. His name is Leonidas Papachristou, by the way, and he's a good-looking guy. I imagine his bedside manner's as sweet as this honey cake," he said.

He drank some more beer, then added, "I saw your eyebrow twitch, by the way, with interest."

"For the doctor?"

He nodded.

"Don't be daft," I said, smoothing down the eyebrow with a honeyed finger. "I'm not here for a holiday romance, remember?" He said nothing, licking syrup from the corners of his mouth. "And I'm definitely not interested in Greek men either. Let's get that straight. Or Greece, for that matter. I'm definitely not you!"

"Oh! That must be a consolation for you anyway, to be anything but me," he said sarcastically.

"I didn't mean it the way it sounded," I said, lying.

"Look … You'll feel different about Greece, if not me, in a few weeks, or even days."

"Even if I fell in love with the place, I've still got to leave in three weeks, all going well. That was the deal."

"Okay. No bother," he said, with a Greek-style shrug of resignation. "In the meantime, make yourself at home, Bronte. Have a siesta if you like. The bathroom's downstairs beside my bedroom. I've given you the top bedroom up here. You get a nice view over the olive groves. I'll be out for an hour or so at the *kafeneio*."

I felt my shoulders suddenly relax. I was eager to have some quiet time alone. He carried my suitcase into the bedroom, through a side door off the sitting room, which I hadn't noticed when I arrived. Then he went downstairs to get ready to go out. My room was long and narrow and fairly monastic, with a single bed on the far wall, a wardrobe and an old wooden chest of drawers on the main wall opposite the balcony doors. On top was a vase of fresh wild flowers, a curiously feminine touch.

I opened the balcony doors and unhooked the blue shutters, pushing them wide. As I stepped out, a wave of heat engulfed me. The sun was beating down on the balcony. The space was tiny, just big enough for the rush-seated chair and small metal table. An intimate space for one, or two at a crush. I liked it. As the house was built on a gentle slope it seemed higher here than it had from the road and the view was unexpectedly grand, looking straight over the ruffled heads of hundreds of olive trees towards Kalamata. To the right was a mountain with a rounded peak and a zigzag road carved onto the face of it, a small village clinging limpet-like to its upper reaches.

I sat down briefly, becalmed by the heat. Yet nothing was tranquil about the scene. It buzzed and boiled with noise: the rasping of cicadas, the melodic tolling of goat bells, striking different notes. I silently claimed this tiny patch of balcony as my solitary retreat while I was in Greece. I came back inside, closing the shutters again.

I opened my handbag to fetch the letter my mum, Marcella, had scrawled quickly to Angus before I left. It was no doubt to wish him a good recovery from his health issue. It showed her forgiving nature. As I hunted about for the letter, my fingers closed over something unexpected. I pulled it out and held it for a moment. It was a sweet image of a saintly character with a boyish face. He was on a russet-coloured horse, a dark cape flying out behind his shoulders. The horse was rearing up and the saint was aiming a long spear at a sword-wielding soldier lying on the ground.

How the hell did this get here? I thought. But the plastic frame was familiar enough, one of twelve. I laughed, remembering the close call on the airport road; the sudden braking and the jiggling of saints on the dashboard. One must have fallen off and into my open bag. I hadn't noticed. I took it into the sitting room with the letter. Angus was ready to leave. He looked smart now: a blue shirt tucked into black trousers and a black jacket. Less ecclesiastical, at any rate. I held up the image of the man and his horse.

"I seem to have had a saint in my handbag," I said. I explained the curious décor of my taxi from Kalamata. His eyes wrinkled at the corners with amusement as he examined the picture.

"Who's the guy on the horse – Saint George?" I asked.

He shook his head. "It's Ayios Dimitrios, or Saint Dimitrios."

I was impressed. "I didn't think you'd be up on Greek saints."

"I'm not acquainted with all of them, but I know this one. He was a crusading saint – from the 4th century AD, I think – who got imprisoned and tortured for encouraging the citizens of Thessaloniki to rise up against the pagan teachings of its Romans conquerors. More importantly, there's an expression used in Greece at the end of October during this saint's feast day when he is celebrated. When the weather stays fine and hot, it's called The Little Summer of Saint Dimitrios, like an Indian summer. It's a lovely time of year – my favourite."

"That's nice," I said, not sure of the significance of all this. "So it's a good omen then, having this crusader fall into my handbag." I felt amused, trying to imagine who the taxi driver would plug the gap with.

"Well ..." he said, staring at the saint as if searching for inspiration. "It probably means ... you're still going to be here in late October. You'll be lucky if you are," he added confidently, as if he were suddenly a minion of the Oracle of Delphi.

"Wishful thinking, but I have a job to get back to. I don't think the editor of the Alba News will be impressed with a long sabbatical right now."

"From what pals in Scotland have told me about the ailing newspaper industry there now, you'd be best to make an early escape." He started toying with his ponytail and looking at his watch. I'd hardly seen Angus in 10 years and now he was making pronouncements about my career and the state of journalism. He caught my churlish look.

"Don't worry, pet. I was just winding you up."

I parried with the letter. "By the way, here's something from Mum."

He didn't look overjoyed and put it down on the coffee table, unopened.

"Okay, I'll be off then. We'll go out for a meal later in the village. I eat out regularly and people will want to meet you, I'm sure."

After he left I made a thin attempt at unpacking and hung up a few clothes in the wardrobe. I propped the saint up on the chest of drawers. I liked the image: the horse rearing up, the saint with his tight brown curls, and a mountain in the background, with a curiously flattened peak. Why hadn't this picture caught my eye in the taxi amongst all the grave saints in black? However he got into my handbag, little Saint Dimitrios was to play a more pivotal role in my Greek adventure than I could ever have imagined on that first tentative day in Greece – which was just as well.

I lay down on the bed, sleepy from the day's journey, the beer and the strangeness of everything. I felt unsure what I was doing here, or what I would achieve, especially after my first spiky chat with Angus. And now there was dinner to worry about. In other circumstances, I'd be keen to eat out on a first night in a foreign country, but I was in no mood to play the visiting, loving daughter of Angus for the Greeks, who placed more importance on family than we obviously did. But I'd be starving by then and I might as well make the most of the trip, I thought.

No matter what Angus was predicting, I'd be here for just the three weeks, enough to sort out his health appointments and for him to get on with his Greek life and me to continue with mine.

Angus had been right about newspapers, however, and it was revealing that while he claimed to have no interest in Scotland any more, he kept up with its political and social changes. The Scottish newspaper industry had been struggling for a few years with a downturn in advertising and a steady decline in readership, like most other papers in the western world. The Alba News was also tanking slightly after a takeover six months earlier and a young English guy from a London daily had been appointed the new editor, which didn't sit well with senior staff, who were mostly Scottish. The paper was a long-established publication with a Scottish slant, given its name was Gaelic for 'Scotland'. It went back to the 18th century and had even sent a reporter to the Battle of Culloden. It doesn't get more Scottish than that. In the past 15 years it had broadened its appeal and gained a new younger readership – until recently.

Along with dumbing down the paper, the new management had threatened to implement cost-cutting measures and redundancies, and there had been the threat of strikes before I left. I still liked the work, particularly the past five years as a feature writer. I'd been given a long rein to pitch my own stories and to travel around Britain for interviews, occasionally overseas. But that freedom was about to be curtailed in the budget cuts. Asking for three weeks' leave, instead of the usual two, had niggled the features editor, Crayton, but luckily I talked him into it, explaining my father in Greece had a health problem and needed my support.

I lay on the bed trying to deep-breathe myself into a siesta, but I couldn't switch off my thoughts. They danced about in this minimalist, unfamiliar room, and I no longer felt tired. I got up and went to the kitchen to make coffee. It was a dreary space; a clunky cooker with scuffed hotplates, and dated wall tiles. The small fridge was well stocked, mostly with booze. I made an instant coffee and wandered around the house with the mug in my hand, looking at Angus's possessions, trying to get the measure of the man I was on an unlikely mission to save.

Every shelf on the bookcases was crammed with mostly English editions, some Greek, one or two Greek language textbooks, and a thick dictionary. I pulled it out. This was a serious book with well-thumbed pages. On the title page was an inscription in English: "To Angus. The ancients believed if you could speak Greek, you were Greek. With love, Polly." Who was Polly? A studious expat friend, perhaps? I closed the book and put it back. After a decade apart, there was so much I didn't know about my own father.

The downstairs area was smaller, fitting into the slope of the land, with two rooms, a bathroom and a small storeroom of sorts. All the doors were open. Angus's bedroom was also monastic, though slightly untidy: a single bed with a Greek-style cover. The other room seemed to operate as a study, with a heavy square desk in front of a small window. The desk was covered in books, notebooks, papers. It was messy. I remembered that when Angus was a secondary school teacher in Stirlingshire, where I grew up, he had a study at home and it was just like this. He had been a good teacher – 'inspired', some people said – but his workspace was chaotic.

I poked about for a bit, opening a few of his notebooks. I saw his characteristic handwriting, small and cramped. There were dates, names and notes I couldn't make sense of. It looked like Angus was busy researching or writing something. He always said he wanted to write a book, so maybe this was it: a memoir about his Greek odyssey.

I had some idea over the years what Angus's life had been like here, not through his own sparse letters but through his mother Lily's younger brother, Peter, to whom he had written regularly. Peter had been close to Angus, a surrogate father in a way, after his own father died young, and a mentor. Peter also kept in touch with younger members of the family, like me. He was certainly privy to Angus's Greek escape and would have understood some of the reasons for it, even if Angus's upbringing hadn't indicated a future wanderlust.

Angus had been born into a modest sheep-farming family in Stirlingshire. It had been his grandparents' farm, where his father Kieran also lived and worked. Kieran had brought his new bride Lily there, and Angus – their only child – was born two years later.

Angus had shown early academic promise. A place at a good secondary school led to a degree in English Literature at Edinburgh University. After a few years of dithering over careers, and some overseas travel, he took a teaching diploma and became a secondary school teacher in a top Stirling school. He met my mother Marcella at a New Year's dance in the city. She was also a teacher and that was their shared passion.

The first years of their married life were happy ones and we lived in a comfortable house in a village just outside Stirling. In middle age, however, something went awry for Angus. He started to drink a bit, though we didn't really know why. If he was suddenly less happy with his lot, he never talked about it. Even in 1990s' Scotland, where the rural character at least was reserved, you tended to keep your misery to yourself.

When Angus was in his late 50s, voluntary redundancies had been offered in line with general cutbacks in the teaching profession. Angus had taken it, which surprised us all, especially Marcella, because he loved his job, and he was valued and popular. No-one wanted him to go. He spent a few years drifting, doing part-time teaching, and when he turned 60, he surprised us all again by announcing he was going on a Greek odyssey for a year to reconnect with the man he thought he once was. It angered Shona and me because of how much it would hurt Marcella. Yet she was surprisingly philosophical. It made us think that perhaps the marriage wasn't what we thought it was.

When anyone questioned Angus's mid-life madness, Marcella would shrug and say, "Oh well, it's just for a year. He'll soon be back when the money starts to run out." And then he stayed for 10 years. My mother slowly got over it, and got on with her own life. She even divorced Angus in the end and remarried, which was another surprise for the family.

I didn't hate Angus for leaving Scotland. He had otherwise been a good father. I tried to be sympathetic and if he'd come back after the first year, the escapade would have just seemed like an ageing guy's folly. But the longer he stayed away, the more selfish and eccentric he seemed, like a novice ascetic who wants to sit in a Himalayan cave indefinitely, counting his chakras.

As the years passed, I felt more antagonistic. Shona got over it. She was older and she had a family to worry about. But I regretted that during the early years of my career on the Alba, when there were stresses as well as excitement with journalism, it would have been helpful to have had a sympathetic father around, a savvy role model. They were 10 years of my life in which something was clearly missing. Now, at the age of 37, I didn't expect to get whatever it was back – certainly not in a Greek hillside village.

3

Greece for beginners

The Kali Parea taverna was the one I'd seen earlier from the taxi, at the back of the square. It was quiet when we got there, with only a few tables outside, occupied by couples. Angus told me that because of the funeral, probably not many Greeks from the village would be going out. The church of the Anastasis (Resurrection) was still open and occasionally people came and went, to light a candle in memory of the deceased, I imagined.

The heat of the day had scarcely dropped but a fresh evening breeze was beginning to funnel its way up the hillside from the sea, making outside dining more inviting. However, Angus insisted we sit inside. He chose a table by the front windows, cooled at least by a large ceiling fan doing lazy revolutions. At the back of the taverna, in a corner, was a table of Greek men, drinking squat glasses of wine and eating from half-a-dozen small plates in the centre of the table, talking animatedly and watching a small TV placed high on the nearby wall.

"They're not from this village," Angus pointed out, as if they were committing a sin by being outsiders. It didn't bother me, however, and I quite enjoyed their liveliness. The taverna owner, Miltiades, was a hearty fellow, with black wavy hair and dark, laughing eyes. He had a big rounded tummy and large meaty arms like two ham joints, and a deep, throaty laugh. He seemed overjoyed to meet the daughter of "*Kirios* (Mr) Angoose" and brought a complementary jug of white wine to the table, and a basket of volcanic bread.

"Angoose?" I asked, failing to suppress my amusement as Miltiades walked back to the kitchen with our order.

"Yes, yes, I know. You'll get used to it. Some Greeks can't say Angus. They don't have the 'u' sound. I thought of changing my name, but what the hell. I'm a bit of an old goose anyway," he said, as if trying to make it clear he accepted his role of disappointing father figure.

"Many would agree with that," I said, ignoring him a moment and sipping the wine. It tasted young and fresh, with the flavour of honey and melon. We shared a plate of moussaka, with its creamy topping, a plate of fried meatballs and a salad. The salad looked healthy, with a mound of tomato wedges, cucumber and olives, but the whole lot was floating in an inch of olive oil.

"Why do they put so much oil on food? It seems a waste," I said, fishing out the tomato pieces and draining them on the edge of the bowl.

Angus looked amused. "Bronte, that is the best olive oil in the world. Taste it."

"Don't worry, I won't be able to avoid it," I said, biting into a tomato and patting my oily chin with a serviette.

Angus knew I had always been slightly picky about food. And Greek food had definitely been no exception, especially with the oil lakes. I like my salad oil sprinkled gossamer fine, like a smirring Scottish rain.

"I mean, *really* taste the oil. Savour it. Here, take this!" he said, pursing his lips with impatience. He tore off a chunk of bread, pressed it firmly into the oil mixture and handed it to me. It dripped across the paper tablecloth. This was going to be a long night, I could tell. But to oblige, I bit off the doused bread, up to the crust. The oil had a fruity, peppery taste, not like the tasteless stuff you get in British restaurants.

"Okay, that's not too bad, I think, but it's still a lot of oil."

He rolled his eyes. "It's local oil from the olive presses round here and it's bloody good for you!"

I stared at him for a moment, thinking how the oil hadn't really helped him. He must have read my mind and gave me a dark look. I thought we might end up scrapping over diets and heart disease and I wasn't in the mood for that. But we fell into silence instead, eating the rest of the food, the first proper meal I'd had with my father in years. I marvelled at how the small rituals of life bind the past and present seamlessly, so that although being with him felt unnatural, everything else had a familiarity that took the edge off matters.

With the lull in our conversation, I lugged into the raucous behaviour of the 'incomers' in the corner. They ate, talked and watched TV at the same time, with one old guy flicking a set of amber worry beads around his knuckles, while smoking with his free hand. A sign at the front of the taverna proclaimed this to be a non-smoking eatery, but I was beginning to realise that rules were bendy things in Greece.

An item on the TV news had all their attention now. It seemed to be about the economic crisis, with footage of riots in Athens, Molotov cocktails being hurled on city streets and rows of black-clad kids shouting at lines of police. Occasionally, one of the men watching the TV would become rowdy, hurling angry comments at the anchor people on the news channel.

Miltiades walked over to our table and refilled our glasses. He seemed to think we were being disturbed by the rowdy guys.

"You must excuse them. It's because of the *krisi*, the crisis." He shrugged his big shoulders. "All the new taxes, all to keep happy the European Union so we get another big amount of the loan. But ordinary Greeks, they still have no maaaaney," he said with amusing exaggeration, holding up his thumb and index finger and rubbing them together, like the taxi driver had done. Miltiades finished with a sigh and walked swiftly back to the kitchen, as if he'd just had a brief walk-on part in a one-act drama.

Angus leaned towards the table. "There is always a table of men in the corner at night, usually from this village. They come to watch the TV and argue over the crisis."

"Don't they have TVs at home?"

Angus looked at me sadly because I was making another ridiculous observation, in his opinion, and showing my ignorance of Greek life.

"Yes, they do, Bronte, but they like to come out and sit together for *parea*, the Greek word for company, like the name of the taverna. *Kali*, good, *parea*, company. Now you're learning Greek. And *parea* is important here."

I ignored the schoolmaster's tone. "Maybe they just want to escape their nagging wives."

"That too. Look, it's quiet tonight, but you can't imagine what this place was like a few years ago. Before I moved to this village, I used to come up here some weekends with friends from the coast and it was always packed with villagers, people from Kalamata and expats, dozens of them. Sometimes there was a group playing bouzoukis and there was singing, dancing. It was well … it's what you come to Greece for … or one of the things. It was a paradise. No-one has the money now for partying, except for the expats – and even they are beginning to return to the UK. Things have changed."

As if on cue, we spotted a group of British expats milling around the square outside, trying to choose the best outdoors table at the taverna, laughing and chatting in anticipation of a good night out. Angus winced when he saw them and I wondered if this was why he insisted on eating inside the taverna. He saw me watching them. "I don't mix with most of the Brits," he explained. "They're okay but it's not what I came here for and if you're not careful you get sucked into their world of bitching and heavy drinking. I did it for a while. Didn't help the ticker, I'm sure."

"Are you going to blame the expats for your health issue?" I said with a churlish tone.

"No, Bronte, of course not, but you get trapped in that lifestyle if you're not careful. But it won't happen again."

We progressed to the dessert: a plate of sliced apple drizzled with honey, compliments of the taverna. We fell silent again. I concentrated on the food, aware suddenly that I was growing weary and my monastic cell at Villa Anemos was calling me. Just then, a middle-aged man dressed in black came into the taverna and slapped Angus warmly on the back. I was introduced to him as the 'daughter' and was given a sturdy handshake. The two men then exchanged pleasantries in Greek. To my surprise, Angus seemed to speak it reasonably well, in a slightly halting accent with a touch of Scottish. While he was chatting, he looked comfortable, happy, almost like a local himself, with his tan and ponytail, his penchant for shrugging and waving his hands about.

It was nothing like the man we knew as kids who had been, professionally at least, a rather serious-minded individual. Outside of school hours, he had been convivial, with a wide group of friends. The only clue he gave to having a more renegade soul was a passion for rock music and playing his electric guitar at weekends, locked in his study with a few musical pals, oiled along by a good few beers.

The man in black moved off towards the group by the TV.

"Your Greek's good. I'm impressed," I said.

"Och, it's not perfect. I've studied it for years and even went to classes in Kalamata, when they used to be free, run by the council. It gets me by."

Angus called Miltiades for the bill and was offered another carafe of wine. Angus declined it.

"I think we're too tired for more wine today," he told me, "and anyway I've got no urge to be blootered these days."

"Your ticker will thank you," I said primly.

"It's not the ticker I'm thinking of. I need my head to be a bit clearer than it has been …" He trailed off.

"Why's that?" I asked, thinking he perhaps needed to keep on his toes with the churlish daughter around.

He gave me a searching look and was about to explain, I thought, but quickly changed his mind.

"Och, plenty of time to talk in the days ahead, pet."

Intrigued, I wanted to probe him a bit more but was distracted. "Don't take offence, Angus, but I wish you wouldn't keep calling me 'pet'. It makes me feel like I'm 12 years old."

He looked hurt, which surprised me.

"Sorry, Bronte. I'm an old fool really."

"OK. Let's not dwell on it," I said, with a light flutter of my hand.

Angus ordered two Greek coffees, which arrived in tiny white cups. I didn't like this dark, muddy stuff on my first trip to Greece, but at least it was always served in mercifully small measures. Angus sipped his coffee with obvious delight, as if it was a rare malt whisky, and again I was intrigued by his new Greek persona.

We walked back to the house in the dark. The cicadas were still rasping in the trees, a donkey brayed nearby and a few chained-up dogs barked a kind of syncopated lament. We trudged along, cocooned in our own thoughts. I was longing for that narrow bed under the watchful gaze of Saint Dimitrios. When I finally sank into it an hour later, the last thing I mulled over before I fell asleep was that final bit of conversation with Angus, about him wanting to be clear-headed these days. I had a strong conviction that there was another reason for me being summoned to Greece. I just needed to winkle it out of him – and soon.

4

The Spartan arrives

A shouty, repetitive voice seeped through the open balcony doors, waking me from a deep sleep. The voice was cartoonish and strangely amplified. On and on it went and finally tailed off into the distance, small and tinny. There was no chance of sleeping in now. I lay a while in bed, enjoying the warmth of the sun through the windows, the sound of a donkey braying nearby. The day promised to be very hot again.

"Who was shouting this morning?" I asked Angus later as he wafted about the kitchen, preparing breakfast.

"Oh that. You'll get used to it. Hawkers go around the villages in trucks. They use loudspeakers to spruik their wares."

"What was that one selling?"

"Oh, let me think .... Watermelons and chairs."

"Oh, of course, why not?" Only in Greece would fruit be paired with furniture.

Angus was putting cold meat and cheese on small plates.

"I take it you won't be looking for porridge?" he joked.

I shook my head. "I bet it's a while since *you* ate it, right?"

He shot me an amused look. "Aye, it is."

I had a sudden memory of being a kid of about 10 and how Angus made breakfast because my mother worked at a different school, further away, and had to leave earlier. He made porridge most days. He liked it very thick. "Stuff you could stot a ball off," he used to say.

"We don't eat much in Greece for breakfast but I can cook you eggs if you like."

"No, this is fine. I'm not that hungry after the big meal last night."

"We can sit out on the big balcony. It's cooler there in the morning," he said, leading me through open double doors. He put the plates on a round wooden table, with a closed sun umbrella in its centre hole. If I thought my tiny side balcony was alluring, this was a revelation. It was a deep balcony running the width of the house, with several terracotta pots full of geraniums in the corners.

The view almost made me feel dizzy; 180 degrees of it from the north Taygetos on our right, Kalamata below and the gulf spread out before us, as well as the Messinian peninsula directly opposite, with its spine of low hills. There was a hazy, balmy quality to the air and the light seemed to shimmer. A soft breeze toyed its way up from the sea. It had a tangy feel, with a hint of salt.

"I know this house is a bit clarty inside, but this view is grand, isn't it?"

I smiled at his word 'clarty', messy, and the fact that even here, submerged in his Greek life, he still savoured his Scots vocabulary. Again, I had the acute sense of this being quite bizarre, sitting at breakfast with Angus after all this time. But in another way, it felt maddeningly normal, which it shouldn't have.

Suddenly the donkey was braying again, the same one I heard when I woke up, and a woman was shouting loudly at someone in the farm compound next door. I'd had a good look at the farm earlier that morning from my balcony, a messy space of olive trees and rural junk, and I sensed there were animal enclosures nearby because of the goaty smell wafting up in the heat.

"Who lives next door?"

41

"Ah, that's Myrto. She has a farm of sorts and a donkey called Zeus, which she seems to argue with a lot, otherwise she's arguing with her stepson Hector, who comes around from time to time. Hector's a sour character, I must say. Don't worry, you'll meet Myrto soon enough. She speaks English and you might find her colourful and interesting, as a journo. Anyway, I thought you might like a walk around the village this morning to get your bearings."

I rather liked sitting on the balcony, soaking up the environment, but I dutifully went off to get dressed after breakfast for the walk and appeared in the sitting room wearing cargo shorts and a T-shirt.

"You need a bit of sun on those legs," said Angus, smirking at my milk-bottle pins. "Maybe you'll manage a tan this time." He was referring to my previous visit to Greece, when I got sunburnt on the first day and had avoided the sun for the rest of the trip. I have the typical Celtic colouring of fair skin and wavy auburn hair – which I have always worn long. My eyes are hazel, like Angus's, with flecks of green in sunlight, and not the cornflower blue of my mother's.

"I doubt I'll have enough time to get a tan going."

"You'll want to swim in the gulf though. It's the best time now for swimming. Not too hot and it's quiet. The place is packed in August, but the minute September arrives, the Greek holidaymakers all disappear back to the cities; kids are back to school. It's as regular as clockwork," he said, snapping his fingers.

"I didn't think Greeks did clockwork."

"They don't, but in some ways they're creatures of habit. In fact, they can be damnably contrary in general. I'm constantly surprised by them. You will be too." *No I won't. I won't be here long enough for suntans or surprises*, I thought.

We set off for the village, walking on the edge of the road and crunching over wild herbs, their pungent aromas filling the warm air. The *plateia*, square, was busier today, with many of the tables outside the taverna and the café already occupied, mostly by men, and some labourers shouting in a language that didn't sound Greek.

"Albanians," said Angus, noticing my confusion. "They do a lot of stone masonry in the Mani. They tend to keep to themselves."

Angus led the way through the square to a steep set of stone steps behind the church, leading to a narrow road. He called this the *Palios Dromos* (old road), from the days when this cobbled thoroughfare was the main residential road in the village, with traditional stone houses, and a few shops, their double wooden doors now sadly boarded-up. Only the old bakery that Angus used was still in operation here.

Marathousa was said to date back to Byzantine times, though all that remained of this period was a small chapel at the top of the hill, kept locked because of its beautiful old frescos. Most of the village dated from the early 19th century, when the surrounding land was cultivated for olives. The 300 or so villagers still made a living from olive harvesting and goat farming.

Along the lower main road were a few stone houses, a general store and an old and once thriving olive press, now unused. It was a compact village, designed to have a clear view down the hillside to the coast and Kalamata, making it easy to spot interlopers in past centuries. From the hillside behind the village, narrow tracks led to high olive orchards and, to the south, the deep ravine of the Rindomo Gorge, where ancient caves were set into its perilous sides.

We walked along the Palios Dromos, where ruined stone piles hunched against renovated houses, many bought by British expats, with handsome front doors and wrought-iron balconies. Despite having lived here for only five months, Angus seemed to know a lot of the passers-by and introduced me as '*kori mou*' (my daughter). He repeated it so many times I finally remembered it. It was ironic that one of the first Greek words I should learn was 'daughter'. Now all I had to do was tackle the word for father, *pateras*. That would take some getting used to.

We came across one expat on our travels, a middle-aged woman whom Angus introduced to me as Cynthia. She was deeply tanned, wearing a long skirt and bright pink top. I sensed that she had been at the table of expat diners the previous night. She had blonde hair in a messy up-do held by clips and combs. My impression was someone artsy and nervous and not quite in her element on this Greek hillside, though I could see her more comfortably organising a village fete in Sussex, where Angus later told me she hailed from. She was a genial soul, however, and seemed to be quite taken with Angus.

As she left, she said, "Come and have a drink with the expats one night at the *kafeneio*, Bronte. They're good company; you'll have a laugh. And get Angus to come as well. He never does now," she added, with a small pout. "Anyway, *yeia sas*, goodbye."

Angus sighed after she flounced away. "Cynthia's been here for years. She came with her husband to live permanently but he's since died and she's stayed on herself. She lives at the top of the village in an old house they were doing up. Don't know how she manages."

"It's brave of her to stay on alone here though," I said.

"She should go back to the UK. She can't manage that old house up there. The Greeks help her out of kindness. A lot of expats are like her. They stay so long that they can't go home again." *Like you*, I thought.

"So you do mix with the expats sometimes," I said.

"One or two, yes."

"I noticed Cynthia was flirting a bit with you."

"Don't even go there, Bronte. I don't get involved with expat women," he replied sniffily. But I imagined that in the beginning he might have, when he was leading the hedonistic lifestyle he'd described the previous night. So, who would he get involved with now, I wondered, or was he just too old for love? Yet with his suntan and reflective shades, he looked craggily attractive, and the Scottish accent added to his charm. Despite his affability, I could see how my mother and he had grown apart in the end because they were essentially very different.

Marcella was born on Mull and went to Glasgow University to study history. She was shy and reserved, apart from when she was in front of a classroom. As a teacher, she was quietly confident. Her Scottish accent was softer than Angus's and sibilant, carrying an aura of the Western Isles and the wild Atlantic shore. Unlike Angus, whose auburn hair and hazel eyes I had inherited, Marcella was very fair, with strawberry blonde hair and a smattering of freckles. She had a fragile, luminous beauty in youth, but in middle years she had grown plainer.

Despite our efforts to make Marcella more outgoing and fashionable, as the years went by, Shona and I accepted that she was happy just as she was. Away from school, she was a domestic doyenne, whereas Angus liked hillwalking and rock music. When he played his electric guitar, my mother would bake cakes, switching the blender on and filling the house with kitchen noise to blot out his riffs. Screaming guitars in one room, blenders in another. Shona and I would flee the house when Angus was feeling musical. Later on, he built a shed at the bottom of the garden and played there. We saw less of him — and we got fewer cakes as well.

Some of Angus's friends had blamed Marcella for him legging it because she hadn't been interested enough in Angus's life, his hobbies, his passions. It was a cruel kind of masculine logic. Had he ever asked Marcella how to bake a pineapple upside-down cake? But there was more to a marriage breaking down than all that. I was into my second day in Greece and already I felt that when I was growing up I hadn't known Angus properly. And the years I wanted to know him, he wasn't there.

We had walked right along the old road towards the west side of the village, where the road curved down the edge of the hill and joined the lower road that wound down to the coast. Angus was puffing a bit.

"The ticker doesn't like walking much now," he said, pointing to his chest as if he had incubated a petulant alien who dictated his life now. "Let's go back by the main road and have something at the café. I haven't taken you there yet. And it's called a *kafeneio*, by the way. I think I'll teach you a couple of words a day. You'll be blethering in Greek in no time," he chortled. Once a teacher always a teacher.

The *kafeneio* was called the Zefiros, named after the Zephyr wind. I had a frappé, a cold instant coffee with a creamy topping, but Angus persisted with his Nile Delta brew. The café owner was almost as short as she was wide, like a voluptuous beach ball. She had a head of thick, coal black hair and curiously small teeth that made her smile seem mischievous.

"I speak some English. You can come here any time and we will talk. I need the practice. My name is Elpida, by the way. Means hope," she said with a shrug. "It's all we can do now is hope."

She wandered off to another table to collect some empty cups.

"Elpida will teach you some Greek too. She's good fun and very patient."

Three weeks to learn Greek. I didn't think so. But there it was again, this urge for Angus to keep me here longer, or not to comprehend that holiday leave usually has a time limit.

"Do the people here know you have this health problem?"

"Not really. I've only been here a short while. I don't want them to think I'm done for already. They'll never leave me alone. The women will want to bring me food and fuss over me."

"Sounds good to me."

"It is, when you're on your death bed."

"But you prefer to keep something to yourself, even here."

"Yes, why not? I'm still a foreigner. We like our space too, don't we?"

After the coffee, he got up to pay. Elpida waved at me. "Come any time. I have free wi-fi too. Your father has no wi-fi in that old house of his," she said, rolling her eyes.

On the way back to the house, we passed the time with disconnected bits of chatter. "Do you still play guitar?" I asked him, wondering if he had shrugged off his old life completely.

"Sometimes. I have one with me, and I bought a bouzouki a few years ago. I'm not much good at it yet."

"Really? A bouzouki?"

I smiled to myself. What a curious man my father was, engulfed in a Greek metamorphosis, the reasons for which I had no great understanding.

Cars passed now and then, mostly battered wrecks or small farm vehicles with chunky tyres, driven by the younger Greeks. One man rode by on a donkey with a bundle of sticks lashed either side of the solid wooden saddle. He waved a thin stick at us and offered a greeting. There was a sense of peace about this location that I might have preferred on my first visit to Greece rather than the more touristy beach haunt where Angus stayed when he first arrived.

In the early afternoon, Angus's landlord, the doctor, arrived after his morning surgery in Kalamata. He rapped at the door and Angus showed him in. The doctor was smartly dressed in a dark suit, his expensive-looking shoes tapping over the tiled floor. It was only then, in his presence, that I really noticed how shabby the house looked, particularly the faded tartan rug over the sofa and the scuffed coffee table. It all resembled the Scottish highland bothies I'd visited with Angus when I was young and we used to go hillwalking. Bothies were small abodes, often no more than rugged sheds in the middle of nowhere, with minimal charm, designed for shelter in foul weather.

Angus hadn't been joking about the doctor's looks. He was extremely handsome. He looked robustly healthy, with glossy, loosely curled black hair, the locks hanging slightly over his forehead. There was a dusting of grey at the temples. His skin was smooth and tanned, his eyes were big and very dark and his best feature, except that the slight heaviness of the lids gave him a hint of aloofness. There was also a little stubbornness in his shapely top lip. Otherwise, you couldn't fault him.

Angus introduced me to Leonidas. "So, I finally get to meet the daughter of *Kirios* Angus," he said, shaking my hand. I felt strong slim fingers, and a firm determination. At least he hadn't called Angus a 'goose' – not yet.

We strolled out to the balcony. "Sit down, Leo, we'll have coffee, yes, or do you fancy a beer, or an ouzo?" said Angus, rubbing his hands and pointing to a chair, as if he were on a night out with his village mates.

"I never drink between surgeries, my friend," Leonidas said, with a sanctimonious glimmer in his dark eyes. He had scruples. That was good.

We sat down and waited as Angus went into the kitchen and rattled about with cups and coffee makers. Leonidas's eyes roamed dreamily over the olive groves.

"I never get tired of this view. It is soothing, yes?"

I agreed. Whatever else might be wrong with Greece, the physical beauty was not in crisis.

"Your first trip to Greece?"

"Second."

"And you like it so far?"

"Yes, but I haven't seen anything yet, apart from walking around the village."

"You must try to go further down the peninsula to the inner Mani. It is very special, very wild."

"I don't know how much time there will be for sightseeing," I said.

"Why not?" he asked, his thick black eyebrows arching up like two lazy cats stretching.

"Well … this is not so much a holiday for me. My father has brought me here because he is worried … about a health condition. You know what I mean, of course."

The doctor played with the cuff of his shirt. "I am not his regular doctor, but I did examine him briefly after he had the chest pains. I suspect he has some heart disease, probably some narrowing of his arteries, causing the discomfort. And he smokes, drinks and eats too many of the wrong things, I imagine," he said in that perfunctory manner that doctors have.

"I suppose if he doesn't watch himself he'll end up having a heart attack."

"Yes, perhaps. For now, I have prescribed some tablets for him, in case he has more discomfort. But I am a general doctor and I suggest he must see a cardiologist. There is someone in Kalamata I would recommend for a more detailed consultation, but for complex tests, he will have to go to Athens because there is very little high-tech scanning available here."

"Your English is very good, Leonidas," I said. His pronunciation was very precise.

"Ah, you must call me Leo. It will be easier for you."

"Leonidas is a lovely name. Wasn't there a Greek hero called Leonidas?"

"Yes, there was," he said, with a tiny lift of his chin. "Leonidas was the King of Sparta who led a small army of Greeks against the Persians at the famous Battle of Thermopylae. He was a hero, but unfortunately he and his men were tragically defeated. But he's still something of a god to Greeks today."

"So, no pressure then being named after a Greek god?" I said with a sardonic grin.

He laughed lightly but I wasn't sure if he appreciated the irony or was just being polite. He had a nice laugh though.

"As for my English, I went to language classes while I was studying and spent a summer working in a private hospital in England when I finished my medical degree. And my girlfriend Phaedra is currently working there and speaks very good English, so it makes it easier for me to learn, you see."

So there was a girlfriend!

"What work does she do?"

"She is a dental surgeon working in a practice in the south of England, in Brighton, and also doing more studies at night."

Dentistry! Not surprising. Dinner conversations in their house would be medical, to say the least, when they managed dinner. I wondered how they conducted a long-distance romance and how she trusted the dishy doctor to rattle around Greece on his own.

"With regards to your father, I can organise a visit to the cardiologist by early next week, if you wish it. It will be a private consultation, much quicker than accessing the public system that is in a crisis also at present. But it will not be expensive. Your father is a good man. I like to do my best for him." He held my gaze a moment. It was comforting that Angus had won some admiration in the village at least.

"That would be very helpful. I'll make sure Angus attends."

His eyes widened with interest. "You call your father by his first name?"

"Em … yes. It's a long story."

Just at that moment Angus came out carrying a silver tray, which must have been the best possession in the house. On it was a large copper pot with a long handle, filled with his beloved Greek coffee. He poured it into the tiny white cups and offered some hard-looking biscuits bought from the village bakery. Like the volcanic bread, they would be another hazard to dental work, which Leonidas's girlfriend would surely abhor. Leonidas crunched daintily without incident, while I broke my biscuit into pieces to avoid amalgam distress. He smiled at me, nothing more than a flicker at the side of his mouth.

"How long will you stay, Bronte?" Despite his pronunciation being otherwise perfect he stumbled over my name and said Brontay and not Brontee. "I have never heard that name before. It is unusual, yes?"

"I was named after a great English writer, Emily Bronte, who happened to also be one of my father's favourites."

He cocked his head to the side and fixed me with his big dark eyes. "Emily Brontay? So, no pressure then!"

"Ha! Very good," I said. He was much more switched-on than I thought, and he had a sense of humour.

"She's not quite as heroic as the King of Sparta. You win!" I said, and found myself winking. How did that happen? I rubbed my eye as if I had grit on my eyeball. He laughed.

"Of course Angus will have told you he was a teacher in Scotland," I said.

"He did, yes. What did this Emily Brontay write?"

"Ah, well. She wrote a very famous book about a love affair between a young woman and a very handsome, wild man called Heathcliff. Wuthering Heights is a romantic story. A classic."

He arched his brows. "I must read this book one day."

"I'm sure Angus has a copy here if you want it."

Angus looked out to sea. "No, I don't think I have. I could get one though, if you wanted to read it, Leo, but I doubt you have that much spare time."

"I always have time for an interesting book," he said, with an earnest nod. Of course he was being merely polite, or ingratiating, I couldn't decide. But the image of Doctor Leonidas sitting in his surgery in his free time boning up on Wuthering Heights was just too amusing for words. I lost myself a moment and snorted with delight and had to turn it into a small coughing fit as a cover.

There was certainly none of the wild abandonment of Heathcliff in Leonidas, but there was an aura of the daredevil in his unruly curls that showed promise. What intrigued me most was that such an urbane professional would have an old village pile like this to rent out. When Angus had told me that Villa Anemos meant Windy Villa, I thought it couldn't be more apt. I imagined the north wind would rake through the roof tiles in the winter. However, the doctor's villa next door was a solid stone house with pale blue shutters, very stylish but not opulent, set further away from the road on two floors with a large top balcony. Below, the garden looked manicured and lush, and you could just see the far edge of a swimming pool. He saw me gazing at the property.

"The house is just my weekend retreat and for summers," he said with a shrug. "The rest of the time I live in an apartment in Kalamata." The comment was meant to distance himself for the affluence of the property, I guessed, but unfortunately it made him seem indulged, especially when Greece was sliding into a fiscal mess and workers apparently had trouble hanging on to their primary homes. He sensed his faux pas and quickly added, "All this land belonged to my father and grandfather before that. This house we are in here was my grandfather's original house and then my father built the one I now have, which I lived in as a child, though I have modernised it. I am afraid I have neglected Villa Anemos now, and Angus has been too gracious in not wanting me to modernise it a little."

"Och, it's fine for me as it is, as I've told you already," Angus said, with a slight grizzle in his voice.

I was sipping coffee but was slightly distracted by the chatter. I drank more than I thought and was down to the bottom of the cup. My final gulp sent a slick of coffee grounds like a riverbed down my throat, bringing on a real coughing fit this time. My eyes welled up with tears.

"I meant to warn you last night not to drink the stuff at the bottom," said Angus with a smirk.

The doctor laughed and handed me one of the paper serviettes Angus had put daintily on the silver tray. I took it and wiped the grounds from my mouth. As I did, I caught that flicker of a smile again. We sat in silence for a moment, enjoying the sunshine, but the serenity was broken by the sound of the next door donkey kicking up a fuss, and the woman shouting.

"I apologise for the noise," the doctor said, rolling his eyes. "That is Myrto with her donkey. They are always arguing. You will get used to it. She is a little eccentric but harmless. She has some goats in there, chickens and so forth," he said, slightly sniffily. He got up. "Well, I must get back to town. A great pleasure to meet you, Brontay."

I thought I would take the Brontay issue in hand and gently told him how it should be pronounced. He had a few goes at it and finally cracked it. I sensed he was quite a perfectionist and didn't like being corrected much, even on so small a point, but he was gracious to a fault. I rather enjoyed his slight discomfort.

"I will arrange something with the cardiologist, and let you both know."

"You can call us on Angus's mobile. I will check it myself regularly. I'm afraid my father has an aversion to mobiles."

He laughed. "Your father is what you call a rebel, yes?"

Unconsciously, Angus played with his ponytail and smiled, without replying.

"Oh, yes, he's quite a rebel. You don't know the half of it," I said.

The doctor left the balcony and Angus followed him into the sitting room. I heard a low conversation and imagined the rent money was being handed over. The front door closed and Angus came back and sat down.

"I wasn't wrong, was I?" he said.

"About what?"

"You know. About Leo," he said.

"He's very charming, if that's what you mean. You made him sound eligible, but he has a girlfriend, working in England."

"Well, I didn't know that."

"I'm surprised he's not married. Quite a catch, I'd say."

"He was married once. Wife lives in Athens with his son."

So, he wasn't a perfect Greek god after all. Good.

"I can see you're interested," said Angus.

"I assure you, I'm not. He's not my type. And a touch arrogant perhaps."

Angus pouted. "He can afford to be. Doctors are the top of the social heap in Greece. And to be good looking as well." He whistled and waved his arm around, Greek-style.

"Let's not mix necessity with pleasure since he's going to get you that appointment with the cardiologist."

"You hang on to the mobile, pet. I don't like the blasted thing."

"What usually happens when people, in Kalamata say, need to reach you? Do they send a homing pigeon up the hill with a message strapped to its leg?"

He laughed and shook his head. "You wouldn't get it, Bronte, but if someone needs me they just call Elpida at the *kafeneio*, or Miltiades and someone there will fetch me. That's how it works in these villages. No-one is that far away. Everyone knows everything here."

It sounded frightening. I decided to avoid the village messengers and stick to the mobile phone. When I was growing up, I never would have thought that Angus would end up in a hillside village in Greece that was clearly stuck in the 19th century. I never imagined he'd end up living alone at 71 either. It seemed to me that anyone's life could take a squinty turn, the way a river in spate can overflow and carve off into a new direction, with no hope of it ever recovering its original course.

5

Myrto and Zeus

Later in the afternoon, after a short siesta, I found Angus on the back balcony under the sun umbrella, trying to read a book. But his attention was taken by a commotion from next door: the sound of buckets being kicked over and Myrto cursing. Angus caught me staring towards the farm.

"I can see you're curious about Myrto, now that Leo has mentioned her."

"Maybe."

"Leo doesn't get on with her, and she doesn't much care for him either. They've got some history, I think, though I'm not too sure what it is. See, there are back stories, vendettas, secrets in these places. It's all here."

"Perhaps the others are a bit jealous of him, with his money and the gorgeous pile next door."

"Yes, but there are other Greeks here with holiday villas. Let's go down, if you like, and meet her," he said, finally abandoning his book.

Myrto's land was secured with a metal fence and gate at the front. When she was in the compound, she left the padlock unlocked, hooked over one of the metal spars of the gate. We went inside, Angus calling her. She came striding through the trees, dressed in trousers, a casual shirt loose over them. My first impression was of rural toughness, though she was striking with it: good bone structure and tanned skin, slightly lined around her eyes, which were pale blue and framed with mannish eyebrows. Her hair was thick and dark brown. She looked to be in her late fifties. She was carrying a bucket with a mound of greenery inside, resembling weeds.

"*Yeia sou,* Myrto, I want you to meet my daughter, Bronte. She's here for a few weeks."

The toughness was softened by a broad smile that showed good, even teeth. She gave me a strong hand-shake with a leathery hand.

"G'day, my dear! Nice to meet you," she said. I hadn't expected the broad Australian accent in her English.

"You're Greek-Australian?"

She laughed. "No, I'm from here but I live a few years in Sydenee," she said, slipping in an extra vowel and elongating the last one. "So, how you like our village?"

"Nice, from the little I've seen."

She looked me up and down with narrowed eyes, as if trying to get the measure of me.

"You married? Children?"

"No," I said.

"Boyfriend?"

Angus had warned me that rural Greeks asked personal questions. I laughed awkwardly.

"Not at present, no."

"We have nice boys in the village," she said, winking at Angus.

"Bronte doesn't want to get married. She's married to her career," he said, smirking at me.

I gave him a glowering look.

"Well, it's true, Bronte!"

I shook my head. It would keep.

"What you do, Bronte, for career?"

"Newspaper journalist."

She whistled lightly through her well-formed lips. "*Poli eksipni.* You very clever then. You write a nice story about our village, yes?"

"Maybe, one day. Who knows?"

"Come sit down under my shady trees."

We followed her down a narrow path of sorts past piles of wood, rubbish and sacks of mystery items I could only guess at. She took us to a clearing under an abundant fig tree that had some overripe fruit still hanging on like fat Christmas baubles. A metal table was set under the tree and some plastic chairs. It was a pleasant, elevated space, with a view between olive trees to the gulf below. Despite the heat of the day, you could feel a gentle breeze from the sea.

Myrto's house was nearby. It was an old village property, similar to Villa Anemos, but with a stone staircase leading to the front door. The windows were covered in old wooden shutters, closed against the sun. Somewhere behind the house I imagined were the goat pens and chicken runs. To the right of us, under an olive tree, the donkey was tethered by a rope to its trunk with a selection of buckets in front of him, an old feta cheese tin overflowing with water and strafed by wasps. This was the beast she niggled at, apparently, and yet he seemed rather placid and fluffy. Myrto noted my interest.

"That's Zeus. I know he looks so sweet there, Bronte, but let me tell you when he gets a crazy idea in his fat *mialo*," she said slapping her forehead, "lightning bolts go flying. He earns his name. Throws me off once and I bust my arm. I don' ride him no more." She wound up with a string of what sounded like Greek oaths. Angus was smiling. I guessed, however, that Myrto could throw a few bolts of her own.

"And I don' take no shit, as they say in Sydenee." She had an endearing habit of shortening words, particularly in negative constructions, and also of mixing up her tenses, but with a preference for talking mostly in the present tense.

58

"You wait. I get some cold drinks."

Before we could reply she disappeared up the stairs into her house and soon returned, carrying a large tray with glasses and a bottle of lemonade. She set everything out on the metal table. There was also a plate of figs.

"Last of the good figs I take from my tree. Best figs in the village." She offered us a few on small plates, with a knife and a serviette.

"We not complete peasants in the village, are we, Angus?" she said, with a wink. At least she got his name right.

I cut a fig in half and ate it. It had a sweet strawberry jam flavour, like no fig I'd ever eaten. I devoured another one, and then another, and drank some cold lemonade. It was heaven.

"Good, eh?" she said, slapping me lightly on the back. "So, Bronte. What you plan to do on holidays? Tour about?"

I nodded.

"You meet any village people yet?"

"Not many. Just the people in the *kafeneio*, and the taverna."

"Ah, you speak Greek already?"

Angus nodded with proprietorial glee.

"Not exactly, Myrto," I said.

"It's bladdy hard language, Bronte! But you doing good."

She flicked her eyes at Angus. "I see Leonidas comes today. You sick?"

"No, I'm fine. He comes every month for the rent."

"Ah, yes, landlord, too. We never forget it."

"The doctor seems very nice," I said, eating another fig.

She gave me a long, shrewd look over her lemonade glass and raised her eyebrows slowly, while slightly shutting her eyes and tipping up her chin. I'd noticed that Greeks seemed to make this gesture a lot. I'd call it a dead expression, neither good nor bad, with the intention of giving nothing away. Sometimes, however, it seemed to imply 'no', or more likely 'no comment' or 'so what!' It covered a multitude of things.

"You don't like him?" I ventured.

She made the gesture again, then threw caution to the wind. "Oh, he is very good doctor and local person. Our families come from the village of Platanos in the old days, up there in the mountains behind us," she said, jerking a thumb towards the high peaks. "Nice little place in middle of nowhere, Bronte. But the doctor and his family have done very good for themselves. His family now what we call the *psilomites*, high noses, or the stuck-ups, as I would call it in English." She laughed heartily and I struggled to stifle a giggle myself. "But here I am on my old farm property, donkey and goats for friends. A proper shithole, as we might say in Aussieland! And the doctor has his beuuuutiful villa next door. He doesn't like the goat smell, the donkey noise," she laughed loudly. She was enjoying herself immensely.

Angus feigned an overly diplomatic expression, I thought. "He's never said anything about that to me," he said.

"Oh, no, he don' say it to other people, maybe. But he would be very happy if I move."

"Are you moving?" asked Angus, looking quizzically at her.

"Not if I have the choice."

"Is Leonidas trying to get you to sell up?"

"No, I don' mean that. Anyway, not so much about Myrto, eh?"

We all sat a while in silence. I ate another fig, bringing the tally to five or six. I'd probably pay for it later. I wiped my mouth with the serviette.

"What took you to Australia?" I asked.

She slapped a hand affectionately on my back once more. "Oh, Bronte, it's a long yarn. My husband Fotis wants to go work with his brother. Building trade. We stay for eight years. Then Fotis dies." She crossed herself hurriedly. "And I come back. That's it. Short version. You come here for coffee one day and I tell you whole yarn. I make good coffee, too. Everyone says so."

"Sure, why not," I told her.

As we walked back to the house, Angus said, "You must go and have coffee with her. She'll spin you a few tales. Not that I've heard all of them. I never stay long when I'm there. But she likes you and she'll probably tell you about Hector, the stepson. Fotis was married before. There's some rift but I don't know what it's all about."

In the next few days I wandered around the village with my camera, taking pictures and exploring hidden corners that were sometimes not what I was hoping for, like the time I came across two men in an alleyway skinning a dead goat. Another day, I found an old woman in a field, dressed completely in black, plucking a fat chicken and singing some kind of wailing folk song. I very rarely saw an expat when I was walking about during the day. I had no idea where they were all hiding, but they all came out at night and flapped around the *plateia* like busy moths. Angus also took me out in his old Fiat a few times to nearby villages and to his favourite hidden swimming cove, a mere slip of pebbled beach with pure pale water and a view of the gulf and Kalamata. I got a sense perhaps of what it was that kept Angus in Greece – but only a sense.

However, each day I could feel myself beginning to unwind. Whole hours went by and I didn't think about Scotland, or the newspaper, but I still checked my emails most days. I was tasked with telling Marcella and Shona how Angus's 'health problem' was going. The lack of a phone and broadband connection at the house meant I had to check emails at the Zefiros, which was a not unpleasant ritual. When Elpida saw me she would sit for a while at my table to chat, offering some snippet of gossip. She was always very interested in what Angus was doing and I could sense there was a desire to riffle a little through his back story. After what Angus had told me about village life, I was on my guard.

But she was also a mine of local information: which saint's feast day it was, and therefore who would also be celebrating and requiring plenty of cake, or ouzo. Every saint in the Greek Orthodox Church has a feast day on a certain date. There is a morning service in the churches named after that particular saint and often a *yiorti*, celebration, afterwards for the congregation in the church grounds with a simple meal. Most Greeks are named after saints and they, too, celebrate on the saint's day with a 'name day', like a birthday. They have a family get-together later, or a gathering of friends in a local *kafeneio*. With so many saints in the church panoply, there is a celebration of some kind in Greece almost every day of the year.

"Soon we have a little *yiorti* up in the hills," Elpida told me. "In the small church of Saint Nektarios. All the village is coming. You come with your father, you will like it. It is special church celebration, the day we honour the holy cross of Jesus, but most important, we baptise the *fournos*, the new brick oven we build. All the people have given money to our village council, and they build oven. Old one kaput."

I quite liked the idea of a proper baptism for a brick oven, dousing it with a bit of holy water, no doubt. I was beginning to appreciate how eccentric rural life was in Greece.

"We will roast pieces of goat in oven. You will like it," she said, kissing the tips of her fingers. I'd never eaten goat. My finicky tastes never veered that way. The prospect of the meal didn't excite me, but I liked the idea of the celebration.

"Okay, thank you very much. I will let my father know," I said.

She laughed and squeezed my cheek between thumb and forefinger, jiggling it as well until it brought tears to my eyes. "Ah, you English, you so ... polite, Bronte."

I don't know if she had any idea that we were Scottish, or even what or where Scotland was, because a few times on my trips around the village I had been asked by locals – as far as I could understand – where I was from, and the word Scotland was met with exasperated looks. Finally, I learnt the Greek word, *Skotia*, but it didn't help the villagers to place the country at all, and several times I was reduced to drawing maps of Britain on dusty paths. In a way, I liked the idea of hailing from a place that was as foreign to the rural mind here as Jupiter.

Amongst my emails was one from Sybil, one of my close friends on the Alba News, and a feature writer.

"Dear Grecian Hen,

I'm jealous as hell of your Greek sojourn. You won't want to come back, not when I tell you the managing editor addressed staff today, in a surprise move. It seems they're about to take a chainsaw to the budget. Saturday mag to be downsized. Features will be no bigger than long news stories. They want to squeeze out a few journos, one photographer, and other staff. We've been told no trips outside Edinburgh, unless everything approved first by Crayton. Poor Crayton, pale and pissed off with life these days. Who isn't? Your father sounds pretty cool. You always made him sound like Hannibal Lecter, but maybe you should cut him some slack. Haven't we all wanted to escape? The doctor/landlord sounds appealing. Holiday romance, hen?

I replied: *"Well, no surprises with the cutbacks, but Crayton will bat for us in features, surely. He's committed. My father is not Lecter (did I say that?), more ageing rock star, ponytail now, chilled. But I feel I'm living with a bit of a stranger. And walking on eggshells comes to mind – sometimes. Keep me posted on work developments. No time for romance, Sybil, not even with a man called Leonidas, named after a Spartan hero."*

Grecian Hen xx

On the weekend, Leonidas called on the mobile to tell us he had organised an appointment with Dr Protopsaltis, the cardiologist, for Tuesday morning. When I told Angus about this, he girned slightly at the suddenness of the appointment.

"You have to do it sometime," I said, beginning to understand why Angus needed some support in Greece, at least someone to keep his medical diary in order.

6

Lipid lush

The cardiologist's waiting room was quaintly decorated with old poster prints of the Greek islands, showing lithe brown youths enjoying the glories of summer in simpler times. This fantasy of raw good health seemed wasted on the crush of patients seated around the periphery of the room, waiting their turn, gloomy-faced and impatient.

Angus was nervous, chewing gum and flicking through magazines. After 20 minutes he was summoned. I decided not to accompany him into the surgery. I felt that a man and his illness should have some space. I thought I was in for a long, tedious wait, but the room livened up with a few arguments at the receptionist's desk, which was diverting, even though I couldn't fathom any of it. I guessed much of it was over payment, with medical fund papers handed over, details jotted down, forms to be signed. Bickering and anxiety.

Leonidas had arranged for Angus to see the specialist privately, though the projected fee seemed low, to a foreigner anyway. When Angus came back out, he settled up the bill in cash − the only person I'd seen doing this. He got a rubber-stamped receipt and we left, walking to the elegant Aristomenous Street, the city's main thoroughfare. It had a long central square for pedestrians and Parisian-style cafés on one side.

I had read in one of Angus's guidebooks that in the 19th century the layout of Kalamata had been redesigned by French engineers after parts of it were destroyed in the Greek War of Independence against the Turks from 1821. Broad boulevards with mansion houses became its trademark when the city was a major trade centre for olive oil. Although much of the city was ruined again in the devastating 1986 earthquake, its former charm had remained in some quarters.

Angus and I decided on a coffee break after a tense morning. We sat outside a café under its shady striped awning. It was fairly crowded. Angus ordered a cold frappé for me, and a beer and a slice of baklava for himself, a confection made up of dense brown layers of pastry alternating with layers of crushed nuts, like a small geological core sample doused in honey. I began to fear for his blood sugar levels.

"So, what's the diagnosis?" I asked.

He pulled a face. "Don't really know yet. The doc did some blood tests. I'll have to wait for the results. I expect my cholesterol will be sky high for a start. It was high the last time I had it tested."

"When was that?"

"About five years ago."

"That long?"

"Yeah, we're not as obsessed here with health as we are in the UK."

"More's the pity!"

"Well, anyway, the cardiologist agrees my arteries are probably knackered, hence the chest discomfort. Like Leo, he says I need something hi-tech to probe the situation, which means Athens." He pulled a sour face.

"Have you never been to Athens?"

"Yes, of course, Bronte, but I go there to enjoy trips around the antiquities, not to have my arteries plundered."

"Quite so, but let's not panic until the test results come through. At least you're moving in the right direction," I said, trying to sound upbeat. But if we were in Scotland now, he'd have been sent off for more tests straight away, and treatment. It would have been so much more straightforward.

"I need to live like a Trappist monk now," he said, skulling his beer. "The doc says I should stop smoking altogether, but I only smoke now and then. And I should cut down on booze. A glass of wine a day is okay, he said, but he didn't say what size glass." He sniggered, then drank some more beer. "And I've got to watch my lipids, as he calls them, especially the bad cholesterol, the artery-blocking stuff. So no more souvlaki and feta cheese, I suppose."

"It's not astrophysics, is it, Angus. I mean, everyone knows all this."

"Yeah. It's obvious, I know," he said, forking up a few stray crumbs of baklava. "A moment on the lips, a lifetime in the lipids," he said, and burst out laughing at his own joke.

I laughed as well, even though I didn't think it was something to joke about. At least he hadn't lost his sense of humour. He leaned back in his chair, his eyes fixed on a table of young people eating a plate of souvlaki with chips and drinking ouzo. I thought I saw just the merest hint of envy in his eyes. I left him to it and went off to the toilet, mostly for a short respite from talk of doctors and lipid surpluses.

When I returned he was finishing off his beer. We watched people strolling along the square: shoppers and street vendors, who seemed to come by at regular intervals, selling all kinds of cheap and counterfeit junk. One old Greek guy in a dusty grey suit was selling worry beads in myriad colours, but no one was buying. Were

Greeks in crisis too poor for a good worry now? We were sorely in need of a better distraction, and soon enough one arrived – Leonidas, striding across the square. I gulped when I saw him heading right for our table.

"*Kalimera*, Leo. Have a seat," said Angus. From the way Angus spoke, it sounded like he'd been expecting him and I wondered how, unless he'd called Leonidas while I was in the toilet. Angus had told me he worked in the same street as the cardiologist, the Kalamatan equivalent of Harley Street. Leonidas sat down and summoned a young waitress, ordering a cappuccino. He offered me another frappé and I meekly nodded but Angus declined another beer, giving me a wink as he did so. Leonidas placed a small, elegant man-bag on the table top, his mobile next to it. His presence seemed to ramp up the atmosphere somewhat.

"So, how do you like Kalamata?" he asked me.

"It has a real buzz, that's for sure."

I liked Kalamata a lot more than the first time I had driven through with the crazy taxi driver. I liked the vibe. Plenty of cafés and interesting side streets that I would explore in time.

Leonidas wasted no time in drawing out the cardiologist's opinion and a medical discussion ensued with Angus, which I didn't much plug into, but I was impressed with the doctor's interest in Angus's condition – or perhaps as a landlord he was just protecting his investment. I mean, who else would really want that old house?

By the time I had lugged into the conversation, I was aware that Angus wasn't really taking his condition very seriously, as usual, and when the talk touched on fats, Angus tried his little joke out again about the lipids. There was a moment of silence, then Leonidas opened his eyes wide and laughed loudly, throwing his head back a little so I had a view of a pristine set of teeth that his dentist girlfriend would covet. It was the first time I'd seen him laugh properly. It suited him and scuppered some of his innate formality. But surely lipids couldn't be that funny?

After Angus had told Leonidas everything about the morning consultation, Angus announced he had some business to see to in the city and if we didn't mind he'd leave us and meet me back at the café in half-an-hour or so. It was the first time he'd mentioned another appoint-ment and I was bemused as I watched him strolling across the square to the row of shops along Aristomenous Street. The idea of entertaining the doctor alone suddenly didn't appeal much. He made me nervous.

He leaned forward slightly in his chair. "Doctor Protopsaltis is playing it cautiously for now, but I think that in a few weeks he will want your father to undergo more specialised tests. But in the meantime, because I know you are looking to his welfare, Bronte, if your father has any chest pains or discomfort, you can call me any time, or take him straight to the hospital in Kalamata." He handed me his business card with a clutch of numbers on it.

"This one is my personal mobile number," he said, pointing a long, perfectly manicured finger at it. "You can call me there any time."

"Thank you, that's kind."

He said nothing but absently ran a hand through his hair, the curls bouncing around his fingers. It was impossible not to admire its vitality and it was distracting. He also seemed distracted, playing with the sleeve of his jacket, glancing every now and then at his mobile, waiting to be called by some patient in distress perhaps. I wondered how in the midst of this economic crisis he had time to leave his surgery at all for no great reason it seemed. In the news that day, Angus had told me that some pharmacies had run out of commonplace drugs, one of the symptoms of the health service buckling in the crisis. I asked Leonidas about this. It struck me that I was not going to be free of medical topics today, so I might as well go with them.

"Yes, it is very bad. Drugs suppliers are not providing many drugs to the pharmacies unless they are given the money first. And many people have no money to pay for doctor visits. Many medical insurance schemes are unable to pay out for consultations and treatments. Every day my job becomes harder. And there are new taxes all the time, and other things that make our lives difficult now," he said.

Until I knew I was coming to Greece, I hadn't paid a great deal of attention to the crisis, despite there having been a slew of scurrilous features in British tabloids about "workshy Greeks" and corruption and so forth. But Leonidas gave me a quick update.

Greece's economic problems had started a decade earlier but by 2009, in the midst of the global financial downturn, the country found itself deep in debt, exacerbated by soaring public sector spending and widespread tax evasion. In 2010, with Greece edging towards bankruptcy, the International Monetary Fund, European Central Bank and Eurozone countries approved a bailout package for Greece of 110 billion euros. In return, the Greek government was forced to implement stringent austerity measures, which resulted in economic hardship, unemployment and violent protests. The economic crisis slowly became a humanitarian disaster.

In the mid-summer election of 2012, the country finally showed its hatred of austerity by giving only a slim margin of victory to the dominant party, New Democracy, and offering instead a spike in votes to the little-known left-wing party Syriza, led by Alexis Tsipras (which would win the Greek elections in 2015). During this black period of austerity and antagonism towards the ruling elites there was also a rise in popularity of an extreme right-wing party.

"There is always talk now," Leonidas added, "that we may never cut our debts and that we will fall out of the Eurozone, returning to, let us say, the drachma. You can't imagine the chaos that would follow. We will be back to zero. No medicines, no new equipment. The system will collapse. Everything will collapse: no food in the shops, no petrol. I fear it."

"Is that why your girlfriend has moved to England?"

He fiddled with his cuffs again. "Yes, but many people are leaving the country now, mainly professionals, like doctors, and students."

"Would you ever leave?" It suddenly dawned on me that that was obviously the plan, to go one at a time to England. He didn't answer straight away.

"I just cannot say right now. It is all very difficult," he said, whatever that really meant. And yet the statement had the same effect as a rag nail that I knew I would have to pick at again, some other time. Certainly not now, when he had a slight stubborn set to his mouth. He drank his coffee and looked around for the waitress. "I must go now. I hope everything will go well with your father. Let me know if you need my help in any way."

"Thank you again, but it's occurred to me … that if Angus should have bad chest pains, can't I just call an ambulance?"

He pulled a face. "We don't have much of an ambulance service in general, but now in the crisis, it is another thing that has been cut back. You will be lucky to get one if you call. Don't bother with it. Just drive your father straight to the hospital."

He noticed my panicked look.

"Don't worry, Bronte. Everything will be fine."

I'm in a country, I thought, with an unreliable ambulance service, looking after a man who is one pork souvlaki away from a heart attack and everything will be fine? My own heart was doing a kind of nervy salsa now. I suppose this could be one of the reasons I was here: to ferry Angus to hospital if needed. On Greek roads? I'd need more than 12 saints on the dashboard!

The waitress brought the bill, Leonidas paid it and got up.

"I must go back to work now. It was very nice to see you again," he said, squeezing my shoulder lightly before he turned and strode away. It felt like a reassuring gesture, one a doctor might offer when he's just told a patient about their incurable illness. But it was not unpleasant, of course.

I waited for Angus, wondering what the hell he'd found to do that was suddenly so urgent. I was playing with my mobile phone when I heard the grating of metal chair legs on paving stones. Angus had returned.

"I thought we might walk up to the old sector of the city near the *Kastro*, that's the castle. There are plenty of small tavernas there, where we can have lunch and a carafe of local wine."

"You're supposed to be cutting back, right?"

"Tomorrow, pet."

"You're calling me pet again."

"Sorry. Habit, that's all."

"From when? From over 10 years ago?"

"Let's not start up. I didn't ask you to come to Greece to have a rammy over the past."

He noticed my frown and softened his approach. "Look, we've got two more weeks together, so let's enjoy it while we can. Let's not argue."

"You're supposed to be too worried about your health to enjoy yourself, aren't you?"

He had his arms folded over his chest. He looked defensive. "Well, we don't have to act like we're in mourning. I'm not dead yet."

"Just as well," I replied. "Because I feel you've got something else planned while I'm here that you're not owning up to."

He didn't reply.

"Well?" I said.

"Let's go to that taverna I told you about. We'll talk there."

So, there *was* something else. We trailed up Aristomenous Street, past fashionable shops, paper sellers, and one bank with a long queue snaking along the pavement outside.

"People are trying to get their money out now in case we crash out of the Eurozone," said Angus, as we walked around the end of the queue, where people were waiting with grim stoicism. For some odd reason I thought about my icon of Saint Dimitrios. It seemed to me that Greece could do with another caped crusader sometime soon.

7

Mission improbable

The Perdika taverna was in the historic sector of the city clustered below a ruined 14th century castle on a low hill. It had some tables outside on the pavement. Inside, a queue shuffled past a glass-fronted display of metal trays brimming with food. Angus told me this was one of the oldest, most popular tavernas in the city. It was nothing to look at inside. The only nod to the past seemed to be the stout wine barrels along the back wall.

The food was what I had come to associate with Greece: moussaka, oven potatoes, fried fish, and mounds of boiled greens, slippery with oil. But I was getting used to it and I was suddenly starving. We made our choices and decided to sit outside under a small lemon tree that offered some shade from the afternoon sun. The meal arrived, with a carafe of wine. I had salted, fried cod and a salad. Angus had a meaty casserole in tomato salsa. The wine was strong and honeyed, the bread thick but not volcanic.

Angus refused to take up our previous discussion until we had finished our meal. "I want you to savour the moment. Be a little Greek. Enjoy the food, the atmosphere," he said, sluicing his bread through the meaty sauce.

By the time we'd finished our leisurely lunch, most other diners had drifted away home for their siesta. The city grew quieter: only a few shoppers trailed about with bags of food from a nearby market, a *papas* in his stove-pipe hat walked majestically, his robe lapping the tops of his shoes. Even the street vendors had gone. The city oozed a thick, sleepy ambience. A noisy group of diners at the next table had already gone, leaving a collection of plates, many with small portions of leftovers. Yet no-one seemed to be in a hurry to clear the mess. After a while, stray cats appeared, leaping onto the table and helping themselves.

"I hate that about Greece, the way they let swarms of cats onto tables. It's a filthy habit. I don't know what's with the waiters today. They usually clear the tables straight away," said Angus.

So, not everything about Greece was glorious in his mind. As we sipped the rest of our wine, a dirty ginger cat hoovered up a plate of leftover meat, eyeing Angus all the while.

"Och, that one's got to go!" he said, picking up a hunk of bread. With one deft movement, he threw it, hitting the cat on the head. It shrieked and leapt away. A solitary old Greek guy sitting at a nearby table shouted out, "Bravo!" Angus laughed and the two bantered for a while until the waiter finally arrived and cleared the table. Angus ordered more wine and ignored my sanctimonious look.

"So, okay. Tell me now, why I'm really here," I asked.

He took a long, indulgent swig of wine and I could see how much he was enjoying it, dragging out the Greek 'moment'.

"Honestly, Bronte, I did ask you here because of the health issue. I kept thinking if my condition suddenly got more urgent, I might even have to pack up and get back to Scotland. Still might have to."

"Okay, fair enough," I said, not believing for a minute he'd want to go back to Scotland unless he was nailed up in a box.

"And there is something else that I need your help with. It's to do with Kieran."

We both went quiet. He wasn't looking at me. He was playing about with the salt cellar. I should have guessed all along that this summons to come to Greece had something to do with his late father Kieran, even after all these years.

"Oh, Angus, I thought you'd exhausted the subject long ago!"

He frowned. "I know. But I've come across some new information."

I felt a stab of disappointment — pity as well — over this endless mission.

When Angus embarked on his 'odyssey' at the age of 61, it surprised many people he knew. What didn't surprise his family, however, was that he picked Greece for this mid-life escapade. For us, Greece wasn't just the sunny holiday magnet it is for other Brits, it was a country that had been locked into our family's psyche since the Second World War. It had shaped our destiny, more so Angus's.

Just before Angus's young mother, Lily, had found out she was pregnant, his father Kieran joined the war effort. Until then, he had worked on his parents' Stirling-shire farm, where he and Lily also lived. He had been late in joining up because as a farmer's son he had special dispensation to remain on the farm, all to do with the imperative of the nation producing enough food to fuel the war effort. But by the end of 1940, he had been desperate to enlist, and do his bit for his country. He enlisted in the Royal Army Service Corps (RASC) and was sent first to Alexandria in Egypt and then to Greece in March 1941 — but he never returned.

He was one of an estimated 60,000 British and allied troops in the Greek Campaign against the German invasion who had to retreat from northern and central

Greece in the face of overwhelming Nazi forces. Many of these troops had ended up in the southern Peloponnese awaiting evacuation by sea and had launched a brave rear-guard action in Kalamata in late April 1941. This became known as the Battle of Kalamata, and more chillingly, the 'Greek Dunkirk'.

As an RASC driver, Kieran had been caught up in this battle and had later gone missing, presumed dead. His disappearance was made all the more difficult since this was a military campaign in Greece that had not been well documented after the war. It was a campaign the British armed forces didn't want to remember – ill-fated and badly conceived, with a tragic outcome. Not the finest moment of the Second World War.

In 1940, Greece had been brought into the Second World War due to the Italian offensive by dictator Benito Mussolini, an ally of Adolf Hitler. Mussolini sent five heavily armed divisions over the border into Greece from Albania, which the Italians had held since 1939. In October 1940, the small but heroic Greek Army managed to drive the Italians back into Albania. However, Hitler drew up plans to invade Greece in April 1941, through Bulgaria, to achieve a hold on southern Europe in readiness for his planned invasion of Russia. Hitler sent four Panzer divisions, the Luftwaffe air force and his elite parachute corps.

Fearing the outcome of the German invasion, the British government under Prime Minister Winston Churchill sent a force from Egypt to Greece in March 1941, comprising British, ANZACs and a few thousand other Commonwealth troops. However, the Greek Campaign on the mainland had been disastrous, due to poor planning and communications, the poor state of the road system and the speed of the German offensive, with around 3,000 British and allied troops killed or wounded.

By mid-April, as the Germans secured northern and central Greece and Athens, the allied troops were forced to retreat, engaging in a huge evacuation by sea, called Operation Demon, which began with embarkation from ports in the northern Peloponnese. As the ports came under heavy fire from the Luftwaffe, the remaining troops fled further south, ending up in Kalamata, the end of the road, awaiting evacuation by Royal Navy warships.

During the seven nights of the operation, around 50,000 troops were evacuated, with 9,200 leaving from Kalamata. The operation had been fraught with difficulty at Kalamata because it had to be done under cover of darkness — due to devastating German bombing raids but with virtually no RAF cover.

On April 28, the Germans finally entered the city in force, with the remaining allies putting up a spirited fight against them. The action was centred in the port area of the city that night, and mainly involved a small heroic band of New Zealanders who refused to heed talk of surrender. An attack was led by Sergeant Jack Hinton, armed only with grenades and a rifle but who routed out the Germans, allowing the allied force to briefly recapture the port area, with 41 Germans killed and 100 taken prisoner. He was later shot and taken prisoner himself but was awarded the Victoria Cross – the highest military honour for bravery.

The allies fought on during the night but by morning the troops, under the command of Brigadier Leonard Parrington, surrendered to the Germans. By now the British warships had departed and around 7,800 troops were left stranded in Kalamata, many of whom would become POWs. Parrington informed the troops on April 29 that "…any officer or man is free to make his own escape", so basically it was now every man for himself.

Around 300 of them fled down the nearby peninsulas, looking for a means of escape to Crete by boat, 160 miles to the south. Kieran was believed to have been one of them. Some of these troops managed to get away but many were captured or killed in daily Luftwaffe raids or while in hiding. Many were reported missing in action and their remains were never found.

The War Office had informed my grandmother Lily that Kieran had not been evacuated, or listed as a prisoner of war. He was last seen alive with some other RASC troops south of Kalamata, but where he went from there and how he died was never known. Like other families with loved ones missing in action in Kalamata, our family had been stymied by a dearth of information on this part of the Greek Campaign.

Angus's odyssey in Greece may have had something to do with a mid-life crisis and a personal sense of failure, but our family believed it was probably underscored by his search for closure over his father, and how and where he actually died. This had been all the more heartbreaking because of the knowledge that Kieran had apparently died not even knowing his wife Lily had been pregnant when he left for the war effort. Although Angus's family understood his bid to find closure, what made it hard to accept finally was that the search for Kieran had gone past its logical limit, with no more useful information coming to light.

"This quest over Kieran is just a damned excuse," Marcella would say, "for a long mid-life romp. He's a daft old bugger!"

We pieced together Angus's life in Greece from the letters he'd written home, mostly to his uncle Peter. We heard about some of his jobs, like the private English lessons he gave for a while to help to stretch the redundancy money. When Peter died two years ago, he left a small inheritance to Angus that allowed him to keep his life in Greece going a bit longer.

Angus gave me a grim look. "I know what you're thinking, Bronte. Why carry on with this useless search? But it's like this. I did talk to a lot of people about the Battle of Kalamata when I first came here. I hooked up with veterans at the remembrance day held in the city every May – all of that. I started Greek classes and did some research in the library here. I got nowhere. The reason is that the Battle of Kalamata was total chaos, everyone who was left behind who wasn't taken prisoner of war had to flee for their lives, as you know. Some veterans even believed the failure to evacuate everyone from Kalamata was hushed up by the top brass in the British armed forces because it was an organisational mess.

"Apart from one or two fairly recent books with veterans' accounts of the battle, which I have read, and re-read, no-one has really documented the whole thing. There is no telling exactly how many people died in the southern Peloponnese, trying to escape, as opposed to dying in POW camps or on the way there. Or where people died. Each year it gets harder to research. Each year the veterans' numbers dwindle, with the only survivors in their 90s now. However, in the past couple of years, some veterans' groups have started up websites and Facebook pages. I've seen most of them and that's where the interesting stuff can now be found."

He gave me a funny look. "Yes, I know what you're thinking, but just because I don't like using mobiles doesn't mean I can't surf the net."

"I never said anything …. Go on then."

"More stories are gathered all the time and put on these sites, often by the veterans' families. Amazing tales of bravery and hardship: men lining up in their thousands on Kalamata beach every night, waiting for the landing craft to pick them up to take them to waiting ships. Mostly it was the fighting units that got out first or the officers or signalmen, the important guys. The RASC – the drivers, mechanics and so forth – were generally among the last. There are tales of daring escapes down the Mani with soldiers looking for small boats to take them out into the gulf with the hope of being picked up by a returning warship. Some did sail from Souda Bay in Crete to the gulf for a few days after the surrender at Kalamata.

"While I was searching one site, an account caught my eye. It was uploaded by the daughter of an English veteran called Thomas, who was also in the RASC. She had found a diary he must have written years after the war as a way to remember what happened, but she hadn't seen it until the poor guy died early this year and she was sorting out his belongings. The account she uploaded was only a section of Thomas's diary concerning the Battle of Kalamata, his escape attempt and capture by the Germans. He later became a POW. I've got a copy of his account here," Angus said, pulling a folded piece of paper out of his pocket. He had obviously come prepared.

"But briefly: Thomas wrote about heading down the coast with a group of mostly RASC lads looking for a boat to get to Crete. They had a few ANZACs with them, a Greek Cypriot as well, who helped them talk to locals, and a couple of Yugoslavs. They passed coves on the way, where there were scores of other allies trying to do the same thing but with little success. Finally, they came to a long beach, not far from the end of the coastal road. Here they befriended a local Greek, with the Cypriot acting as an interpreter. He told them the Germans were moving down the peninsula fast and the allies would probably be rounded up before they found a seaworthy boat. He had a different idea about escaping ..."

Angus unfolded the paper and started to read: "*The Greek was a farmer, as nice a bloke as you'd ever want to meet. He said he knew the mountains and they were safer. We wouldn't get picked off as easily by the Jerries. He pointed to the mountain area, some distant peaks, high bloody things, some thick with snow. There were some villages up there, well out of sight. The Jerries wouldn't bother us there, he told us, and then we could advance from there through the mountains, due south. I remember thinking – blimey! It would take about a week to hike up there. All the same, the Greek told us the name of one of them. None of us would have remembered one village from another with their strange Greek names but it's funny what things stick in your mind. I remember this one because it sounded like the philosopher Plato. I had a grammar school education so it wasn't lost on me. Platonos, I think it was. The Greek told us to head straight up from the coast through the olive groves, keeping to the northern side of a deep gorge. At the base of the mountains, there was supposed to be a track of some kind that led up to this village. Well, the boys weren't keen and pinned their hopes on a boat, except for two of the RASC boys who were Scottish ...*"

Angus stopped for a moment, to see how I'd taken this bit of information. I deadpanned it and he continued. "*These boys wanted to have a crack at it. They were used to mountain terrain I'd say. I don't remember much about those poor lads now or their names except for the way one of them looked. Tall thin bloke with a thick head of auburn hair, good looking. A plucky sort, he was. He must have made an impression cause I still remember him to this day. We tried to talk them round, tried to tell them it was better for all of us boys to stick together, but the tall one was keen for the mountains and off they went. I never heard of either of these lads again. I guess they didn't make it.*"

Angus handed me the paper. "What do you think, Bronte? It sounds like Kieran. Tall, auburn hair. And he was confident on the hills; spent a lot of time as a young lad rambling on them, like most rural Scots. All right, it's not a lot to go on, but it's the best, most specific information I've ever come across."

"There must have been lots of Scots in the Service Corps, and plenty with auburn hair," I said.

"Yes, but you know, from the old pictures of Kieran, how thick and bonnie his auburn hair was. You'd remember it, wouldn't you? Kieran's father, Tom, said the men in the family, mostly, had that amazing hair. And remember my hair was similar when I was young, and you've got it too."

"Well, it's a funny thing for this Thomas to remember, in the midst of a terrifying escape, the colour of someone else's hair," I said.

Angus smiled. "Well, some of the accounts of veterans I've read are full of strange details, like one soldier remembered a guy in his battalion who carried gold nail scissors around with him like a lucky charm. There's a heightened reality in times of war. It's the odd little things people remember. Like Thomas also remembering the name of the village, Platanos, even though he spelt it wrong, but it has to be the same village in the mountains that Myrto came from, as do a lot of others in Marathousa. There's no other village around here with that name."

"If the guy that Thomas mentioned really was Kieran, do you think that he and the other soldier might have made it to this Platanos?" I asked.

He shrugged. "Och, I don't know anything. Who knows? Maybe they set off and changed their minds, or got picked up by the Germans. We know from War Office records he was definitely in Kalamata during the battle, and if this guy in Thomas's story is our Kieran then this narrows him down to a specific part of the Mani. That's why I decided to move to Marathousa. I discussed this with an expat called Rupert, who knows the Mani well, and knows a lot about the battle. He agreed that Platanos would have been the ideal village in which to hide out because it's right back in the mountains and only accessible by a mule track. There are a few other villages further into the mountains but they would have been too hard to reach quickly. But if you were to draw a rough line from the beach that Thomas mentioned, which must have been Santova beach – the one near the bottom of the lower road from Marathousa – and continue the line just west of the Rindomo Gorge, you would roughly come to the foothills of the mountain range. And if you managed to ascend, you would eventually come to Platanos."

"Perhaps the two guys just hid out in Marathousa? That would be an irony," I said.

"They may have passed through it, but I don't think they would have hung around. There were Germans swarming all over the north Mani a few days after they occupied Kalamata. I've heard stories of how the locals in Marathousa were terrified of the Germans rounding them up, so they hid in the caves along the steep sides of the Rindomo gorge, which was a dangerous undertaking anyway."

"Realistically though, the pair could have gone anywhere in the mountains," I said, feeling light-headed at all the possibilities. I had seen a map of the region and knew that the spine of the Taygetos mountains ran the whole length of the Mani, petering out near the tip. In a cove there lies the fabled cave of Hades, doorway to the underworld. In 1941, the whole place must have felt like a portal to hell.

"Rupert also told me that there was a link between Platanos and Marathousa since many villagers had come down from the mountains to lower villages like ours from the early 19th century onwards after the Greeks won the War of Independence. They were looking for an easier life basically and the lower villages were suddenly more secure from interlopers and there was land for the taking. Rupert thought that villagers with the mountain link would probably be able to help me with my research. Ironically, the one old guy who might have been the most helpful was Yiorgos, who died recently. The fact that Kieran was here fighting for their country makes him a hero in their eyes, but the mountain people are often guarded, with foreigners, at any rate."

"Have you told anyone there about Kieran?"

"No. I want to tread carefully. I've just mentioned the issue of allies possibly hiding out in the mountains. Nothing specific. But I get the feeling they don't want to talk much about the war, not when they've got a crisis on their hands. I haven't been to Platanos yet. That's what I plan to do next. Go up and see if there's anyone there who remembers war stories – not that there are many villagers left. I've gathered that much at least. Anyway, this is where you come in. With your sharp journalistic brain, I thought you'd be able to help me push my research further and solve the mystery of what happened to Kieran once and for all."

"Oh, starting with the easy stuff then," I said, sarcastically.

"Yeah, why not?" he said, twisting his ponytail around.

"I can try to help, but you're the one who speaks Greek."

"Sadly, my Greek might not be up to this challenge. But two minds on the job will be better."

"What about Rupert. Can't he help you a bit more? He seems to be the expert."

He puffed air out through pursed lips. "Rupert is back in the UK. He isn't very well."

I had a sudden thought. "Is all this what you've been scribbling down in those notebooks in your study?"

"Oh, pet. You've been poking around on my desk!"

"I didn't read anything but I noticed the books. And there's the 'pet' word again."

He ignored the reproach. "Okay, yes. I've been doing plenty of leg work these past months. Making notes."

I was impressed. "So how do you propose to start this search?"

"I've started already. I've ordered a four-wheel drive for tomorrow, to drive up to the mountains."

"That's quick. When did you do that?"

"Today, while you were chatting with Leo."

"I see. So, let me get this straight. You want us to drive up into the mountains and look around for some old guy of 90 who might remember a couple of British soldiers during the war? Some guy who might have hidden them in his wood shed?"

"Aye. Something like that," he said with a wry smile.

"And you want to do this, despite being a possible heart attack victim?"

"Oh, fuck all that! The cardio doc will give me a load of tablets and I'll be fine. The heart issue has been a wake-up call. I'm getting old. There will never be a better time to find out about Kieran. And now you're here. I've got some moral support," he said.

My faced flushed slightly with aggravation. Suddenly I had forgotten Kieran and the Battle of Kalamata. "You want *my* moral support, Angus? What moral support did you give me when you left and came to Greece? I was in my 20s, trying to crack into a bloody difficult profession."

He rubbed his hands over his forehead and looked agonised. "Och, Bronte. I know what you're feeling. I've been a right bam sometimes, but this is not the time to spear the donkey's arse, as gran would say."

"When is the time?" I hadn't meant to snap but it amazed me how much rancour bubbled just below the surface. He just did that Greek thing with me: flicked his eyebrows up and half-closed his eyes. No comment.

"Tell me one thing. When you left 10 years ago, was it all about Kieran really, or was it other things?" I asked.

"Who knows, Bronte? But one day we'll talk about it, I promise," he said, evasively.

I let it go. I didn't have the energy to bicker and, by the looks of him, neither did he.

"Let's make tracks. The city's beginning to empty now."

Angus had parked his Fiat in a side street nearby. He knew what streets were good for half a day's parking and, anyway, he said few cars ever got booked. It also didn't bother him that he'd been drinking because there were few police patrols around. This was southern Greece, a place that even other Greeks called 'wild', where rule-breakers seemed to be able to sleep at night.

As we drove back to the village, I mulled over this improbable mission, dodging heart attacks and perilous mountain roads. And there was I thinking that all I had to do here was escort him to heart specialists. How wrong I was. We bumped along the same route the taxi driver had taken me on, past the switchback bends but slower, the engine straining up the inclines. I had a longing suddenly for the line-up of saints.

"What I don't understand, Angus, is why you didn't tell me the truth when you wrote to me recently. Why did you turn it into a medical drama?"

He kept his eyes on the road and didn't answer straight away.

"I thought … if I told you the whole truth, you wouldn't want to come. You'd think it was useless and that I was a daft old bastard."

"Yep, I'd have thought that. Thinking it right now."

"And you'd think, 'Why should I help him after all this time?' Right?"

"Yeah. I'll admit I'm wresting with that too," I said, crossing my arms over my chest, feeling grizzly as we took a few more bends on the road. The car engine sounded asthmatic. At one severe bend with no guard rail, I noticed a small shrine with a lighted candle inside. He saw me staring.

"That's where a collision happened last year. Some poor guy got incinerated in his car."

"Oh, that fills me with confidence. Thanks."

Angus's Fiat was in fact better than some of the cars I'd seen around the village, which looked like they'd survived a wrecking ball. He told me people didn't have money any more for MOT or tax and they just drove these heaps to and from their farms, as few police ever bothered to go to Maniot villages unless they really had to. I knew how they felt!

I was relieved when we pulled up outside Villa Anemos. As soon as we got inside, Angus made coffee and we sat outside on the balcony. It was quiet in the late afternoon while everyone slept. Only the cicadas kept up a shrill reminder of summer's heat and sweat. As we drank our coffee, Angus handed me a book.

"It's one of the best books, in my opinion, about the battle, just to refresh your memory, and gives a bit more background on how the allies escaped."

The book was simply titled The Forgotten Allies: Stories from the Battle of Kalamata, with a photo on the front that I took to be an old one of Kalamata beach. Unlike the vista of today, with its cafes and apartment blocks, this one had thick olive groves running down close to the shore. I assumed he thought the book would inspire me on this mad mission.

"Okay, I'll read it, but I'm still not sure how we can get to grips with this search when I only have a couple of weeks left. Just thought I'd mention that."

He rubbed a hand over his chin. "I agree it's not long, but we can make a start and see how we get on. Luck may be on our side. I might talk to Leo about our mission. I haven't so far, but it would be good to pick his brains, since his family originally came from Platanos as well, though he was born here."

"Did you call him today when I was in the ladies' toilet?"

He nodded. "But not to blether on about heart disease – to kind of set the scene, to work our way into his good books, with the mission in mind."

Set the scene? He was shrewder than I thought.

"It was generous of him to come – busy doctor and all that," I said.

"He's been a lot more attentive since you arrived. I think he's quite taken with you, Bronte."

I shook my head in disbelief. "Really? Aren't you forgetting his dentist girlfriend, the tooth fairy?"

He sniggered. "Ach, don't worry! No-one could possibly be in love with a woman who gawps at molars all day long." I laughed at his totally inane comment.

"Don't be too sure! And anyway, have you turned into a matchmaker now?"

He looked shocked at that. "I might tease you about Leo, but I wouldn't dare match you up with anyone, Bronte. As I've said, you're married to your career."

"And you would know, of course!" I snapped back.

He winced and held his hands up. "Okay, I deserved that. I'm sorry. But just tell me: are you on board with this mission, or not?"

I sighed. "Is there a choice? It's just the degree of difficulty in solving this … mystery."

"But you're a journalist. You do this all the time, unpick mysteries, track down people for comments."

"The people are usually alive though. It makes things easier."

"Good. I'll away then and have a wee siesta. I'm knackered."

I was relieved when he went downstairs. We hadn't had the big rammy that I feared was coming. I was stung by his words though. I knew he'd followed my career at times and referred to my stories in some of his rare letters, but my love life was something he knew nothing about. I wasn't wed to my career but it eclipsed everything else in terms of its success. A few years earlier I'd won a couple of journalism awards for feature writing, but I wouldn't be receiving plaudits for my love life.

My last love affair was with a sexy guy called Rory, who played bass guitar in a Scottish rock band. I'd interviewed him for a feature and it was love at first sight. Rory was dark-haired and swarthy. Irish heritage. And he had an Irish temperament as well. Brilliant and quixotic. I went to as many of his gigs as my job allowed, put up with temporary hearing loss and passive smoking in badly ventilated venues. We were unofficially engaged when he gave me a hastily-bought ring with a moonstone until he had time to get me the real thing with a big "muckle diamond" as he put it. Then he went on a tour of Australia. Two weeks into it, a text arrived: "Sorry, sorry, I'm a complete toerag but I think I'm not ready for commitment after all. And I don't deserve you." I sent him a text back, saying simply: "Well fuck off then!"

My friend Sybil told me I was blinded by Rory's bass guitar and his blarney. She said she saw the apocalypse coming long before I did. I'd never been great at relationships. They didn't last because I picked the wrong men, obviously. A psychologist would say I did that because I expected them to let me down — just as Angus had. I tend to think some people aren't fated to meet their soul mate. I believed I was becoming one of those people, at 37. One day at work, I confessed my fear about finding the right partner to a male journo friend, who was older and wiser. "There's no such thing as the right partner. All there is are people walking past you, day in and day out. You've already passed 'the perfect man' – you just haven't looked at him properly. You've got to be open to love. It's not always going to be obvious; the grand moment. It can come from the most unlikely direction. It's whether you recognise it or not. Or whether you let it walk past you."

I didn't know what he was blethering on about, to be honest, but one day I might, perhaps. In the meantime, I gripped at the concept of fated love, only because it didn't require anything of me at all.

I took the book Angus had given me and went off for my own siesta and to think some more about Mission Kieran. How could I refuse to help? I had grown up seeing pictures of young Kieran, with his thick wavy hair, his hazel eyes, like mine. When I thought of the Taygetos mountains that we lived in the shadow of, I felt overwhelmed. If Kieran had made it up there, how terrifying the last days or weeks of his life must have been. He was just 25. I had probably not given enough thought over the years to Kieran's disappearance. It was so long ago, and it happened overseas. But to be here now with the possibility, slim though it was, of finding his final resting place would be immense. It would give everyone closure.

8

Ascent to Platanos

On the mountain road, the small four-wheel drive slithered and bumped over heavy scree, spitting stones out behind the vehicle. To the left was a craggy rock wall, to the right a sheer drop to a wooded gorge below, with no guard rail. Beyond that, the Messinian gulf sparkled and winked in the bright morning sun. I began to wish I was swimming in it, instead of being half-way up a mountain with a man suffering from dodgy arteries and probably delusions as well. Angus slowed the vehicle over the bumps, inching forward until we were away from the rock shower. I could see sweat beading on his forehead and I asked if he was okay.

"I will be when we get past this feckin' bit of road. There was a storm up here in the summer, and it obviously loosened some of the earth banks. It looks like no-one has bothered to clear the road."

The journey had started well after we picked up the four-wheel early from Kalamata. The weather was hot but not unbearable, the sky an indelible blue with a long scattering of fluffy clouds, as if they'd been rolled out like dice. It promised to be a good day, until we started to ascend the western flank of the Taygetos mountains, leading to Platanos. The hairpin bends were stacking up against us and occasionally a roadside shrine clung to the edge in honour of some poor devil who'd perished.

Finally, the tarmac road became a dirt track, winding deeper into the mountains. Angus was silent with concentration. He looked like he was ready for a rock concert rather than an ascent on Everest, dressed in a black T-shirt and jeans, denim jacket and baseball cap with *Ellada* (Greece) written across the front, his ponytail hanging out of the cut-out in the back. He was wearing an old pair of black Ray-Bans.

After one last bend, we reached a high plateau, where the road straightened out. The land was rocky, scrubby, with flowering bushes. We passed a battered metal sign for Platanos, but the village wasn't in sight yet. There was a small fresh water spring at the side of the road, with a tap dripping into a marble bowl. We got out to stretch our legs. Angus filled his water bottle and splashed his face. It was pleasant in the sun and the air was fragrant and cool.

It felt like old times, hillwalking in Scotland. Angus, Shona and I had done a lot of walking from our childhood, like Kieran. When Shona went to university, it was just Angus and me out tramping the hills around central Scotland. We took backpacks with food and water and often sheltered in small bothies when the weather was poor. When I went to university, I came home every few months and for holidays and we still walked, but much less as time passed. Perhaps Angus had started then to lose enthusiasm for his old pursuits, just as he lost the urge to teach.

Further along the road from the spring there were two ruined stone houses at the bottom of a long ridge covered in firs and oaks. The houses were set a fair way apart but were the only properties at this edge of the village. Behind them and between were fenced animal enclosures, now empty and given over to wild fruit trees and weeds. Finally, we arrived at the village itself, built from the bottom edge of the same ridge. The road cut through the top end of the village, with most of it built to the right, where the land flattened out over a fertile plateau. The houses were solid stone constructions, with thick outer walls and protected courtyards to withstand the perishing mountain winters. Many were now wrecks, their roofs fallen in, the walls like skeletal remains sinking into the ground. Occasionally, in the midst of ruin was a renovated house, with neat repointed stone and pitched roofs, wooden balconies with planter pots and new shutters, firmly closed.

The village was fairly large but, squatting in the shadow of the Taygetos peaks, it seemed like nothing more than a small eruption of human endeavour. The peaks towered ahead like sentries. The highest, Profitis Ilias, which Angus told me was more than 7,000ft high and snow-capped in winter, was now a bare, geometric shape, as if the Egyptians had colonised the Peloponnese once and dragged blocks of stone here to create a pyramid. Other peaks ranged behind it, one after another, with sharp precipitous flanks, way into the distance towards the end of the peninsula, where they would finally peter out in desolate fields of spiky cactus, which characterised the *Mesa Mani*, the Deep Mani.

Angus told me that among the various explanations for the name 'Mani', some academics suggested it came from the female adjective of the word *manos*, meaning dry, treeless, waterless. It felt like we had reached the roof of the Mani here, and it would be hard to find a more remote place than this.

Angus parked on the road where another, larger, spring water outlet was set into a long arc of stone, with several taps over stone troughs. Perhaps animals came to drink here, or villagers congregated to do a weekly wash. The area had been richly served with water and much of the land seemed fertile, promising self-sufficiency in past years. Across the road was a sign pointing down a cobbled pathway to the *plateia*. Several houses bordered the path and at one crumbling wreck we saw an old couple sitting on a stone banquette chiselled into an outer wall, warmed by the sun. They were thin and hunched together, dressed in amorphous sun-faded black attire, the woman's head swathed in a black scarf. They resembled two bundles of rags left out in the sun for an airing, only their eyes glistened, alert to this intrusion.

Angus said good morning. They nodded, nothing more.

"There probably aren't many people here now. I've heard some of the old places have been done up by the families of the original owners, ones who left for Kalamata and Athens. They're used as holiday homes now, but only in the summer. I think only a recluse would want to live this far up," said Angus.

We arrived at the *plateia*, with a monumental plane tree in the centre. Angus explained that the Greek for plane tree was *platanos*, which accounted for the name of the village, and had nothing to do with the philosopher Plato. On the *plateia* were the remains of an old taverna and a *kafeneio*, with a poster on the front window for a musical evening five years earlier. The wide front windows offered a clear view inside, a glimpse into another era, the walls covered in old photos. A wood-burning stove sat in the middle of the room and rush-bottomed chairs and metal tables were set out, as if waiting for the regulars. I could even see items on the dusty counter: a metal box, pens, a few stubby wine glasses, an empty ouzo bottle. It was as if the owners had finished for the day, locked up and never came back.

The *plateia* was cool and quiet, with wooden benches set under the shady branches of the tree. At the southern end, over the roofs of houses, the dome of a large church peeked out, and beyond that the outline of the mountains. The place was deserted, but just as we decided to walk back to the car, the sound of a door creaking made us jump. We turned around to see a man at the wooden doorway of an old shop. The sign above it said *pantopoleio*, general store, written in a folky script, with the faded painting of a loaf of bread and a carafe of wine. It was perhaps the only store for miles around. The man was middle-aged, with a long, tired face and strangely pale blue eyes, not unlike Myrto's. Perhaps a mountain attribute. He wore a suit that seemed a few sizes too large. Angus spoke to him briefly, and I could tell from the man's responses he had a difficult rural accent.

"He's asking us if we'd like to come in to his shop. He can make us some coffee."

We trailed in after him. The shelves were stacked with rows and piles of dusty produce: tins and plastic packets, bunches of desiccated herbs, hessian bags filled with beans and lentils. It sucked the air out of the place and left you feeling slightly light-headed. At the far end of the shop was a scored wooden counter with an ancient cash register that probably didn't work. I couldn't imagine anyone bothering to ask for receipts in this place. The man, who introduced himself as Pavlos, ducked through a curtain to a back room to make coffee, bringing it out on a metal tray in small cups, with tall glasses of water. I really would have to learn to like Greek coffee.

He sat on the other side of the counter. He didn't drink anything himself, but puffed on a cigarette, blowing lazy smoke rings towards a stained wooden ceiling. He and Angus talked for a while and my eyes wandered around the wall behind Pavlos. The space that had once been white was yellowing and was decorated with an interesting montage of church circulars, posters, handwritten notes, bills – all stuck in chaotic order – and a calendar with a saint's picture above the month. The month showed May. There were black and white photos of villagers as well, mostly group shots, and the effect of the wall was a kind of rural storyboard depicting the final years of village life before extinction.

Angus turned to me. "Pavlos says this shop was built in the late 1800s. His family took it over in the 1950s. It used to provide goods for the whole village and, with the *kafeneio* and taverna, was the real hub of Platanos. Now it only opens on certain days in summer. In the winter there are only about eight full-time residents left, though the number swells to around 60 in summer, when people come back to their holiday homes, including foreigners."

"Do they shop here?" I asked, casting an eye around the creaking shelves.

"No, they get in their four-wheels and go down to the nearest town, which is Kambos, to do their weekly shop, or to Kalamata. As the old Greeks die, the village is slowly dying as well. In a year or so he says he may have to shut the place for good. It's the usual story with these villages."

Angus continued his chat with the man for a while and when the conversation reached a lull, Pavlos sat back heavily in his chair, giving us a strange, inquisitive look.

"You seem to be getting a lot of information there," I said, feeling hopeful.

Angus looked drained. "I'm starting to struggle a bit with his dialect though. It's a hard job trying to make sense of things. I could do with a translator. I've just asked him whether he's ever heard about any British soldiers hiding out here in the war. He says as a kid he remembered hearing stories from the villagers about a few allies trekking through the mountains, but he doesn't know whether they stopped here or not, or if anyone in the village helped them. Well, I didn't think we'd be that lucky, first off. He says there is no-one living here now who was more than a kid during the war, like the old couple we passed, even though they looked 100," he said with a wink. "There were a few old-timers in their 90s, until recently, but they have all gone to live in other locations with their families, or else they've died. He says many villagers have left in the past decades for Athens and for places like Australia and America. They rarely come back, or if they do, it's for a special reason, a saint's day."

"Did you mention Kieran?"

"Yes, briefly. He said he was sorry, that was all, and he was grateful to the allies, but it was a difficult time for everyone."

They spoke again briefly and Angus wrote his name and mobile number on a piece of paper, handing it to Pavlos.

"He's going to ask around a few village contacts and call me if he comes across anything useful."

"Call *your* mobile? The one you never answer?"

"Well, yes, that's the best I can do."

Before we left I asked if I could take pictures of his shop. I didn't think I would ever come across a place like this again. Pavlos shook our hands and wished us well. He leaned on the door frame of the shop, smoking, as we strolled back towards the main road. I had a strange feeling that he never stopped watching us until we were out of sight.

"Is he the only guy we can talk to today?" I asked.

"Looks like it, which is a pity," said Angus, sounding weary. "I don't know what it was, but I felt Pavlos was reticent to talk. Perhaps he knows more than he can say. I just wish my Greek was up to all this."

When we reached the car, Angus walked to the nearby spring outlet and splashed his face with the cool water, as if trying to ramp up his mood a bit.

"You're not feeling defeated already?" I asked.

He shook his head. "Not defeated, Bronte. I'm panicking. I wish I'd done all this years ago, when there were more people around here."

"You didn't have all those internet stories then, so you would never have thought to come up here."

"Aye, that's true, but I still have the feeling I've left it all a bit late."

We stood for a moment by the spring, enjoying the solitude of the place. A gentle breeze was twirling leaves around the empty space and bees and hornets were droning over the overflowing water troughs.

I had goaded Angus about feeling defeated already, but I felt the same just from the first impressions of Platanos. The closed houses and shops, the lack of people. It augured badly for the mission. We needed years, instead of weeks, to undertake it. And a bit later, the feeling would be heightened.

"Let's just drive on for a bit. It's grand just to look at this mountain scenery. We might as well get something out of the day after hiring this thing," said Angus.

The ridge that lay along the eastern edge of Platanos began to peter out and on a gentle rise that was partly cultivated we could see stone circles that Angus said were old threshing circles that had been used up to late last century, when the villagers grew wheat to make flour. We passed nothing else, apart from a few animal enclosures and sheds. Further on, past a copse of wild pear and almond trees, that seemed to grow in abundance here, we came to a dilapidated farm building with a battered flat-bed truck parked beside it. There was a fenced field with goats tethered to trees and a fierce-looking dog. Close by, we saw a man standing by a water trough. Angus stopped the car.

"This has to be the last guy standing today. Let's go and talk to him," he said, adjusting his baseball cap and smoothing his ponytail, as if grooming were at all required in this far-flung place. We picked our way down a narrow dirt track towards the farm. The man eyed us shrewdly, under a big straw hat. He wore a long plaid shirt, muddy down the front, and stout boots. Angus spoke to him for a while. The man looked ill at ease, glancing from one of us to the other. When he spoke he had a gravelly voice, like a low bark, as if he'd spent too much time out here on his own with farm animals. I didn't like the look of him at all.

Angus turned to me. "This guy is one of the few villagers who stays during the winter. He probably keeps his eye on things, with the help of that feral mutt over there," he said, flicking his gaze towards the slavering beast straining against its chain. "I've just asked him the same things I did with Pavlos, but I didn't say Kieran was my father. He doesn't know anything about allied soldiers. He was born just after the war. He's taking a philosophical approach, tells me to forget about the past, about the battle. 'What happened, happened.' Now there's the crisis to worry about. He tells me that trying to dig up the past will be useless and no good can come from it. Time to move on, he says, and I think he means that in a literal sense, as in 'push off'. Angus turned his back to the man and rolled his eyes. "Let's go then."

"So soon?"

"It's useless, pet. This man would rather grapple with razor wire than talk to us."

We headed back towards the car. When we got there we turned around to check out the farmer. He was still standing where we left him, staring at us hard. I felt I was acting in a low-budget spaghetti western.

On the road back to Kalamata, we didn't see another vehicle the whole way. At the bottom of the mountain road, the village of Ayios Yiorgos (Saint George) clustered round a tiny, scruffy square. There was a *kafeneio* and a taverna that were both unremarkable, yet Angus had a mind to eat lunch in the taverna, claiming he was famished from our mountain 'expedition'. I was, too, but I wasn't drawn to the taverna, with its greasy plate-glass frontage and the two grizzled villagers sitting outside at a wooden table. They watched our approach with the same suspect glances we'd witnessed in Platanos, as if we'd come to annexe their village.

The Maniots, as I had just read in one of Angus's travel books, were tough people who had a violent history, with warring clans in past centuries building tall stone towers clustered on hilltops to repel interlopers with land-grabs in mind. It was all very reminiscent of Scottish highland struggles, or Sicilian vendettas. Even the pugnacious Turks during four centuries of occupation had not managed to conquer the Mani, though there had been frequent incursions into the area. Suspicion of interlopers, it seems, was branded onto their genes. Metaphorically, some of them seemed to be still living in towers.

Angus noticed my lemony expression as we entered the taverna.

"I asked Pavlos about lunch places and he mentioned this taverna." It was a dubious recommendation, coming from a man whose *pantopoleio* was sadly nothing more than a folk museum now.

A sign on the door promised that no dish would cost more than four euros, and Angus laughingly called it 'the crisis café'. The inside space had a wood-fired stove and half-a-dozen tables and chairs. A middle-aged man with a bushy moustache came out of a doorway and seemed affable enough. Angus let him yammer away in his fractured English, probably too exhausted from all his Greek.

The guy ran through the whole menu verbally, from entrees to desserts – every last bean and lamb chop –

which was amusing as I couldn't imagine he could rustle up half of what was on this extensive 'menu'. He was having a laugh perhaps. He ushered us through a side door to an outside terrace, which was more pleasant. It was shaded by a grapevine now bereft of grapes. It looked out towards the wooded bluff of the mountainside, where a few goats were scrambling about. Two Greek men sat in one corner of the terrace, eating and smoking.

We took a table in the opposite corner. I can't say my appetite was sparked by the place, especially when I slipped off to the toilet and found a mingin' space buzzing with fat flies, and no soap at the basin. Angus must have noted my sickly expression when I returned and tapped the back of my hand. "Don't worry, pet. Lots of rural tavernas look like this and they're absolutely fine," he said, with raw confidence.

Angus had ordered and when the meal arrived it was surprisingly tasty: pieces of oven-roasted chicken with peppers, chips perfectly fried, and a mountainous Greek salad. We shared a carafe of white wine.

"See, it's not so bad here, is it?" said Angus, giving me a shrewd look and quaffing his wine.

"No, not bad at all," I said, swirling my bread through the olive oil in the salad, having forgotten my recent funk over oil lakes. "Anyway, how do you think we did today, up there?"

He shrugged. "Och, I don't know. It's a bit like being an archaeologist, isn't it? You assume there's something to be found, but it's a case of knowing where to start digging. We're going to need more help to track down info. I've always found Kalamata Library to be helpful but in the past I've only researched the war, and not mountain villages. Maybe I've missed things. Time to go back, I think."

"Didn't you say you'd talk to Myrto and Leonidas?"

His face looked sour. "After my experience today, I worry that maybe everyone from Marathousa will feel the same as they do in Platanos. No-one will want to dig up the past. Myrto can be thorny. Maybe you can pick Leo's brains."

"Me?"

"Why not, pet? You're more charming than me."

"Well, that's a no-brainer, isn't it? And you're calling me 'pet' again." I wondered if the moniker wasn't just a tiny act of defiance on his part.

"Sorry. I keep forgetting," he said, summoning the owner for the bill. He wandered over to the table and scrawled the amount on the paper tablecloth. It was pretty cheap: nine euros. Angus only had a 20 euro note. The guy took it and pulled a wad of banknotes out of his pocket, peeling off a 10 euro note. Angus flicked me a look of surprise at the sight of all this cash. There was no offer of a receipt. It was easy to see why tax and VAT revenues in Greece were going down the pan.

"First time our village?" said the owner.

Angus nodded.

"You been up the top there to Platanos? What you think of village?"

"Not many people about these days."

"Nobody wants to live in mountains now. Always a hard life. And once there was no road, only the *kalderimi*."

"Where is the *kalderimi*?" asked Angus, his eyes sparkling with enthusiasm.

"If you drive back out the village and take the road to the right, just over the little bridge, you go maybe five, ten minutes, you come to very nice area with a church of Ayios Yiorgos. Not far from here you find sign for the *kalderimi*."

Angus noticed my puzzled expression and explained that the *kalderimi* was a great feat of rural engineering, a cobbled stone pathway, of which there were many in the Mani, connecting villages, and built to last. According to the taverna owner, this one was the longest in the region.

"You go up there one day," said the man, with a wink, "slowly maybe, 'cause you no young any more, eh? Take your lovely daughter. *Kalderimi* goes straight up mountainside to Platanos. Villagers once bring mules and donkeys down it for their fields in winter. Then back up again, spring," he said, waving his arm around to indicate the effort involved.

Angus was keen to see this *kalderimi* and wasted no time following the man's instructions to the signpost. We didn't need to walk to the start of the track, however. It was possible from the road to make out the stone outline of it as it zigzagged perilously in sharp angles all the way up the rockface, hundreds of feet high. Here and there the track and some of the stone walls that buttressed it were obscured behind fir trees and bushes, which meant that from a great distance, the construction would have been almost invisible to the naked eye. We later discovered the *kalderimi* had been built around 1900 over an existing, rough donkey track. It was the only year-round access route for people and livestock before the modern road was built.

"This is great, Bronte. Remember in Thomas's account of the escape down the Mani when the local Greek told the soldiers there was a track leading up to the mountains? This *kalderimi* is definitely *that* track since it does go up to Platanos, as we've just been told. This would have been the easiest, quickest route to it. This means it was definitely possible for soldiers to have walked from the coast all the way to the mountains. But a long slog, I admit."

He gazed up at the track with a curious longing. "I'd dearly love to ascend this *kalderimi* one day, Bronte."

"Well, you can if someone adds in a Stairmaster, or you can ping yourself onto Myrto's donkey." I couldn't think which feat would prove harder.

We set off on the drive home, feeling slightly more uplifted. The discovery of the *kalderimi* was probably our only success in the whole day.

The Zefiros *kafeneio* in the early evening had its usual vibrancy. There were a few tables occupied inside, with Greek men playing a board game and watching TV. There were some Greek families outside, and one rowdy table of expats enjoying a few carafes of wine.

I sat outside so I could watch everyone easily while I checked my emails and enjoyed the cool breeze that snaked its way up from the gulf, carrying salty, herby aromas. It toyed with the plane tree above, making a pleasant susurrus through the leaves. I supposed that many Greek villages nestled under plane trees but it was ironic that this village had a plane tree in its *plateia* as well, as if it really were a sister village to Platanos, yet in no other way did it resemble the outpost we'd seen today.

Elpida saw me and came straight over. I only wanted an instant coffee but she brought me some cake she'd made that day. I wasn't hungry after lunch at the Crisis Café, but the cake was good, not too sweet.

"Rivani," she said, "Everybody likes my rivani, Bronte." She sat down at the table, as was her habit.

"How is Angus today?"

"He's good. Gone out to see friends tonight."

"And today, where you go today?"

I wondered if she'd somehow seen us driving off in the morning.

"Just some sightseeing."

"Where you go?"

"We were in …"

I was about to say Platanos, but then I thought it wasn't a good idea to let everyone know yet that we were digging up family history in the mountains. And telling Elpida was the same as getting one of those village hawkers to give it a blast on their loudspeaker.

"We were driving along the coast road."

"Ah, nice. Seeing the sights with your father? And what he does other days?"

"Em …. he reads a lot."

She laughed. "Reading? Once, no reading. Once, he used to come up here every weekend from where he lived on the coast. We had music. Bouzouki. Lots of dance. He liked a party. Sometimes he played his guitar and sometimes just a little bouzouki, for fun, after a few glasses of ouzo," she said, with a vibrant smile showing her small teeth. She looked like a terrier who'd just dug up an old bone.

"He played here? Really?" I already knew he had a bouzouki but actually playing it here stirred my imagination. I had a strange image of Angus with his ponytail, playing and singing in Greek.

"Your father is what we call *leventis*. Means brave, bold man. We Greeks like this kind of man."

Okay. Whatever! I thought. It was funny how the Greek view of Angus didn't quite chime with mine. But I was learning something new every day.

"Where is your husband, Elpida?" I asked, realising I had never seen him, only one of her younger sons, who helped out in the *kafeneio* when he wasn't at school.

"He works in Kalamata in a taverna in summer. Times are tough. He earns more money there than here, in the crisis," she said, making that gesture of rubbing her thumb and forefinger together.

"So you're the boss here?"

She slapped me affectionately on the back. "You got it right, Bronte. And I am tough," she winked. "Don't forget the celebration on Sunday. You tell Angus to leave his books and come, okay?"

"The foreigners, will they come?" I asked, glancing towards the table of expats.

She grimaced. "One or two maybe," she said softly. "The *xenoi*, foreigners, don't like our celebrations so much. Don't like the church service. Standing for hours and kissing the icons. But they like the roast goat. And the wine, Bronte." She laughed heartily, her ample chest bouncing up and down. I could tell she was itching to reveal a lot more about the foreigners but wouldn't because, after all, the expats were loyal clientele. I had no doubt she knew a lot too. If ever I wanted to write an exposé of expats in the region she would be my go-to woman.

"Everybody comes to this celebration from village. And even Doctor Leonidas comes too," she said with another wink. My face flushed and I wished she hadn't seen that. She gave me a long, analytical stare. It felt like emotional dermabrasion. Then she was on her feet again, a genial smile, bustling away to another table.

It wasn't quite what she thought it was with the mention of the doctor. It was merely that her questing, gossipy nature made nearly every subject a minefield. Yet, since I was tasked with grilling Leonidas about Platanos during the war, his appearance on Sunday would be most fortuitous.

9

Crosses to bear

The chanting reached us through the trees from over a hill in the still morning air. It blended seamlessly with the environment, sounding ancient, assured, as if it had been conceived at the dawn of time. As we drew closer, the chanting began to mix with the mortal sounds of people chattering, kids scrambling about, chairs scraping on hard surfaces, the chink of crockery, and the divine aroma of roasting meat and incense. The air seemed to fizz with joyful expectation.

Once we crested the hill, the church came into view, a small white building with a backdrop of the Taygetos mountains in the distance. It would have been hard to find a more extraordinary position for a chapel, hidden in the hills behind Marathousa. It had a small forecourt, where rows of chairs were set out for those who couldn't find a space inside. To the right of the church was an orchard circled by olive trees. To the left was the new *fournos*, a solid brick oven with a chimney puffing a ribbon of dark smoke into the air. A young man wearing a stout apron and holding a pair of kitchen tongs stood guard at the *fournos,* holding court with several tables of men nearby, their religious observations having been attended to earlier perhaps.

Other men were huddled under a tall olive tree, smoking and talking quietly. There was obviously a protocol here that everyone understood, yet underlying the church ritual and the social imperatives there was a seam of unstructured movement: villagers walking in and out of the church, gossiping, fidgeting, yawning vibrantly. It should have been contradictory and distracting but it wasn't; the ritual and the chaos seemed to co-exist very well. And maybe that was uniquely Greek. I couldn't tell.

I could see Elpida sitting on one of the chairs outside. She waved and patted an empty seat beside her, but before I could make my way there, Myrto scooped me away by the arm. She looked rather handsome in her Sunday clothes: a black dress, gold jewellery, a black bag hooked over her arm. Her hair was swept into a knot at the back of her head, pinned with a tortoiseshell clip. She wore a little make-up. She looked nothing like the woman I had seen the other day in her farm compound.

"You come with me, Bronte. We will squeeze inside and later get a blessing. It is the day we honour the holy cross of Jesus."

She directed me towards the door of the church, while Angus kissed the icon outside, waved at me and made his way towards the men under the olive tree. Myrto propelled me into the church, using an elbow to skilfully divide the crowd in the central aisle, as if it were made of butter. We slithered further in. I could see the *papas* over the heads of the villagers in a bright gold and red robe, swinging a censer, the clouds of aromatic incense rolling over us and up towards the dome of the church. There were rows of men to the right, women to the left, in an antiquated nod to Byzantine ritual no doubt.

Myrto stopped for a moment at an icon on a wooden stand, decorated with a garland of flowers. She kissed it and urged me to do the same. It was an icon of Christ on the cross. I bent low over the glass front and noticed the imprints of many kisses, the odd smear of lipstick, and the neat freak inside me decided to air-kiss it instead, which I did with a gusty gesture, like an overawed Oscar winner.

Myrto spied two old women about to vacate their chairs and somehow, with practised ease, managed to shoehorn them out of the way while grabbing the chairs for us. I was glad to sit down, away from the crush of people. Along the wall of the church sat very old women in high wooden seats. They were impassive, thin as coat hangers, in black clothes. They had a timeless patience about them, having survived many such long services, many trials as well in their lives. The ancient Greeks invented the concept of stoicism, and centuries later it was still being sired in the deepest corners of the Orthodox Church.

The service was interminable. After a while, the drone of chanting and the clouds of incense made me sleepy. I was close to dozing when the sight of a well-dressed man in a dark suit with lustrous black curls, gleaming under the chandelier, snapped me out of it. Leonidas cut an impressive figure in a crowded church and everyone turned to look. Like Angus had said, he was almost a minor deity, but adoration seemed to glance off him as he made his way to a seat in the men's section, given up for him by a younger worshipper.

At the end of the service, everyone lined up in the aisle to receive a blessing from the *papas*, standing at the front of the church. Myrto again grabbed my arm and pulled me into the aisle. Out of the corner of my eye I could see Leonidas leaving his seat. He offered a regal nod in my direction and that twitch of a smile, as if my presence as a foreigner had been logged and approved.

Myrto directed me to where the *papas* was thrusting a large silver cross towards each worshipper's face for a pious kiss and then pelting them in a strange manner with a large bunch of greenery doused in holy water.

An arc of water strafed my face, bringing with it the sweet smell of basil, and I had no defence against the cross colliding with my lips, as it had with dozens of others. At the moment when I should have felt blessed I was counting up how many viruses I'd just come in contact with, and if I'd survive without a cold — or something worse.

Out in the sunshine, Myrto was still holding my arm as I mopped basil water from my face. She was fussing over where to sit, checking out the rows of tables, with rising panic in her eyes, as people sprinted out of church, corralling their family members and making a dash for tables in shady positions, as if this was some new and exotic version of musical chairs. I had no idea a *yiorti*, church celebration, was going to be this entertaining and slightly crazy. Elpida also appeared at my side and took hold of my other arm, insisting I sit at her table with her family and friends since it was she who had first told me about the celebration. I felt like the new girl at school in danger of being pulled in two as the women fought over me. In the end, Myrto dropped my arm and sprinted off to commandeer a table under an olive tree, waving me over when she got there, shouting my name vibrantly.

"So sorry, but I'm sitting with Myrto. She asked me before," I explained to Elpida, tipping my head towards Myrto's table.

Elpida looked peeved. "Oh. But you must come and talk to me later, before you go. You must not spend all the time with *xenoi*." She patted my shoulder and strode towards her own table. I already knew that *xenoi* meant foreigners and wondered if she considered Myrto a foreigner because of her years in Australia and her independent rural lifestyle. However, when I reached the table I discovered that Cynthia, the expat woman I'd met on my second day, was also there.

Cynthia was in a floral dress with her hair tied behind in a loose ponytail. She had too much make-up on for a rural knees-up, but apart from that, she seemed pleasant.

"*Chronia polla*, 'many years', as we say," she trilled loudly when I sat down, air-kissing me on both cheeks. Myrto sat on the other side of me and several other people filled the rest of the table, village Greeks, I imagined. I looked at my watch. It was only 10 o'clock and I felt exhausted already.

"Angus is over by the *fournos*, captured by his male friends," I told Myrto.

"Don' go over there, Bronte. They like to be alone, smoking and talking their politics, drinking wine. The women never go there. It reminds me of Aussie barbecue: men on one side, women on the other. Not just the Greeks, everybody. That's why the Greeks feel at home in Aussieland," she said, laughing heartily.

I could see Angus talking animatedly with his Greek buddies, waving his arms about, as if he'd known them all his life. If I'd taken a picture of that scene and sent it to Marcella, would she have trouble believing it was the man she had married? I didn't doubt it.

Soon after we sat down, food was ferried across from the oven – sizzling pieces of roasted goat on small metal trays, for each table, oven potatoes, bowls of salad, bread, and carafes of wine. I still wasn't sure about goat meat. This would be a first, but I was ravenous. Everyone tucked in with gusto because a village feast during the crisis must have been a rare treat. I tried a sliver of goat meat and found it quite delicious. When Myrto saw me smile with delight she forked more goat onto my plate from the metal platter.

"Eat up, Bronte, you never find nice boy if you skinny like a mountain rabbit," she said, causing others at the table to stop and stare. Even if they didn't understand, it was her cajoling manner that caught their interest. Cynthia giggled and I decided to ignore the wind-up, my head bent over my plate, enjoying the morning feast and the wine under the dappled shade of the olive trees. I felt gloriously relaxed all at once. There was an appealing simplicity about this gathering. Was that what Greeks were best at, I mused, deriving pleasure from good food, health and family? We could learn a lot from them, especially about family ties.

As I glanced around the dozens of tables, I noticed one set slightly apart from the others. It must have been the top table. The *papas* who took the service sat at the head of it. He looked young, with very black hair tied in a knot at the nape of his neck. He had changed back into his everyday black robe. He was laughing and others had joined in, including what seemed to be village elders, and close by, Leonidas too, facing in towards the rest of the other tables. He had his jacket off and his white shirt had the sleeves rolled up. He was wearing reflective sunglasses, tucking into the goat meat with relish and drinking wine.

Myrto and Cynthia were chattering in a lively fashion though I wasn't paying attention. I could sense, however, that Myrto had at some stage taken Cynthia under her wing, possibly when her husband died. After we had all eaten, several women at the table got up to leave, taking some of the leftovers with them in plastic bags, which earned them critical looks from some of the other matrons, though not from Myrto.

"No-one can resist roast goat, Bronte," whispered Myrto, tapping my arm. "And especially not in the crisis, eh? Not like the Aussie barbies, yes? I see many times – big lamb chops and steaks, big as plates, being thrown to the family dogs. Too much for everyone. Aussieland, eh? Land of plenty waste. But here in Greece, we make a face at people picking up food, not wanted, from the table. But okay out of the bins, eh? *Po, po, po!*" she said, waving her arm around and chuckling. "I go now, Bronte, just to see few of my village friends. I come back to you later, okay?" she said, rubbing my shoulder as she left.

"How are you enjoying your stay in Marathousa, Bronte?" asked Cynthia, topping up our glasses with wine.

"It's very pleasant, but there's a lot to see and not much time. I have just 10 days to go."

She looked surprised. "So short, oh my! What a pity."

"What made you come to Greece?" I asked her, falling into the occupational habit of the journalist in not being able to resist interviewing every person I met.

"Running away from life, Bronte, simple as that. Charles, my husband, and I had been both married before, you see. We met at work and left our respective partners for each other. We had one child each. They were independent by then, well, at university. We left them to get on with their lives and came to Greece to avoid all the guilt and anxiety, and judgemental relatives. That's the potted version. And we were very happy here, I must say."

"What about your kids? How did they take it?"

"They were miffed to start with, but then they started to come out regularly to see us. It was fine. The thing is, Bronte, the expats here are all very nice. They are fun, actually, but they are all running away from something: divorce, decrepit parents, rebellious kids, bankruptcy, something. We get washed up here and though it's very pleasant, as you can see, we end up not being able to leave."

It all echoed what Angus had told me on my second day.

"Why not?"

"It's complicated. The longer you stay away from Britain, the harder it is to go back. Some of the expats would rather walk over broken glass than go back. You should talk to them. You're a journalist, right? You will get some good stories, believe me. I can introduce you to all of them."

I groaned inwardly at the thought of spending my last week or so listening to expat escape stories, though I had no doubt they would be fascinating.

"Thanks, but I just don't have enough time left."

Cynthia gave me a sympathetic smile. "Let me know if you change your mind," she said, excusing herself and wandering off to speak to a few of her Greek friends. It seemed to be the custom here that as soon as the meal was over, there was much socialising between groups. I stayed alone, however, preferring to watch others. I looked towards the top table. The *papas* was still holding everyone's attention. Leonidas was not there. He was striding through the olive trees, straight towards my table. I took another gulp of wine and tried to look casual.

He pulled out Cynthia's chair. I caught an aroma of wine, something herby, the tang of lemon, like an aftershave. He gave off a charge of good health and energy. I felt rather self-conscious. I wasn't so ignorant of Greek ways that I couldn't imagine a lot of villagers turning their heads in our direction, wondering what Leonidas, the doctor/landlord, was doing with the lone foreigner. I sensed Elpida's eyes on us, tight like wing nuts.

"I am glad you could come, Bronte. Have you enjoyed our celebration?"

"Very much," I said, pushing my wine glass around the paper tablecloth. He took the nervy mannerism to be a call for more wine and poured me some from the carafe and some for himself, clinking his glass against mine.

"Good health!" he said. "And talking of that, I have spoken on Friday with Dr Protopsaltis, your father's cardiologist, and he expects the results back this week. His secretary will call you."

"I don't suppose anything will be conclusive yet."

"The doctor will have a better idea by now of some of your father's main risk factors, but he will need more tests, I imagine."

"I won't be here for the tests, unfortunately. I have to return in 10 days." Making that point now made me realise how quickly the time had gone already and nothing much had been achieved.

"You can't stay a bit longer?" he asked.

"Not really. The newspaper I work for doesn't usually like us taking more than two weeks at a time. And I've already twisted my boss's arm to get an extra week off."

He didn't say anything. He was rubbing the side of his chin with his left hand. I looked at the long fingers. They were elegant and on the little finger was an engraved gold signet ring. It looked classical and certainly expensive.

"But your father's health. It's more important, yes?" he said, his eyes darkening a moment, as if a cloud had crossed the sun. He was judging me, I felt.

"Than work, you mean?" He nodded. "Of course," I said, though it was only partially true. In the time Angus had been living his own merry life here, my career had come to have huge significance in my life. I wasn't going to jeopardise it now, but I couldn't share that with Leonidas. He wouldn't understand. But I added, "We have a more rigid work environment in Britain. And I have to work."

"I understand. My girlfriend, Phaedra, tells me her work life is very different in England. Many rules, I think."

"Does she like living in England?" I asked, just to shift the emphasis from myself.

He started to answer the question, about how she liked this and that, and hated other things and so on, and my eyes started to wander around the other tables. It's hard to listen to an attractive man talking about his girlfriend, even a man you have no real desire to snare. He must have finished talking about Phaedra. I turned towards him and realised that he had been asking me a question.

"Sorry, I didn't quite hear that."

"Why don't you ask your boss if you can extend your holiday? Tell him Angus's cardiologist has recommended you stay because your father needs you at present."

"Don't tempt me now, Leonidas," I said, as a kind of throwaway line.

"Are you easily tempted?" he said, after a heartbeat of silence. He stared at me, and in the depths of those big dark eyes I perceived a glimmer of mischief, augmented by one thick curl of hair bending over his right eyebrow. Yet again I marvelled at how, beneath the carapace of Greek propriety and medical blethering, there was a gremlin at work, or so I imagined. Each time, it took me by surprise.

"It depends ... what I'm being tempted by," I said, with a coquettish flap of my eyelashes that was wholly unintended and made me feel rather foolish, as if I'd been possessed by some yammering sprite of my own, emboldened by too much wine and goat meat. He smiled as if he'd just caught me out.

To hide my embarrassment, I changed the subject and decided it was time to mention Kieran. I told him briefly about Kieran's involvement in the Battle of Kalamata, and how he'd fled the city, and what Angus had discovered from his recent research: the slim possibility that Kieran and another soldier may have trekked from the coast to Platanos to avoid capture by the Germans. I told him we didn't know the outcome of his escape, but he was later officially listed as missing, presumed dead. He looked astonished by the time I'd finished the story.

"Your father has never told me this story. I had no idea your grandfather fought in the Battle of Kalamata. I am very sorry to hear that he lost his life fighting for us. And how curious ..." he said, trailing off, as if he'd lost his train of thought.

"Curious?"

"Yes, that he might have gone to Platanos, of all places. Amazing! My own family come from this village."

"Have you heard of British soldiers hiding out in Platanos? Perhaps some of your family may have spoken about it?"

He shook his head. "No ... I am afraid I have never heard about this. My family were simple farming people. My grandfather kept goats. In the sixties – before I was born – he moved the family down to Marathousa for good, as many people did, for a better life. Some of the more distant family members stayed on a while but now they have all gone. So, you see, our links with Platanos have been broken."

"It must have been a hard life in those days."

"Yes, it was. Before the family moved, they spent the summers in Platanos and came down in the winters, often with all their animals, for the olive harvest on my grandfather's land in Marathousa and went back up in the spring."

"They came down on the *kalderimi*, right?"

"Ah, you know that word now. And you've seen it?"

"Yes, we have, from the village of Ayios Yiorgos."

He nodded, but said nothing, his long, thin fingers folding and refolding a paper serviette, like a macramé experiment.

"I realise it's going to be difficult to find anything out. We need to talk to someone who is now old enough to have been there during the war as a kid at least. Or someone who knows something, anything," I said.

He pursed his lips. "The difficulty for you and your father is that many of the mountain people are shy talking about the past, and about life there. They had a difficult time, even before the war and the German occupation. And after the war we suffered the civil war in Greece, which was actually worse. Even if some of the villagers in Platanos could remember British allies escaping, they might not want to talk about it. Perhaps they also feel some guilt because, in the end, they couldn't help them. The Greeks put up a good fight against the Germans, but we were too small a force, so we were very relieved to see the allies here. We saw you as liberators. And then there was the catastrophe of many of you being left behind and killed or taken prisoner. Greeks felt bad about that."

"Perhaps if you can think of anyone from Platanos who might be able to help us, you can let us know."

"Of course, Bronte. I will ask my father, Gregorios. He lives in Kalamata now. But, to be honest, I don't think he will have any useful information." He shrugged and raked his hand through his hair, repositioning the errant curl.

"Thank you."

"By the way, where is Angus? Did he come with you?"

"Yes, he's over with the men by the oven."

He turned and looked for a moment and I could almost read what was going through his mind: Angus knocking back wine, having the sly cigarette, as if he had the arteries of a newborn baby. But at least he made no comment.

"I am afraid I must go now, Bronte," he said, looking towards the top table that was beginning to empty. He got up and shook my hand firmly, saying *"Chronia polla"*, many years. I watched him striding back to his friends and thought how much he improved on acquaintance; a few layers were peeling back just a little. But it was time to fetch Angus and head home, as the tables were being cleared up. I walked over to the table by the oven. He was having a laugh with the men but when he saw me he got up. He looked slightly sheepish but definitely tipsy, but no more than the others.

"Did you have a good meal, Bronte?"

I nodded. "I think I might leave now, but you stay if you're having a good time."

"Och, no. I better not. I'll only get blootered. I'd like to have a swim today. What about you?"

"I've been desperate for a swim. Let's go then."

We set off back to the house. He was in a good mood and I didn't want to tell him the blood test results were imminent or that Leonidas was no help with 'Mission Kieran'.

10

The wisdom of the coffee cup

The pebbled cove we picked was near the village of Paleohora, hidden from the main road, down a narrow track. In Paleohora, the area around the clifftop had been settled even in ancient times and Homer had referred to this region in the *Iliad* as Iri. There had also been a Byzantine fortress on the clifftop, which had since crumbled, but nevertheless the village had history − and in modern times. Angus believed that this was one of the small coves on this stretch of coastline where the allied soldiers had gathered in April 1941, looking for an escape boat. The notion that Kieran may have come to just such a place on his tramp south gave it extra poignancy, though the beauty of this shoreline must have meant little to desperate troops fleeing for their lives.

Kalamata sparkled in the distance at the head of the gulf, but back in 1941 it would have been ripped apart by air attacks, gunfire and chaos. To the right were the peaks of the Taygetos and the nearest, Mount Kalathio, towered over the eastern edge of the city, with the village of Ano Verga near the top. Some of the allies were said to have hidden out in this village for a time, but their fate would have been perilous, as the village was clearly visible from below and too close to the city. Platanos, on the other hand, was further south and much further back.

As I swam in the gulf, a fair way out from the shore, while Angus slept on the beach after his boozy lunch, I had the best view of the hinterland behind this stretch of coastline, and the mountains. While the olive groves all the way to Marathousa were visible, and some outlying hamlets, there was no trace of the high mountain villages. After a while I forgot about the past and just enjoyed the feeling of complete solitude, swimming in the cool, clear waters. I could get to like this aspect of my Greek sojourn. Even the sun on my skin felt good, in a way it never had before.

When I got back to the beach, Angus was sitting on his towel, dripping with water from a quick wake-up swim on the shoreline.

"Let's go and grab a coffee," he said, drying himself.

We got dressed, and walked around some rocks to an adjacent cove, where a *kafeneio* had a narrow patio beside the water covered with a bright awning. It was pleasant to sit at the edge and watch fish darting about below.

"I once caught an octopus here," he said. "Actually, 'caught' is the wrong word. It simply crawled out of the sea and attached itself to the seawall. A young one, I think. The owner here prised it off and cooked it up for lunch. It just shows you that even the shrewdest beast can lose its radar now and then and get marooned."

"Is that your allegory for the day, professor?"

He laughed. "I do miss teaching. You know I gave English lessons to Greeks after I arrived here. It was enjoyable. I was offered a job in one of the big *frontistiria* in Kalamata – a kind of tutorial college. But I turned it down. I preferred to freelance. I did a lot of olive harvesting too. There was always plenty of work if you wanted it. Different now, and the price of olive oil has dropped."

We sat for a moment without talking, while the waiter put our coffees on the table: a Greek one for Angus, of course, and instant for me.

"If I can say so, Bronte, you're looking much more relaxed." He gave me an appraising look. "When you first came, you looked so pale and rather stressed, if I can say that."

I shrugged. "Okay, you're probably never stressed because you lead a different kind of life to the rest of us."

He frowned. "Don't start now."

I didn't respond but I could never resist an opportunity to vent my bubbling frustrations on Angus.

"I spoke to Leonidas today. I told him all about Kieran and that we'd been up to Platanos, as I assumed you'd not got round to telling him," I said.

"Aye. To be honest, I haven't seen as much of Leonidas as you think."

"Anyway, he was shocked to hear about Kieran, but he wasn't hopeful we would find what we're looking for. You know something? I got the feeling he didn't want to talk about it, like the others we met. That's what we're up against."

Angus drank his coffee, then stopped and turned his cup upside down on the white saucer, tapping the bottom of it. I frowned, watching, as black liquid began to seep from the rim of the upturned cup.

"I've got less than 10 days to go, to help with Mission Kieran, and you're doing … whatever it is you're doing …." I said, waving my hand at the cup.

"I'm reading my fortune. Greeks read the future in the images the coffee grounds leave as they drip back down the sides of the cup," he said matter-of-factly. A few moments later, he turned the cup the right way up and peered inside, making small appreciative noises.

"See that," he said, shoving the cup in front of my face.

I peered inside. All I could see was a mess. "See what?"

"Look more closely."

"Don't be daft!"

"Go on, you might be surprised."

"Ach, give it to me then," I said, just to keep him quiet. I peered around the mess of coffee grounds. I could see a few shapes: a jagged mountain peak and, beside it, something resembling a tiny star, or perhaps a cross. Maybe. Or was it what I wanted to see?

"I see nothing," I told him.

"You're lying. You saw what I did, a mountain peak. I know you did."

I laughed. "No I didn't!"

He gave me a churlish look.

"Okay. I saw a mountain peak – and a cross."

His eyes lit up. "A cross too? Well that is a good omen, Bronte," he said, scanning the inside of the cup again for the thing he'd missed.

"I wish you'd be sensible now instead of carrying on like some wannabe mystic. Ten days to go, I told you. What do you think we'll achieve in that time?"

He didn't answer. He put the cup back and crossed his arms over his chest and stared out over the water. Despite my small strop about the time I had left in Greece, a certain resolve had already begun to creep into my head while I was swimming in the blue waters of the gulf earlier. It had been so relaxing that I had the urge to swim there again and again.

"This might surprise you, Angus, but given the task ahead of us, I have considered emailing the features editor to ask for an extension to my holiday, using your health as the excuse, of course."

"That's grand, Bronte. I think you're finally hooked on the hunt for Kieran." He rubbed his hands together.

"Somewhat, of course."

"And you're starting to like the place, I can tell. You're getting over your sunburn phobia and looking very healthy, my dear. And your food phobias, especially the foreign stuff. Don't frown ...!" He was enjoying himself now.

"Okay, leaving my phobias aside a minute, I might have asked for more time off in the beginning if you'd told me the truth about what you were doing here, about your quest to find Kieran."

"Sorry, you're quite right," he said, feigning some seriousness and rubbing his hands over his stubbly chin. "But we've been through that issue already. I didn't want to put you off."

"I'm not saying I'll get an extension. The features editor will go mad when I ask for more time off. I'm not looking forward to it, to be honest."

"Try it, and see what happens. Say I'm at death's door. Another three weeks or so would be really helpful."

I was actually thinking another week or so, but what the hell! The more I considered it, the more I liked the idea, for all kinds of reasons.

"Apart from the mission, it's nice having you here, Bronte. I know you think I haven't missed you, and Shona, over the years, but I have, believe me," he said, with a catch in his voice, the light-heartedness of a few moments ago swept aside.

"Then why didn't you come back, years ago? Why maroon yourself here?"

"I don't feel marooned."

"I know I've asked you this before, but was your odyssey all about Kieran really? Tell me, please!"

He hesitated a while before he spoke. "No, not all about Kieran ... I don't think so, not in the beginning, anyway. Marcella and I hadn't really been close for years. I think you all knew that, even if we never actually talked about it. I was bored, jaded. I just wanted to do something mad before I got too old."

"And it just happened to be Greece?"

"Where else would I go? I'd been here a few times when I was a student, as you know, trying to get some notion at least of the place where Kieran had perished. Later on, it was the obvious place to come for a long adventure and, yes, while here I did do some research, to no avail, of course. We've been through all this." He gave me an exasperated look. "Once I'd been here a few years though, I liked it, and what did I have to go back to? And now Marcella's remarried."

"Can you blame her?"

"No, I guess not."

"I don't know, it all sounds a bit vague. Why do I always feel like you're not telling me everything?"

"I am! Sometimes there isn't a neat reason why people do things. That's what you want as a journo, isn't it? You ask a question and I give you a good sound-bite and you're happy. Real life isn't quite so tidy. I don't know why I left really. What was going through my head then. I can't put it all into words. I don't even know if I want to. But maybe one day I will, then I'll tell you. But it doesn't mean I didn't miss you."

In a way it would have been easier if it really had all been about finding Kieran. Even a grand obsession would have been better than the blethering on about world-weariness, and the suspicion that he just couldn't be bothered with his old life any more, or us.

"Cynthia in the village says that all the expats are running away from something," I said.

"And you want to know what I've run away from, right?"

I nodded.

"Okay, how's this for a sound-bite? Myself!" he said, folding his hands over his chest.

I laughed. "You can do better than that!"

He shrugged. "I'm serious! Myself. The person I was brought up to be. Maybe I didn't like that person much. Here, I've become the person I want to be."

"So you've reinvented yourself as a Greek?"

"If that's it, then I'm well pleased. The Greeks have the best attitude to life of any people I know."

"Are you happier here?"

"Happiness isn't part of the equation, but I want to be at peace somewhere along the line. Now I'm older, I think I will be ... once I solve the mystery of Kieran."

I shook my head. It always came back to Kieran in the end. I would get no further today. It would have to keep for another day.

"Let's pay up and head back," I said. "I'll go to the *kafeneio* tonight and email the features editor."

He tapped the back of my hand lightly. "Thanks, love. I appreciate it."

That afternoon I succumbed to a siesta, the aspect of Greek life I had adopted with relish. The shutters were half open and I lay on the bed and looked about me while I waited to drift off. The room had a strange familiarity already: simple, unadorned with the icon of Saint Dimitrios on the wooden chest of drawers. Joining it was a framed picture of Kieran that Angus had given me, perhaps to inspire our mountain quest. It had been taken a few years before the war beside a Scottish loch. He was sitting on a rock by the water's edge. He was laughing, his thick auburn hair blowing back from his face, showing a fine, chiselled forehead, one of the things that made him look so distinctive. He had smiling eyes and a cheeky grin. He was someone I would have wanted to know. He was someone the family hadn't talked about enough – but how could they? He had been less than a shadow in our lives, almost a fantasy. Until now.

Despite the fear that we would get nowhere with our mission, as each day passed, Kieran's 'shadow' grew form and depth. It was attaching itself slowly to my life, whether I liked it or not.

"Dear Crayton," I wrote, from my outside table at the *kafeneio*, sipping wine from a chilled carafe, for inspiration of course, because I was struggling, trying to get the right tone for the grovelling missive.

... *"I hear there are changes going on at the Alba, including the features department. Sorry to hear it. This email, therefore, won't be reaching you at a good time, but I am afraid I have to ask if I can please have another three weeks added to my leave. My father's health is less certain than I expected. He is suspected of having heart disease and needs to undergo tests, probably in Athens, in the next week or so, to confirm the extent of the problem. He may even have to return to the UK in the end. I don't know yet. The medical situation here is dire because of the economic crisis, I'm afraid, so it is all taking longer than expected to sort. Sorry if this is inconvenient for you. Please let me know if my request is possible.*

With all best wishes,

Bronte

That should do it, I thought. It sounded convincing, without too much hyperbole and grovelling, apart from the lie about the tests being lined up for the next week or so. But he'd be a heartless man if he refused. Crayton wasn't really, but the new editor was, by all accounts, and management in general. But I reasoned that if features were having a smaller role in the paper, then one less scribe for a few more weeks shouldn't be a problem.

11

Myrto's lament

The metal gate on Myrto's compound was unlocked, so I pushed it open and went inside, calling her as I did. She appeared through the olive trees, holding the end of a hosepipe.

"*Kalimera*, Bronte, good morning," she shouted as she aimed the hose into the deep feta tin that served as a water trough for Zeus. His ears flicked back and forth while she talked vibrantly to him in Greek.

I asked her how she was and she replied in her thick Aussie/Greek accent, "As we say in Aussieland, I'm flat out like a lizard drinking!"

I'd never heard this expression for being busy and it made me laugh, doubly so because it sounded so bizarre in Myrto's accent. She laughed as well, slapping her hand on her thigh. She finished with the hosing by placing her thumb on the end of the pipe and spraying Zeus lightly with water. I don't know if he loved it or loathed it but he brayed loudly several times and she mouthed a few obscenities at him, a routine that seemed perfectly normal to me now.

"Come with me, I make you coffee." She motioned with her hand towards her house. "Don' worry. I make good coffee, Bronte – not that mud stuff Angus makes." I wondered if Greeks did anything else apart from making coffee.

I followed her into the house. The first room was the kitchen, a plain space with a flagstone floor. There was a two-ring electric cooker set on a wooden counter top and a small primus stove beside it with one ring, which she called her *petrogazi,* for making Greek coffee. A tall, dark dresser took up almost one wall, stuffed with crockery. In the corner of the room was an open fireplace with a chain hanging from the inside edge of the chimney with a hook attached, a kind of old-fashioned set-up for cooking in a heavy pot. The last time I'd seen this contraption was in a crofting museum in the Western Isles of Scotland. She must have noticed my eyes darting around the room.

"Yeah, Bronte, look how Myrto lives in Greece, like a pioneer woman. If you saw my kitchen in Aussieland...." She whistled and waved her arm around. "Not like this one. And now no money to fix this shithole!"

She laboured over the *petrogazi.* I glanced through an open doorway into a big room, not unlike the open-plan sitting room in Angus's house, with the shutters closed and a heavy aura about it.

"My *papou*, my grandfather, he builds this house, Bronte, and comes down every winter to escape bladdy cold winters in Platanos, like everyone. He does his olive harvest and goes back in spring, and then one day he doesn't bother to go back. Too tired. Later dies and my father takes over the house. Then father dies and I inherit house and land as oldest child. Then my uncle Babis from Kalamata sets up my marriage with friend Fotis and later we go live in Aussieland. Easy story, eh? Glory be to God," she said, with not a little sarcasm. I loved the way that Myrto, when she was recounting a story, would tell it in the present tense, as if it had just happened. It was probably easier that way but it was one of her endearing foibles.

She put the coffee cups down on a small laminated table, where two rush-bottomed chairs were set.

"Tell me, Myrto, I heard you yesterday from my room. It seemed like someone was giving you a hard time," I said.

"Ach, that was Hector, my stepson. Hector, he likes to go ape-shit now and then with things."

I smiled, greatly amused by more of her Aussie expressions.

"About what?"

"Ach, it's like this. I inherit this house and land with trees from my father. Six hundred trees. Big land. But Hector, he owns half now. His father Fotis, not a good man. Not a good marriage. I already older than other girls when I marry. I isn't a looker. Know what I mean?"

I found that hard to believe, as Myrto had a strong, rather handsome face. Maybe that wasn't in fashion when she was young.

"Just when the family are thinking I will be spinster forever, I get landed with Fotis. He is married before and one son, Hector, who is then 21. When we marry, Fotis comes to live here with me, son stays in Kalamata. He works in taverna. Then Fotis wants to go to Aussieland, but son wants to stay in Greece. So, Fotis worries about the son now. Poor boy, no security for later and he makes me sign over half my land to Hector. Not this bit with the worm-eaten house and sheds. The other half, Bronte, with most of the olive trees and nice grazing for the goats. The best bit."

"Could he do that?"

She shrugged. "Men still the boss in Greece, Bronte. And you can do anything with solicitor and some money. I am not happy. This land is mine. Is in my blood. Family land. I argue with Fotis over the land. 'Let the boy wait,' I say. 'If you die first, later I leave the boy everything in my will. All his.' But he goes mad. He says if I don' do what he wants now he will kill me," she said, drawing a finger across her throat.

"No, surely not," I said.

"Yes, Bronte, I tell you the truth. He kills me if I make problems over it. My uncle Babis, he tells me not to come the raw prawn, as we say in Aussieland. I am old boiler when I am *nifi*, bride, so poor Fotis deserves something. So he wants land for Hector. But my uncle, he tries. He tells Fotis that Hector can have half land in his name, but he must never sell it while we all alive. It is an honourable agreement, cause we are all family now. If we come back to Greece, Fotis and Myrto are free to work the land and harvest the olives. If Fotis die, same for Myrto. Hector agrees. Not interested in olive trees then. So off we go to Aussieland. I think, what does it matter? I never coming back, I suppose."

"Why Australia?" I asked her.

"Fotis wants to go help his brother. He is builder, doing up old wrecks in Sydeneee. Pah!" She rubbed her thumb and forefinger together. "Lot of money in building, eh? Not for us. We never get rich in Aussieland, Bronte. Only the brother gets rich. But I do everything Fotis asks. I am always in wonder of him. Little village girl, and he is a guy from Kalamata. Man of the world, handsome, a bit. Shrewd. Always in a suit with his *komboloi*, his amber worry beads. But underneath he is *malakas*. You know that word? Very important word. Means w-a-n-k-e-r!" she said, with great emphasis.

I spluttered over my Greek coffee. She laughed loudly. I made a mental note to add it to my Greek vocabulary.

"What happened to Fotis?"

She put her palms together and rubbed them furiously, as if trying to rid them of something noxious. "He kaput in car accident in Sydenee, driving home one night," she said, jerking a thumb towards her open mouth to indicate he'd been drunk.

"I come back to Greece afterwards – eight years ago. Nothing to stay in Aussieland for. Again, Myrto's all alone.

Hector never comes around. He don' bother me. I go on with the olive harvest, hiring Albanians now and then to help. I make enough to live and with small pension. Hector sticks to deal, he doesn't bother about land, or never helps with harvest either. While we away in Aussieland all the trees go wild. It takes years to sort out. He never checks the house. It is full of mice and bugs when I get back. He is lazy *malakas*, like Fotis. Ach! These days Hector comes to his land just to fool around, shoot birds, dump old cars and junk. You can see it all there, up near the road."

I had seen it amongst the olive trees from the road out of the village. It was something I was getting used to here, the rural junk that lay around everywhere.

"What does Hector want now?"

"Everything changes with the crisis. Years ago, he buys small share in a taverna in Kalamata. It does okay, now with crisis, it struggles. He is broke. Now he wants to sell his piece of land. Forget family agreement. If he sells I lose most of income. There are only a few dozens of olive trees round the house. So Myrto up shit creek without that land. Nobody thinks Fotis is going to be kaput in accident. Nobody knows we are going to have crisis in Greece. Nobody plans."

"Would he do it? I mean, break that agreement?"

"Pah! Hector, like father, has no honour. And in the crisis, I see people selling family houses, land, doing many crazy things. We are desperate people now."

"What can you do?"

"Nothing."

"But you handed over your land under duress, surely? Under the threat of death, remember."

"No-one takes anyone to court in Greece. Too much red tape, too expensive, too many delays. Corruption. Simple people like me, we don' go to court in Greece with envelopes stuffed with money like the high noses," she said, streaming off in a torrent of Greek, of which I recognised not one word, apart from *gamoto*, the Japanese motor scooter word. She said it several times.

"I'm so sorry for you, Myrto."

"Ah, me too. Gives me big bladdy headache, Bronte."

"Do you have family who can talk to Hector, like your uncle?"

"He is old now, Bronte. I have only younger sister, who lives in Athens. She is not interested in olive trees and goats. Troubles of her own."

"What about the other men in the village? It's such a close community here. Can't they frighten Hector off?"

"Pah! You think anyone gets involved in my drama, my land? Everyone has troubles. No. Myrto is alone."

She shrugged her shoulders and pulled a face, her mouth a deep grimace. She took a blue spotted handkerchief from the top pocket of her shirt and wiped it over her face. I saw her wipe away a tear. I felt mortified.

"Someone will help, surely? What about Leonidas the doctor? He will be on your side. He won't want the land, so close to his, to be sold off to anyone, maybe to a foreigner, for a development."

She made a vibrant windmill gesture this time. "He don' care! He probably like all the land to be sold. He don' like my little farm, my goats, the smell. He likes his lovely villa there with view and everything around him to be just so." She grimaced.

"You don't get on with the doctor, do you?"

She twitched her eyebrows upwards – no comment.

"I can't explain more now. I say too many things already. But I see life different. Myrto is different. I move to Aussieland and have a new life. People talk more free. Like happy cockatoos. Everything out in the open. In this village, many people have secrets, and for everyone else, it becomes their job to find what it is, and then it's not secret any more."

Before I left I decided to tell Myrto a few secrets of my own, describing our trip to Platanos, and the disappearance of Kieran. She listened intently, with what seemed to be rising shock in her eyes.

"*Po, po, po,* Bronte! May your *papou,* your grandfather, rest in peace," she said, crossing herself and wiping her eyes again. "And you think your *papou* was hiding in our village during that war?"

"We don't know. It's a long shot, Myrto. We don't have much to go on."

"Angus never say this to me. Why not? This is amazing fact, Bronte." But her amazement quickly turned to concern. She leaned over to take my hand, examining my rings first, twisting them around, deep in thought.

"Bronte, my advice is to forget about it, and Platanos. It will be hard job to find out, like you say, and if you do, maybe it's not what you want to find."

"What do you mean? Do you know something?"

"No, no. How can I know anything. My family comes down from the mountains like Leonidas's and we don' know everything about life up there, only what the old folks tells us. Now there's nothing up there. If your *papou* hides up there, and dies there, you don' find nothing. Too long ago. You opening up worms, Bronte."

I smiled despite the gruesome aptness of the expression. "You mean opening up a can of worms."

"Yes, yes. I mean that. My English is stupid sometimes," she said, palm-slapping her forehead.

"No, it's very good Myrto, really. You must be exhausted from all your English today."

She ignored the comment and patted my hand. "You have nice holiday, go home and forget."

It wasn't what I wanted to hear, but after our day in Platanos, and my chat with Leonidas, it didn't surprise me.

"Ah, you look sad now, Bronte. Greece giving you the heartburn, eh? When I am in Sydenee, I cry every night for Marathousa. I cry for olive trees, and *yiortes,* and for Easter week, and *mizithra* goat cheese. I can't wait to come back after Fotis dies. Now I am in the village, I think how good life was in Aussieland. Now it is too late."

"Everything will work out, Myrto, You'll see."

I gave her a hug as I left. I liked her a lot. There was something solid and decent about her, and more than other villagers at least she had lived in another place, had gone to the edge of familiarity and back again. It gave her a kind of wisdom that I found appealing, even if it had an oddball spin on it.

When I got home, I found Angus sitting outside on the terrace, drinking beer and staring at his mobile phone, which was unusual. He looked up when I approached. "Just got a call from the heart consultant's secretary. They have the results now. I'll have to go and talk to him soon, apparently," he said.

"When do you want to go?"

"I'll arrange it for some time in the next few days. You can come with me and we'll hit the reference library as well. Get some more info on the mountain villages."

I told him about Hector. He frowned. "I never thought he'd sell the land. It's not really his. Everyone in the village knows the story of how Myrto was forced to sign the land over, but somehow I think they blame her and think she was bonkers to do it. Easy for them to say. Not easy when you're a lone woman in this macho society, even today."

I was glad Angus took Myrto's side, at least. What I didn't tell him was that Myrto had also advised us to leave Mission Kieran well alone. Its opponents were beginning to stack up. Was the mission doomed?

12

The custard muse

The reference library was an elegant, high ceilinged space in a public building on Aristome-nous Street. Its collection of books about Greece, and Kalamata in particular, was said to be one of the most unique in the country. Angus waited to talk to a young librarian at the information desk who spoke good English, though it was not the contact he had used here before, a fact that seemed to disappoint him. She found some books for him on the mountain villages of the Mani, with photographs, and brought them over to the table, where we sat side by side.

"If you have trouble understanding the Greek, ask me and I will help," she said.

"I doubt we'll find anything specific in these books about allied escapees, but you never know," he whispered. It was only 10am and I was certain we'd be here for hours, scouring these books.

We'd had an early start that day, arriving for a 8.30am appointment with Dr Protopsaltis. This time I went into the consultation with Angus for fear he might try to underplay his problems. Angus's blood test showed very high cholesterol that was a definite heart attack risk, along with high blood pressure. He was told yet again to give up smoking and to cut back on alcohol, and he had a script for several tablets to get things under control and protect his heart. The doctor wanted to see him in a couple of weeks.

"If you don't get all these things under control, you are walking a tightrope, my friend," he said, and we knew what that meant: that a heart attack could be imminent. Ideally, he thought that in the coming weeks, Angus should go to a private hospital in Athens − it was much quicker than the overtaxed public health system − and have an angiogram to see what was happening to his arteries because he suspected they would probably be narrowed in places.

Angus was not well pleased with any of it. "I'm cutting down on the bad stuff, more or less," he said peevishly, as we walked back to the *plateia* beside Aristomenous Street. "But I don't have time right now for tests in Athens. We've got to get a move on with Kieran."

On the way to the library, we stopped at a pharmacy for his medication. There were angry scenes inside the shop that day due to a shortage of some drugs, though thankfully not the ones Angus wanted. Some of those waiting were arguing loudly with the pharmacist. One woman was crying.

"What are they saying?" I asked.

Angus shook his head. "There's a woman here needing chemotherapy drugs, and there are none. Apparently, many patients are having to source their own chemo drugs because the oncology departments in many hospitals can't provide the treatment. People are dying here now of cancer because of lack of drugs. The EU has turned Greece into a third world country."

Angus's health prospects here suddenly seemed a lot grimmer. "Putting Kieran aside a moment, don't you think you'd be better off coming back to Scotland with me, soon, to sort out your health problem?"

"Och, that would be logical, wouldn't it, and maybe it will come to that," he said mournfully, "But I don't relish the idea of resettling in Scotland with winter on the way. And besides, I love it here."

"I know, but this country's falling to pieces."

"Och, let's not talk about dreich stuff now. I'll just end up feeling skunnered," he grizzled.

I smiled at the word 'skunnered'. It's an essential Scots word for being pissed-off and jaded big time, the way Scots are with their lot in life, their weather and their status as a small nation always having to fight its own corner. I imagined most Greeks were pretty skunnered as well, and it made me think, not for the first time, how alike the two nations were.

As we sat in the library, Angus nudged my arm. "Look at this, Bronte," he said, smoothing a page in one of the old reference books. "Pictures of Platanos."

Platanos in the late 19th century didn't look all that different, apart from the fact there were people in most of the village shots, which made me realise how much of a ghost village it was now. The villagers were mostly gathered in groups, sometimes dressed in stout farm clothes, sometimes in crumpled suits, and the women in black, as if they'd just been to a funeral. In one shot, there clearly had been a funeral. It was a bizarre photo of around 30 people in the forecourt of the big church, with a coffin balanced on a kind of trestle table, with the lid off and the outline of a black-clad woman inside, her thick hair springing up above the rim of the coffin.

Angus read out some of the information about the village, as much as he could glean with his Greek. The village had been in existence since the early 18th century as a farming outpost with some 25 families (a few hundred people) but its real attraction seems to have been its remoteness. The *kalderimi* track was not completed until the early 20th century, so previously it would have been a perilous journey for an interloper taking this route from below and in most respects the village was more or less cut off from the outside world.

During the 400-year Ottoman occupation of Greece, although the Turks never dominated the Mani, it was subjected to regular violent incursions, but the local groups of *kleftes*, bandits, who traditionally hid out in mountain villages, waged their own guerrilla-style war on the Turks. One band of *kleftes* were said to have hidden out in Platanos and finally settled there after the end of the Greek War of Independence in the early 19th century. Angus was disappointed that there was very little to glean about Platanos in the 20th century. Despite the completion of the *kalderimi*, the village remained something of a remote outpost.

When Angus returned the books to the main desk he explained to the librarian that he was keen to find some interesting snippets of information about the villages during the Second World War and the aftermath of the Battle of Kalamata.

"I don't think we have any more books to show you," she said. Angus turned and gave me a dismal look, as if we had just wasted a whole morning. But then she added, "I do know someone who might be able to help you. He was a university professor, now quite old, but I think he has an interest in the battle. He lives not far away. I have his number. Would you like me to call him?"

"Yes please," said Angus, looking more perky than he had all morning.

The librarian turned away to make the call. Angus whispered to me, "It's a strange thing about life, how timing can suddenly change in your favour. I've been here a few times over the years to find books about the battle and my usual contact was very good. I never spoke to this woman before but she was obviously the only one who thought to mention the professor."

After a few moments the librarian said, "I have called him. He is happy to see you, even this morning if you want to go. The only problem for him is he is not sure if his English is good enough for you. He does not use his English much any more. He is old and has not been in good health. I know you speak some Greek. Will you manage?"

Angus sighed. "My Greek isn't that fluent and I might struggle a bit. But I'll try, and thank you for your help."

"I hope you find what you want."

She gave Angus the name of the historian, Professor Adrianos Zografos, and his address, which was nearby, close to the Cathedral of the Ipapanti in the old sector, just below the ruined Frankish castle. As we left the library, Angus seemed to have a new spring in his step. He even got his mobile phone out.

"I'm calling a Greek woman I know in Kalamata. I think I'd like her to come with us and help with the Greek, in case the professor's English really is bad."

"A friend?"

"Yes, Bronte. Men and women can be friends, even here." He gave me a withering look and dialled a number already in the phone's contact list. So the mobile wasn't such an alien piece of equipment.

"Hi, Polly. It's Angus. How are you? I wanted to ask a favour. Are you busy right now? I need someone to come with me to talk to an old Greek guy. Remember I told you I was thinking of going up to the mountain villages, all to do with Kieran, my father? I've been on a trip with my daughter Bronte. ... Yes, that's right, she's over here at the moment. I'm trying to get somewhere with that research I was telling you about. .... Is that okay? Great!" He gave her the address and pinged the phone off.

"Polly? Didn't you say she was Greek?"

"Short for Polyxenia. I used to teach her English years ago when I was giving the lessons I told you about. It's a safer bet to take her along. I don't want to give this old guy a hard time with his English. And I don't want a struggle with Greek today."

It dawned on me that this must have been the Polly who gave him the Greek dictionary I found on Angus's bookcase.

"Polly's very nice to drop everything and meet you at a moment's notice."

"One of the things you have to learn about Greeks, Bronte, is that they are spontaneous ..." he said as we trailed along various streets in the direction of the old sector. I felt one of his mini lectures coming on. "... Greeks don't make arrangements for weeks ahead like we do. If you make an appointment like that to see a Greek socially, chances are they'll just forget. But if you ring someone and say, 'Let's have a coffee right now', they're up for it. They live in the moment. I wish the Brits were more like that."

So he had his little rave as we walked along about Brits and Greeks and how refreshing it was to live in a place where one was constantly surprised. Before long, we were in the old sector. First, we made a curious diversion to a cake shop. It was a traditional place, with faded family photos on one wall, and a huge glass-fronted display case filled with mouth-watering cakes.

"This is Skiadas. It's famous in Kalamata and does the best *galaktoboureko*. It's a kind of pie with crisp filo pastry on top and a thick custard layer inside." He licked his lips. "I might as well make an occasion of this and buy one."

"What about the diet, the lipids?"

"Oh fuck the lipids!" he said, raising his voice, just as an old guy, his shirt sleeves rolled up to the elbows, appeared from a back room, oblivious to these curses amongst the custards. Angus spoke to him in Greek and I could tell from their familiarity that this was a place Angus frequented. The old guy took one of the round confections Angus had described from the display, placed it in a box and tied it up with a great flourish of ribbons.

We finally reached the *plateia* called 23rd of March Square, where the opening shots of the War of Independence had been fired in 1821. Nearby was a street of two-storey buildings in an older style to the ubiquitous apartment blocks, with elegant wrought-iron balconies on the upper floors. A woman stood beside a blue front door. She waved when she saw us, offering a big, exuberant smile. Polly was, I guessed, in her late 50s but young-looking and shapely, with shoulder-length black, wavy hair, probably dyed, but expensively so. She had sunglasses pushed back on her head. She was wearing jeans and a long top, with a sweater tied over her shoulders. When Angus introduced us, she kissed me on both cheeks and I caught a whiff of something expensive.

"I see you've brought something very fattening with you," Polly said, eyeing up the cake box.

Angus laughed. "You know me."

She smiled, showing a set of very big white teeth.

Angus rang the professor's buzzer beside the blue door and it clicked open. While we were climbing the stairs to his first-floor flat, he suddenly appeared on the landing. A small man with thick grey hair and an infectious smile. He was wearing smart black trousers and a neatly pressed white shirt. He showed us in. The apartment had a sunny front sitting room with a balcony, from which you could see the dome of the cathedral. There were Greek rugs on the floor and old photos and maps on walls. It was every inch a Greek academic's home, with a comforting atmosphere.

143

Angus told the professor he had brought Polly along as translator because his Greek wasn't good enough. Although the professor claimed the same for his English, he was being excessively modest. His English was very good and only now and then did Polly have to help him out with a difficult explanation.

His eyes lit up at the sight of the *galaktoboureko* and he spirited the cake off to the nearby kitchen to cut it into fat slices, which we ate first, accompanied by tall glasses of lemonade.

"Thank you, *Kirie,*" he said to Angus. "How did you know this was my favourite. But it is everyone's favourite, is it not? My dear wife Dimitra, when she was alive, would buy this always for a special occasion. Many people you know have asked old Mr Skiadas for his family recipe but he won't say. It is *megalo mistiko*, a great secret," he said, chuckling. Then he turned to me. "This is the best *galaktoboureko* in Kalamata. Your father is very indulgent."

The room became silent as we ate the custardy confection. Angus devoured his slice with relish, as if this was the last lipid of his life. When he had finished I saw him wink at Polly and she smiled back, picking primly at her own slice. I didn't know what was sweeter at that moment: the confection or that look they exchanged. Once the empty plates had been transported back to the kitchen, Angus explained the reason for the visit: the story of Kieran's disappearance after the Battle of Kalamata, and how he may have fled to a high mountain village, like Platanos, for refuge. Adrianos listened quietly and when Angus had finished he shook his head sadly.

"First of all, I am very sorry for the loss of your father. It was a very great sacrifice that the British and all the allies made to help us in that terrible time. Many Greeks lost their lives too, of course, but that battle was a desperate thing. So many allies trapped here and unable to be taken away to safety. There have been some stories from Mani of villagers helping these allies, even under threat of being shot by the Germans. Mostly, they were in villages closer to the coast. But I must say there is so much that we still do not know about this time. Very little has been written about the battle. I am afraid also our public records department in Greece has been very poor at collecting documents pertaining to the whole of the war and the German occupation."

Angus nodded in agreement. "Do you believe that some British soldiers could have made it up to a village like Platanos?" he asked.

Adrianos shrugged lightly. "It is possible, I suppose. But I have not heard anything very specific on this, I am afraid, except for one story I heard many years ago. I was a professor of history at the University of Athens but I used to spend all my summers in Kalamata with my wife and children. We had a house near the sea then. My old family home. If I may digress ... I was just a boy during the war but I do remember the terrible Luftwaffe raids and how the Stukas would dive-bomb the city with their screaming sirens," he recalled with a shudder.

"So, on the summer holidays, I used to collect information about 1941 and the battle. I had the ambition of writing my own book on the subject, but I did not manage it. Life has a way of distracting one. I had four children to amuse during the holidays. But I remember one of my son Andreas's friends spending some days with us one year when they were teenagers. And the boy told me that his father was originally from one of the Taygetos villages, though not Platanos, I think. His father had said some soldiers, British, I think, had come to the village after the battle and had been helped by the Greeks. I think they stayed for many months. But what happened to them afterwards, I don't know. There are many stories from the war that now seem rather vague, after so many years, and difficult to prove. So, my friends, anything is possible. But I am afraid none of this is very helpful to you perhaps. I am sorry I have no more to share, about the villages at least," he said, looking at us with a mournful expression. Angus tugged on his ponytail and gave me a look of quiet frustration.

"Your task in finding out about your father," Adrianos said, looking at Angus, "will not be an easy one. There is still frustration over the past, and particularly over the civil war, when Greeks on the left and the right were killing each other, when the communists, who had fought to help free the country of the Germans, wanted to seize a greater role in post-war government. We have not forgotten these dark periods of our history. And now we have the crisis and Greeks once more feel occupied and pushed about. You are trying to uncover a shred of our history among so much."

"I agree. It's an impossible task and we may have to give it up. There may be nothing to find out now," said Angus.

"Do you think, *Kirie*," said Polly, who had looked pensive throughout the conversation, "that although most people in Platanos have moved away now to different places, or died, it is still possible to find some-one, anyone now, who may have been in this village at that time, or someone related who knows more?"

"You would be looking for someone quite old if they were there during the war," Adrianos said. Turning to Angus, he added, "But I sympathise with your cause, and the degree of your difficulty, and the fate of your brave father. I know a great many people in Kalamata, espe-cially the older ones, and a lot of the places where they still congregate: the *kafeneia,* and *ouzeries* where I used to go to drink in younger years." He smiled and his eyes glistened with memories. "So, at least I can make some enquiries for you. And we shall see." We all looked at each other and tacitly decided it was time to leave. He shook our hands warmly and said he would be in touch.

"Well, that was a very pleasant meeting with Adrianos, even though we didn't get any further with our research," said Angus as we stood on the pavement outside the professor's house.

"We can't expect too much, Angus, you know that. We're just chipping away at things. What else can we do?" I said.

I felt rather dispirited myself and again wondered at the wisdom of this mission, especially on a sunny day when we could have been swimming in the gulf. Polly had to rush away on another errand and suggested we all meet up for lunch one day.

"That would be lovely, Polly. I'm sorry if we wasted your morning," said Angus, kissing her goodbye.

"Not at all. It was interesting and so nice also to meet Bronte," she said, kissing me on both cheeks. "You are very pretty, my dear, and you have wonderful hair. Maybe you will be able to persuade your father to have his lovely hair cut a bit shorter, yes, without the pony's tail," she said, with a mischievous twinkle in her eyes.

It seemed a rather familiar thing for an ex-student to say and Angus must have noticed my surprised look. As we walked back to the street where the car was parked he said rather breezily, "Polly has a playful nature, as you can see."

"Is she married?"

"Divorced, but only lately. She has two daughters."

"So, an attractive and unattached woman. A good catch for an old guy?" I said, goading him a little.

"Don't even go there, Bronte. I'm not in the market for a relationship right now," he said, in a snippy voice.

"No, I don't suppose the old ticker's up to it," I said, relishing this kind of niggly banter that we increasingly fell into now, even though there was generally a darker undercurrent to it.

Once more I got the sense that I didn't really know my father at all. Sometimes I almost felt like I'd been in a coma for years and had woken up to find I had a father I didn't remember.

13

A poltergeist wind

The email from Crayton, which I read on my laptop in the Zefiros, was brief and a bit cool: *"Sorry to hear about your father's health problem. Bad time to ask for an extension on your holiday, as you said. I have discussed this with the editor. He was not well pleased, but has under the circumstances generously offered another three weeks. That's the best we can do. In return, we would like you to write an in-depth feature on the Greek crisis, include all facts and figures, talk to a range of people, get plenty of colour. Can it be ready before you leave Greece? With pics, of course."*

Another three weeks. That was beyond my expectations. Too generous for the Alba, even though it had been turned into an assignment rather than compassionate leave. Ho hum! Three weeks ago I wouldn't have cared either way, but now I felt a sense of relief that I had more time, now that we were hammering on with Mission Kieran.

I had nothing much planned for the day and thought I might talk Angus into driving down to the gulf for a swim. It was scorching weather for late September, with a hot, dry wind blowing.

Elpida arrived with a frappé and a slice of cake. "You look pleased today, Bronte. Good news?"

"My boss back in Scotland has just given me another three weeks off," I replied, beaming.

"Just like that?" she said, snapping her fingers. "Why you don't ask for more weeks before. Why now?"

Elpida was a shrewd birdie, there was no doubting it. I had not forgotten I wasn't to tell everyone in the village about Angus's heart issue and the research we were doing, although I felt I could trust Leonidas and Myrto. I hoped I was right on that score.

"Well, em … it's a kind of trade-off. I get more time here but I have to write a story about the Greek crisis."

She sat down at the table, waving her hand around, holding a fork in it for my cake.

"You need three months then, Bronte, to get whole story on crisis."

"Okay, tell me what you think. That will be an excellent start."

She put down the fork and I hoed into the cake. Then I reached into my bag and took out a notebook. Might as well make a start, and no-one could talk like Elpida when she was on a roll. She shared her thoughts about the crisis, about new taxes, VAT hikes, and how everything had gone quiet in her business, how Greeks were cutting back on celebratory meals and evenings out. August was the busy month in the village and the last chance of the year to make big money. This year the takings had been abysmal.

"If things get worse, Bronte, we will close. This *kafeneio* has been in my family for 30 years. We can't go on forever as we used to. But everyone suffers." She told me a story about one of her village friends, who lived in a small house with her sister. Both were unmarried. Previously, they had their mother there as well. Then she died. Now they had lost the help of the mother's pension and had nothing to live on.

Elpida held out her arms in disbelief. "What you think they do now? They have nothing. But their father had been good and left both small sums of money for when they marry. They have to use this now. They will never marry now. No-one will want them. Ach, *panayia mou*, holy mother!"

She pulled her chair in closer to the table so that I knew she was about to impart some fresh gossip.

"You know Leonidas, of course? I see you talk very nice with him at the *yiorti* at Saint Nektarios church, yes?" she said, narrowing her eyes at me.

"Yes, he was sociable," I replied.

"He has very nice Greek girlfriend in England."

"I know."

"Oh, so you know everything already. Good. So, he has girlfriend in England. She works as dentist. So now I hear that he too is planning to leave Greece to work as a doctor in England. Too ambitious to stay here in the crisis," she said, with certain disdain.

"I don't think he's made up his mind yet."

"Oh yes, he makes up his mind. He is going, yes," she said, most emphatically. "I move about the *kafeneio* and I hear everything, sooner or later," she added, with a wink.

I didn't doubt it. And what Elpida didn't know about village life wasn't worth knowing. But I sensed her impetus was more about mischief than anything approaching malevolence.

"You can't blame him, with all the problems in the health sector now," I offered.

"Yes, but his girlfriend Phaedra is beautiful too and her father has plenty money. He is doctor too, for children. He has nice villa in Koroni, on the other peninsula, and ..."

She was distracted by another customer and went off to serve them. I would have to wait until another day for the rest of it. I think I got her drift. But it was interesting that so far Leonidas had only ever said he wasn't sure about moving to England. Now he was going, apparently. Though whether it was for his career, or for the love of well-connected Phaedra, probably only Elpida would ever winkle it out. She would have made a great journalist, I mused.

I finished my coffee and sat for a while, feeling strangely fatigued. Elpida and I had talked for nearly an hour and I had made plenty of notes. More than ever I was longing for a swim. I decided to find Angus and see if he could drive us down to the cove. When Elpida came back to the table to pick up the money for the coffee she narrowed her eyes at me. *What now*, I thought.

"You looking tired, Bronte. You need siesta. Today we have the *sirokos* blowing, the hot African wind. Makes all people feel *treloi*, crazy, and tired. Me too. You go home, have a rest."

There was something about that day that I remember well. It was hot, but more than that, the air felt tight and there was a metallic taste in the air. I felt a migraine coming on, which I rarely ever experienced. Yet instead of the pain, I had an aura of coloured, dazzling lights that started in a tight circle at the centre of one eye, working towards the outer edge. I decided to go straight home. She was right. I needed a rest.

I found Angus in the kitchen, making lunch for himself. I told him about my extension on the holiday. He looked pleased, and gave me a hug. It made me wince.

"You look tired, Bronte. What's the matter? Maybe the thought of another three weeks with me doesn't entice you after all?"

I smiled. "It's not that. I'm pleased. But I've suddenly got a migraine. Funny lights in my eyes."

"Oh," he said, stepping back a little and looking at me. "You better lie down. It's the African wind. It stuffs you up completely."

It was three o'clock when I finally lay down on my bed with the shutters firmly closed. While the aura was slowly disappearing from my sight, I felt light-headed and quickly slipped into a deep sleep. I dreamt of Platanos, of walking through dry fields with the peaks of the Taygetos ahead of me. I passed an old stone house; walls, with the roof caved in, the floors inside collapsed into the basement and a smell of rank vegetation.

Under the lintel of the front doorway I saw a handsome old man, with thick grey hair and a beard, dressed in black. He walked from the house, through long grass, heading towards a distant field. Then he stopped and called to me by name, over and over. I ignored him. He beckoned me with an outstretched arm. The more I ignored him the more urgent his look, as if I were in danger. I had a notion that it was Kieran, as he might have been as an old man, but I wouldn't follow him. As I got to the doorway, the walls began to wobble and stones came loose, raining down on me. Still the old guy called me, over and over …

I woke up startled, with the sensation of not knowing if I was still asleep or awake, my name still ringing in my ears. Villa Anemos seemed to be moving as well, as if someone had picked it up and given it a good shake. The bed was rocking and as I lay, staring wide-eyed around me, I heard an eerie noise, like wind moaning through the house, as if it had been invaded by a poltergeist. Then it stopped and all was silent. A few moments later I heard a tapping noise and Angus's face appeared as he pushed the door open.

"Are you awake, pet?"

"Yes, come in."

He sat on the end of the bed. "We've had an earth tremor."

"Was that what it was? I thought it was part of a strange dream I was having." I didn't tell him I may have dreamt about Kieran as an old man – a disturbing vision of things that might have been.

"I couldn't sleep," Angus said. "I was in the study when it happened. We've had these tremors all through the summer. Some people say it's a good sign that the earth is kind of letting off steam. But I always think it's an indicator of worse to come. It's made a right mess of the bathroom."

"What do you mean?"

"The floor tiles have buckled. Half of them are broken. It's a bloody mess in there. I'll have to let Leonidas know. Don't get up if you're still tired. I'll tidy up in the bathroom. That's why you had the migraine. I always think you can sense when a tremor's on the way. It's odd, hard to explain."

On Saturday, Leonidas arrived in the morning with a tiler to look at the bathroom floor. We had cleared away the broken tiles, leaving a large space with the concrete exposed.

Leonidas was full of apologies. "I am sorry, my friends, you have to put up with this," he said.

"You can't be blamed for the earthquake, Leo," said Angus.

"Well yes, but those tiles were very old. But do not worry, Petros here will be able to fix this. He has plenty of tiles to match the old ones for now. Later on I will have the whole bathroom redone. It's time."

Angus shot me a look of irritation. I knew that he would rather have his ponytail cut off than put up with renovation faff.

"This job will take a few hours maybe and will be noisy and dusty. Are you both planning to go out for a while?" Leonidas asked.

"We are now," said Angus, but without rancour. He looked at me. "Do you want to go down to the beach for a swim, Bronte?"

The idea was very appealing. I had been tormenting myself over another swim, but before I could say anything, Leonidas butted in.

"You are both welcome to come to my house, if you like. You can swim in the pool. I am just there doing some little repairs. It's very quiet. Please be my guest. I feel very bad for your trouble here."

Angus shot me a look, and I could tell he didn't want to go, but didn't want to insult Leonidas. I didn't find the idea very appealing either, for all kinds of reasons, but I did like the idea of having a look at the villa close up.

"You go to Leo's house, Bronte, and you can interview him for your story," he said, flicking his eyebrows up provocatively. I ignored the gesture, but the idea of the interview was good, as I needed a lot more material for the feature.

"Do you have time for that, Leonidas?" I asked him.

"Of course, Bronte. But what story?"

I explained about my extra three weeks and the trade-off.

"Well done. More time to discover our region. And you can swim afterwards, if you like."

"Okay. I'll just get my things." I went to my room and collected my bag with the notebook inside and my camera. I brushed my hair and tidied myself up a bit, but not too much. However, I had no intention of swimming when the only costume I'd brought was an unflattering black one-piece, which was okay for swimming with your father in the sea, but not at Leonidas's house. I could do without that embarrassment. I would have to buy something more appropriate soon, if swimming invitations were to be a regular occurrence. When I was ready,

Leonidas walked ahead of me. At the front door I turned to wave to Angus and he winked at me.

"You are a wicked man," I said softly, shaking my finger at him. He just laughed.

A pathway at the side of Leonidas's house led to a stout wooden gate, which opened onto the lower back patio, where the pool was. It was quite a large pool, the water crystal clear and sparkling in the sun. There were very smart loungers beside it and a table with a large canvas umbrella spiked into the middle.

"We can sit here and talk. Can I offer you a drink – coffee, a frappé? I have a small studio with a kitchen down here. It won't take a minute."

"A frappé then, thanks."

A small studio as well? Very nice! I thought. The house was traditional in style, with thick stone walls that had obviously been repointed and smoothed. The old wooden shutters were pale blue. It was elegant. The floor above had a wide balcony, with a low stone wall around it. He returned with two frappés on a tray and mercifully no volcanic biscuits or pastries. Leonidas put up the umbrella over the table to cut the glare. It was pleasant here, with the same lovely view that we had, except that his gardens were lush with fruit trees and shrubs, and it had a more serene ambience, apart from the moments when Myrto's donkey started braying in the distance, followed by a barrage of loud Greek curses.

Leonidas rolled his eyes. "I cannot ever forget, Bronte, that I am in the middle of a Greek village when Myrto starts to fight with the donkey. And it has a temper to match hers. She used to ride him around the village, but one day he was in a very bad mood and stopped suddenly. She fell off and broke her wrist."

"Why does she keep it then?"

He shrugged comically, with his shoulders near his ears. It was a dismissive gesture. "Maybe it is for the company. And he carries things about for her. He is useful."

I mulled over what Myrto had told me: that Leonidas would probably be happier if she wasn't there. It did seem that way, or maybe there was a lot more to it. A journalist likes to see both sides. Currently, I could only see hers.

"So, what is this story about exactly?" he asked.

"I'm writing a piece for my newspaper about the Greek crisis. I wondered if you could talk me through some of the excellent points you raised recently in Kalamata about the ailing health system."

He was cautious at first, and insisted I didn't use his name in the article. He talked for quite a while, but not hurriedly, giving me time to keep up with my shorthand and drink my frappé. He gave me great information as he had before, but embellished it with even more details about drugs shortages, hospitals running out of money, people dying from common complaints because they couldn't access treatment quickly enough. It was all distressing stuff, but it would be good copy for Crayton. I had more than enough material and yet I wanted something a bit more personal, candid. I was thinking about what Elpida had recently told me.

"You told me once before that many Greek doctors are leaving now to take up jobs overseas. You implied you might be tempted to do the same. How do you feel about that now?" He was holding on to the handle of the frappé glass, twisting it around. He seemed uncomfortable.

"I admit it is very appealing, but I can't say for sure yet. It's a big step." He looked away.

What was wrong with this guy? Why so much dithering? I thought.

"You really can't decide whether to move to England? And with your girlfriend there as well?" I said, looking straight into his eyes. I hoped that might pin him down, finally.

He pushed the frappé glass away and lowered his voice, as if someone were within earshot. "Okay, I will tell you this, but it's strictly between us – please. As you will have found out already, in a Greek village even the trees have ears."

I smiled. Was it just Elpida's ears he was worried about?

"I have a plan to move to England with Phaedra. I have applied for a position in some medical centres in the south of the country. I am very sure I would get one of these, but it's not confirmed yet. Phaedra has gone first, as you know. She is settled now, I think. For me it would take longer. I have an ex-wife in Athens and a son. Apollo is just eight. I will not see so much of him if I go to England so, for this reason, I am wanting to be very sure about this move."

"I can see that would be a problem, with your son," I said, chewing the end of my pen and beginning to think that Elpida hadn't quite got the story right. Or perhaps he was just procrastinating for reasons only he seemed to grasp. "But if you don't go in the end, how will your girlfriend feel? What will she do?"

"I don't know," he said, daintily scraping his perfect top teeth over his bottom lip. "Perhaps she will want to come back, or perhaps she will choose England over me." His eyes flickered towards me, with a hint of dark confusion. *As if she would*, I thought, but I said nothing.

"Believe me, Bronte, no-one chooses to leave their homeland to work overseas if they can help it. But now in Greece, there are many people in a difficult position who leave to improve their lives, and sometimes leave a partner behind for a while."

"I understand, but few couples would want to live apart, as you are doing. Distance doesn't always make the heart grow fonder. I think sometimes it kills romance in the end," I said, goading him a bit to see what was behind his steely defences.

He gave a defiant lift of his chin. "Phaedra and I have a strong understanding. We come from similar backgrounds. We are well suited. In these difficult times, we know that we can't just let our hearts rule our heads."

He saw my eyes flicker with surprise, and quickly added, "Of course, I don't mean that quite as it sounds. We are very attracted, of course, and she is beautiful. But you see, when I married, I picked my wife mostly because of romantic notions. I was swept away by her. She was an actress, not well known then, and she was still living in Kalamata. We had a child and then suddenly she became more successful and was offered a TV role, based in Athens. That was not the main problem. It was closer than England at least," he said, smiling. "We had already grown apart very quickly because we were very different; wanted different things. I should have seen that but I just lost my head, as you say. This time, I wanted a steadier relationship. Even though Phaedra is miles away, we have stronger ties. Does that make sense to you?"

It didn't really. But I was intrigued. Leonidas may have been chasing a sensible blueprint of happiness, but the more I got to know him, the more I saw flashes of mischief beneath the common sense. The man who had teased me slightly at the village *yiorti* was not a man who would be a slave to marital templates. Perhaps he was just confused. After all, he had moved from a glamour goddess to a dentist. And what would Phaedra look like, I wondered? A beautiful but bespectacled swot in a white coat wielding a power drill instead of the latest fashion accessory? Again, he noticed my slightly unbelieving look.

"You don't agree?" he asked.

"Oh, I can't say anything about love and what works. I have had some disastrous relationships. I don't choose very wisely. Now I have become lazy. I leave it to fate to sort my love life, then nothing is demanded of me," I said, shrugging Greek-style.

He laughed. "I can't say I put so much faith in destiny. Life may be too short for that, but I hope it is kind to you at least, Bronte." He tipped his head to the side, as if he were trying to get the measure of a misguided patient. Yet I sensed he didn't want to pursue our chat about love any longer.

"Would you care to have your swim now? The water is warm enough, I think."

"I'm afraid I didn't bring my costume," I said, and quickly changed the subject. "Have you heard about Myrto's battle with her stepson, Hector?"

He blew air out between his lips and shut his eyes for a moment. Another difficult discussion. I almost felt sorry for him.

"Ach, that business. They have been arguing for a while, but I think it will never happen. Hector is too lazy to organise a sale of the property."

"Myrto thinks he is determined. He needs the money."

"Myrto should never have handed over the land. It was her grandfather's land in the beginning. She had no right to sign it away. She was a very stupid woman," he said rather sharply. I gave him an arch look. "Okay, I am sorry. Of course she is not stupid but, really, there was no need for her to do what she did, or to marry the husband. She made bad choices and now she suffers from them," he added, with a little hint of Greek machismo.

"She wasn't a young woman. Maybe she felt pressured to marry finally," I said.

"Perhaps, but what we are talking about is her family's land. It is something precious to a Greek. Look, we left Platanos when my father was a young man. There is still a family house up there, an old wreck. Every year it crumbles a bit more. It would be better to sell it, but I could never do that. One day I will fix it up. It is part of our history," he said firmly.

The chat about Myrto, or perhaps about love, had put him in a spiky mood. Time to go. I put my things in my bag.

"I fear I have been too outspoken about Myrto," he said.

"No, not at all. What do I know? I'm just a foreigner here," I said, a little too regretfully.

He reached over and patted the back of my hand lightly. Although I took it as a brief, avuncular gesture, like the day at the café when he squeezed my shoulder, his long fingers had a warmth and sensuality about them. I would be lying if I said I didn't enjoy that brief touch. Then he withdrew his hand.

"Perhaps you would like something else to drink? And my sister has made a lovely cheese pie for me. She always thinks I will starve here on my own. Perhaps you would like to try it, with a glass of white wine, maybe?"

His big eyes had a look of quiet appeal, or perhaps he felt guilty for his small strop over Myrto. Damn the man for being so contrary! It was tempting, but I was going to be sensible and not stay and polish off half a bottle of wine (probably), and a mouth-watering pie, with Leonidas, all of which I would undoubtedly enjoy.

"Thank you, but I really must get back now."

"So soon?"

"Afraid so, but thank you for the interview."

"It was nothing really. I like people to know what is going on in Greece now." He walked with me up to the garden door. I said goodbye but as I started up the path to Villa Anemos, he called my name. I turned around.

"I was just thinking. If your work permits, perhaps you would let me show you a bit more of the Mani. The peninsula further down is wonderful. Otylo, Limeni, Areopolis. This is where the real Maniots live. It's very wild. And there is a very nice fish taverna in Limeni, by the water, which I think you will like."

He painted a very nice picture and I heard myself saying, "Oh, that would be nice some time." But I doubted I'd be able to go. Angus would keep me busy enough with the 'mission' and there would be no time for sightseeing, or anything else.

But more importantly, what would Phaedra think of Leonidas escorting another woman round the Mani, dining by the sea, while she was up to her elbows in root canals in rain-lashed England? Did I really care what Phaedra thought about anything? I had a growing sense of unease inside me that, actually, I was just beginning to.

14

Evangelismos

The following Monday, Angus awoke feeling dizzy. He was sitting at the balcony table under the umbrella with his sunglasses on, looking like he'd been on a taverna crawl the previous night. He was drinking his second Greek coffee.

"Call Leonidas," I said. "He told us we could ring any time there was a problem."

"You call him, pet," he said, with a lemony expression on his face.

"It's your body. You should talk to him," I said, irritated as always by his aversion to dealing with health issues. I felt my first frisson of regret that I'd just signed up for another three weeks of playing matron.

"Och, he'll just give me loads of medical dread and I'll feel skunnered for the whole day. I can't take it today," he said, like a petulant luvvie.

"Okay then, give me the phone."

He pulled it out of his pocket and handed it to me. He now had Leonidas on speed dial. After a short delay, he answered the call, sounding a little harassed. I apologised for disturbing him.

"Is everything okay there?" he asked.

I told him Angus was feeling unwell. Leonidas believed the cholesterol-lowering drugs the cardiologist had prescribed were probably giving him side-effects. "Tell your father to take the tablets at night as instructed and things will improve, but he must be patient. And no drinking, if he can."

"Yeah, right. He won't like that, I'm afraid. Thanks and sorry to interrupt."

"Not at all. I am happy to help."

I was about to hang up when he added, "By the way, Bronte, perhaps you recall that I proposed a trip down the Mani? I am thinking that this coming Saturday would be the best day, when I am free. And perhaps Angus would like to come too. It will be relaxing for him."

"Okay, thanks. I'll ask him and let you know." I hung up.

Angus took off his sunglasses. I noticed his eyes were bloodshot. "Ask me WHAT?" he snapped.

I sighed. "Ask you … ask you … if you'd care for a double hemlock with your coffee because you're so bloody crabbit today, that's what!"

"Okay, very funny, pet, but if you could even manage to fix me a double hemlock, I'd certainly drink it. It would be easier than putting up with all this medical faff," he said, replacing his sunglasses and looking sullenly towards the gulf.

"Leonidas says you must persist with the tablets, that's all. No-one said it would be easy. Take them at night, he said, and you'll feel better if you don't drink at the same time."

"Okay. I'll drink in the morning."

"Very droll," I said, shaking my head. "Perhaps you should go back to bed for a while. You look rough."

He rubbed his hands over his whiskery face. "I feel rough."

I decided not to mention the Saturday tour with Leonidas just yet. It would only make things worse because I knew he wouldn't want to go.

The mobile phone chirped. I answered. It was Professor Zografos. I handed the phone to Angus. He sat for a while, nodding and smiling. His mood had completely shifted. "Oh, that's pretty amazing," he said. "I guess you just struck it lucky. Okay. Give me the address and I will sort something out. Any morning, you say? Thanks, Adriano. *Yeia sas*." He ended the call.

"Adrianos says he's been asking around in all his old haunts in Kalamata and he's already found out about an old guy who lives in a village above the city, to the east. He doesn't have a phone apparently but I've got the name of the village and some rough directions. Adrianos says this guy comes originally from Platanos. He's in his late eighties now, but he's pretty lucid and knowledgeable too about the village, though he doesn't go back there any more. Adrianos thinks he will be helpful."

"That's great, Angus. This could be a breakthrough. When do you want to go and see him?"

"First thing tomorrow perhaps, if I'm feeling up for it. I must call Polly though. The old guy has no English and it may end up being an ordeal, like talking to Pavlos the shopkeeper, remember?"

"Sure. That will be nice if she comes," I said, wondering how Polly liked this role of favoured translator, and if perhaps Angus was more interested in Polly than he cared to admit.

The village of Evangelismos was a 45-minute drive to the east of Kalamata in the foothills of the north Taygetos. We had left early to pick up Polly and were now making our ascent on a narrow but well maintained stretch of road past a few small villages. Evangelismos was a traditional settlement, with several churches, a *plateia* and one *kafeneio*. The old guy we had come to see was called Orestes and he lived on one of the back roads of the village but with an exhilarating view down towards Kalamata. It took a while for him to answer the door.

"I hope he won't mind us turning up out of the blue, but this will smooth the way," Angus said, looking down at the box of rivani cake we had picked up in Kalamata. When the front door finally creaked open, a gaunt face appeared, rheumy eyes flitting from one of us to the other, showing displeasure, as if we'd come to offer a subscription to an unwanted periodical. Polly explained our mission but he seemed unimpressed, until he spied the cake box and then his small face lit up. Polly pushed the box towards him. He took it, said something to her and left us for a moment.

"Poor man is quite dazed by our visit, but he's gone to make himself presentable and wants us to sit on his terrace and wait," she said.

The back terrace was accessed via a side path and we sat outside at a wooden table under a faded umbrella. We heard a lot of banging and rattling coming from inside and some 15 minutes later Orestes emerged, looking slightly more dapper in dark trousers and a striped shirt. His hair was neatly combed. He was carrying a tray with cups and saucers and plates and went back inside, returning with a large *briki* full of Greek coffee, and the cake box.

Angus chatted to Orestes in Greek while we had morning tea, but for the discussion about the Battle of Kalamata and the escaping allies we'd agreed Polly should do most of the talking. She and Orestes spoke for quite a while, though he stopped now and then as if to gather his thoughts. At one point Polly interrupted him and turned to us, with a look of excitement. She said Orestes had just confirmed that a British soldier had been hidden in Platanos after the battle by a neighbouring family.

"So finally we have some proof we're on the right track — a soldier in that village," Angus said, looking towards me and smiling.

Orestes told Polly a dramatic but distressing tale that turned out to be the first breakthrough in our search for Kieran. We learnt that Orestes was 12 when the Battle of Kalamata took place. He lived in a house at the northern end of Platanos, where there were two houses set on their own not far from a small spring, which we had seen the day we visited. The larger house was owned by a man called Panayiotis Maneas, who had two sons. Dimitris was the youngest at 14 and he and Orestes were friends. Orestes remembered the invasion of Kalamata late in April 1941 and how the Luftwaffe had regularly bombed the city and surrounding area. The Greeks had at first rejoiced to see the allied soldiers arriving in Kalamata, only to learn that they were in retreat from the German advance further north and waiting in their thousands to be evacuated from the beach. He also remembered the stories of soldiers fleeing down through the Mani, looking for a means of escape or being hidden by Greek families.

He had never heard of any troops escaping to the high villages like Platanos, until the day Dimitris confided in him that his own family were hiding a British soldier in their house and he was sworn to secrecy. In the following weeks, Orestes had sometimes seen the soldier, dressed like a Greek shepherd, roaming about the hillside where Dimitris and he often grazed their goats. It piqued his interest and he was keen to approach him, yet he never did, for fear of frightening him, or angering Dimitris, who might think him interfering. He knew where the soldier went when he was outside, usually to a large cave at the top of the ridge, where Orestes and Dimitris often took their animals during the heat of August. But Orestes never got his opportunity to befriend the soldier.

At the end of May, Orestes was shocked to see a patrol of Germans. They must have come up the *kalderimi* from Ayios Yiorgos. Orestes had been near the top of the ridge that bordered the village, with some of his family's goats. He was a long way from the houses below when he saw the soldiers in the distance marching up a narrow path towards the summit of the ridge. He moved the goats off towards a rocky outcrop and hid. Not long afterwards, he heard shouting and then gunfire and the sound of the Germans hurrying down the hill. He stayed out of sight for a long time, terrified they would find him and shoot him. When he was sure they had gone, he left the goats and ascended the path.

What he found there haunted him still, he told us. He discovered the body of the British soldier on the ridge, where the land began to slope into a ravine. He had been shot twice, once in the back as if in mid-flight, once in the forehead. Afterwards, Orestes had rushed down in a panic to find Dimitris and his father to tell them what had happened, but they were away for the day. Dimitris' terrified mother was alone in the house.

Earlier, the Germans had ransacked both houses before they ascended the ridge. It was as if they were acting on a tip-off because no-one usually came up to Platanos without a good reason. Orestes' father had been confronted by the soldiers and beaten up, his head gashed by a blow from a rifle butt.

When Panayiotis eventually returned with his sons and heard of the shooting from Orestes, they went straight away to find the British soldier. They had no choice but to bury him on the ridge where they found his body.

Orestes' memory was hazy on some of the details of the murder and its aftermath, but he was clear about how tormented poor Panayiotis had been over the death of the soldier, how he had felt responsible, as if he were one of Panayiotis's own family. The soldier was never spoken of again after that and Orestes was instructed never to tell anyone in the village what he knew.

Orestes described the soldier as tall with dark hair. Dimitris had called him English because he spoke English but he could have been Scottish, or anything else for that matter, as far as Orestes knew. Like Dimitris, he was a poor farmer's son with a meagre village education, who knew little about the world beyond the perimeters of the Mani. Also, he couldn't remember the soldier's name, if in fact he'd ever known it. Orestes told us he rarely spoke to anyone outside the family about these things and it seemed a huge effort for him now in calling it up again. Certainly, it wasn't worth all the sweet rivani cake in Greece – poor man. We felt sorry for him.

"Well, at least we know there *was* a British soldier in Platanos and someone who vaguely resembled Kieran. But what a terrible story, a young man alone on a foreign hillside, hunted down and shot in the back," Angus said, catching my eye. "It's funny how you can feel desperate for closure, isn't it, Bronte, and then when a story comes along like this, one part of you doesn't really want the boy in it to be Kieran at all. Yet we know he died somewhere in this region. If not here, then it was some place equally strange and wretched."

"We knew the search wouldn't be a happy one and we're a long way from knowing if this is Kieran," I said. "All we know about this soldier is that he was tall with dark hair. That could fit half the British Army. And if this was one of the two Scottish soldiers mentioned in Thomas's story – the one you found on the internet – there should have been two soldiers hiding. This could be someone completely different."

Angus nodded. "I wish we'd thought to bring the photo of Kieran that's on your chest of drawers, Bronte. I just never thought we'd get this far, but I've an idea," he said, looking towards Polly, who sat quietly nearby, her hands clasped in her lap. "Polly, can you ask Orestes, if we brought a photo of Kieran here, would he perhaps recognise him as the soldier in Platanos?"

She spoke to Orestes, and the old man shook his head sadly.

"He says it wouldn't do any good. It was too long ago and he only ever saw the soldier from a distance, and then after he was shot, when his face was covered in blood," she said with a shudder. Orestes gave us a mournful look. Angus sighed and leaned back in his chair.

"I think he has blocked a lot of things from his mind actually," said Polly, "but maybe we can bring the photo here one day if you don't have any other success. We shall see. I must tell you, though, that Orestes definitely believes that someone in the village must have informed on the soldier and his whereabouts because the Germans searched the two houses below and then went straight up the hill to the cave, as if they had been told exactly where to go. Lucky for the two families, the Germans found nothing incriminating in the houses."

"A village informer sounds highly likely," said Angus.

"I agree," said Polly, "and it's well known the Germans put a bounty on the heads of the foreign soldiers."

"Does Orestes know where the soldier was buried exactly?" I asked Polly.

"No. I already asked him that but he says that although Dimitris once showed him, he hasn't been up that hill for decades and would be unsure where it was now. Panayiotis's children would probably remember. In fact, Orestes says your only real chance of discovering any more about the soldier is finding them, if you can."

"Where are they now?" Angus asked.

"America."

Angus rolled his eyes. "Well that's not very helpful."

"Not necessarily. Panayiotis and his family left the village in the 1950s. They moved to Athens and then America, where the children still live. But Orestes believes that Dimitris, the younger son, still keeps the family apartment in Athens and comes back now and then. Panayiotis has passed away but Orestes said he once saw Dimitris, 15 or 20 years ago, at a summer *yiorti* in Platanos. He has not seen him since, but then Orestes does not go back to Platanos any more," Polly explained.

"Perhaps someone in Platanos has a contact number for this Dimitris?" I said, rather naively. After our recent visit to Platanos, and our meeting with Pavlos in his *pantopoleio*, I must have had the notion that Pavlos kept a dog-earned record of contact numbers on his story-board behind the counter.

Angus scoffed at my idea. "It's unlikely that one of the eight or so people who still live there would have a contact number for Dimitris. But it might be worth going back to talk to Pavlos sometime."

When we said goodbye to Orestes, he hugged Angus and said something a few times, which I took to be an apology because he hadn't quite given us what we wanted, an identity, or so I imagined. Polly lingered a while at the door, talking to him. After a few minutes, Angus and I strolled back to the car.

"What were you talking about?" Angus asked Polly when she finally joined us.

"Ach! I asked him if he knew who betrayed the soldier. He said he doesn't know. More than likely he just doesn't want to say. Old customs die very hard. Village allegiances are strong."

As we set off towards Kalamata, Angus looked glum.

"What a story Orestes told us – but depressing. I can't bear to think the soldier might have been Kieran. What a shocking way to die. And the Greek family must have felt devastated after hiding the soldier, to lose him like that, and how incredible that they all put their own lives in jeopardy."

Polly sat in the passenger seat, saying nothing, but biting softly at one of her cherry-coloured fingernails. As we got further from Evangelismos, Angus rallied.

"Well, I think we're in need of a good lunch. My treat, Polly."

"Oh, that is a such a good idea," she said, turning towards me with a beaming smile that instantly persuaded me to like the idea as well.

"It's the best I can do for the effort you put in today, Polly, and for your generosity to Orestes," said Angus. She made a face. "I saw you slip a few notes into his hand at the front door. You didn't have to, but I appreciate it."

"I'm sorry, but I felt so badly for him," she said. I was touched by Polly's gesture.

"I think we should go to the Gorgona on the seafront, then I won't have too far to walk home," she said.

"Great idea," said Angus. "I think we need to debrief in salubrious surroundings."

15

Polly, Bronte, Kalamata

We turned onto the main seafront road, right past the intersection where the taxi had stopped on my first day, across from the gulf. It seemed a long time ago now. The Gorgona, the Mermaid, was a traditional kind of taverna, much frequented by Kalamatans for its position overlooking a pristine stretch of beach and for its seafood. We took a table at the edge of the terrace. We ordered a carafe of wine to start with, and I never thought to chastise Angus for filling up his glass. He deserved a drink today, as we all did.

"*Yeia mas*. To our good health," he said.

I turned to Polly. "Thank you for coming with us today and translating everything. Even if Angus probably understood quite a lot, it was helpful to me."

"Oh, my dear," she said, squeezing my arm. "I am very happy to help you both. This is such a big thing you are trying to uncover and, if I may say," she glanced at Angus, who was staring out to sea, "it is not going to be easy. How much further you can go with it, I don't know."

"You're right, Polly. We gained some amazing information but may have also hit a brick wall," Angus said, sipping his wine, twisting the squat glass around between his fingers. "If we want to discover who the murdered soldier really was, it's important to find the family of Panayiotis Maneas, particularly the son, Dimitris. But if he only comes now and then to his holiday house in Athens, how can we trace him?"

"There will be other relatives still living in Kalamata, I think, with that name, who might have a contact number for them. I can search through the phonebook for you and ask around. I know many people in Kalamata. But even if you found Dimitris, would he remember who this soldier was? He would be in his mid-eighties now," said Polly.

"If they had somehow discovered the soldier's real name, wouldn't they have at some point later tried to get that information to the War Office in Britain, or give it to someone who could?" I mused.

Polly shrugged. "These were simple farming people to begin with, my dear. They spoke no English. Would they have known even where to begin? And then they left for America."

"It's hopeless, I know, but we have to push on now, don't we, Bronte?" said Angus.

"Of course," I said, but I didn't feel at all confident, not with just the few weeks I had left.

Our meal arrived and it offered a welcome distraction. One plate was piled high with pieces of calamari, which were light and crispy on the outside and soft and delicious, not the rubbery rings I'd had on my first trip to Greece. The barbecued octopus was succulent. I ate with a good appetite. Angus smiled.

"I like the way you eat everything in front of you now, pet," he said, as if he were an anxious parent and I was a 10 year old in need of bulking up. He just couldn't help himself.

"This country gives me an appetite. And you've just called me '*pet*' again!" I said with emphasis. Polly gave us both an inquisitive look.

At the end of the meal the waiter brought a small plate of fresh fruit: peaches and something else with a peachy colour and a strange texture.

"Persimmon; *lotos* in Greek. You must eat some. If you do, you will never go home again and Angus will be a very happy man," Polly said, laughing gaily.

"Why is that?" I asked her, thinking it would take more than persimmon to make Angus happy.

"Have you read Homer? Do you remember when Odysseus was sailing around the tip of the Mani, near Cape Tainaron, on his way home to Ithaka after the Trojan War? His ship was blown off-course and he had to drop anchor at an island inhabited by the Lotus Eaters. They lived on this sweet fruit, which induced forgetfulness and oblivion. When the sailors ate the *lotos* they forgot their family, their friends and they didn't care to go home again."

"We'll leave all the *lotos* for Bronte then," said Angus, enjoying himself immensely with this tale, as was Polly.

In the sun, her face looked bright and relaxed and she seemed much younger than her 58 or so years. Despite Angus's directive about not wanting a relationship, I felt he was very taken with Polly, as she seemed to be with him. Was this something that had only recently fired up because of Mission Kieran? I doubted that.

"Well, I'll just pick at the *lotos* because, as you know only too well, Angus, I have to go back after my extended holiday," I said.

Polly and Angus both frowned. However, sitting in the taverna with the gulf spread out before us, gazing at the lustrous water, the mountains towering in the distance, I felt completely relaxed and content, as if I'd already gorged on *lotos* fruit. I was losing my grip slightly on home, or rather on the things that used to obsess me. At the end of our long, leisurely lunch, I decided on a shopping trip and asked Polly where I could buy some tasteful beach gear.

"Well, it's now siesta time in the city, but the shops will be open in a few hours. Why not come back to my apartment with me and wait a while and we will go out together. That will be fun, won't it?"

Angus pulled a face. "Does that mean I'll have to hang around while you girls go shopping?"

"You don't have to stay. I can get a taxi home in the early evening," I said. The idea of spending some time in the city without him, having some female company for a change, was very appealing.

"Good, then I can go out later with some of my village friends and get blootered without any lectures," he said, with a teasing look.

Polly lived on the top floor of an apartment block just off Navarino Street. It was a large, elegant space with a wide balcony at the back that was high enough to have a clear view out towards the hills behind Kalamata. There seemed to be a small orange orchard across the road, curiously stuck between two blocks of flats, which helped to give the apartment a sense of space. She saw me looking at the trees.

"It's part of an old orchard. The owner has kept it and sells the oranges. I hope it doesn't change. This part of the city was all orchards once, olive, orange, figs, right up to the sea road."

I remembered the cover of the book Angus had lent me about the Battle of Kalamata and its picture of olive groves, and it was hard to imagine that possibly this very apartment block was built on land where the allies had fought valiantly to fend off the German invasion.

In other ways, the apartment was a fascinating window into a different life than the one I'd grown used to in the village. This was the haunt of someone educated and independent. It was decorated with icons, old prints, Greek rugs and tapestries, and on one wall there was a fine built-in bookcase, heaving with Greek books, English books and a smattering of others. It was a space that was comfortably intellectual.

Polly was different from other Greek women I'd met, in that she didn't want to talk much about her life, personal things, and all I gleaned about her was that she had divorced six months earlier and she had two daughters, one living in Australia, the other in Athens. We sat on the back balcony and she brought out a large pot of coffee and placed it on a glass-topped table.

"What do you think about my father's quest to find out about Kieran?" I asked.

She exhaled air gently through her lips. Her big eyes looked slightly mournful. "Between us, I think it is a near-impossible task. It would take a while to locate Dimitris, unless you become very lucky."

"I know. I don't have much time now and Angus seems to do his best to ignore this fact."

She looked at me over the over the top of her coffee cup. "I hope you don't mind if I say something, Bronte, but as a student of Angus's, I did get to know him over the years. I am sensing that you and your father have … some anxieties together, am I right?"

"You could say that."

"I imagine you must be angry with him for being here so long; that you feel a little abandoned. I would."

"It's been difficult, yes. If I knew more about why he left Scotland, and why he stayed away, it would be easier. But he doesn't want to talk about it."

She put her cup down. "Perhaps he's not sure himself why he left."

"Is that what he says?"

"In a way."

"I don't go for that. He's far too intelligent to do something mindless without a reason."

She looked sympathetic, but I found it rather awkward talking about personal issues with someone I didn't know well, and I resorted to my own fondness for turning the tables.

"How long did you have lessons with Angus?"

"For a few years. But not now. I had not seen your father for quite a few months until we met the other day at Professor Zografos's house."

Polly had what you would call a rather patrician face, a long nose, dark brown, almond-shaped eyes and a nice forehead. She must have been stunning in her youth. She had a face that was pleasant to observe, full of interesting angles that would probably never really age. She was also very smart, and had the shrewdness of a lot of Greek women I'd met. She knew how to change a subject as well as I did.

"So tell me, Bronte, what are you planning to buy at the shops. Clothes?"

"Mainly. I packed in a hurry. I need a swimming costume, a dress, sandals and so forth."

She gave me a curious look. "But you are only here another few weeks, like you said. A summer wardrobe? Surely you don't need it."

"We are being invited to things, Angus and I. I have nothing to wear."

"Village things?"

"Yes, and now Angus's landlord has invited us out on Saturday for a drive down the Mani, lunch in some smart taverna, I think …"

Her eyes widened. "Leonidas Papachristou has invited you out?"

"Yes, but both of us."

She whistled. "You will need to shop then."

"What do you mean?"

"I am joking!" she said with an impish grin.

"I think you're probably not joking, Polly, and I know what you mean. To be honest, I find him slightly intimidating."

She pouted. "Yes, I have met him several times. He is as you say and proud perhaps. All doctors here are the same. They have a great sense of entitlement. But you must go. I can think of two dozen women who would jump at the opportunity to be in your place."

"Including his girlfriend, the dentist in England?"

She laughed lightly and made a windmill of her arm that meant, in this instance, 'so what?'

"She can't be serious about him. A woman doesn't go out with a man like Leonidas and then disappear to England," she said, with another gesture that I had often seen, a kind of exaggerated grimace, palms held out at the same time, that indicated disdain or doubt.

I blushed. "I'm not looking for romance, Polly, I can assure you. I'm just being sociable."

She wagged her elegant finger at me. "But maybe the romance is looking for you."

"I don't know what that means."

She laughed. "It could mean that your moment in the sun has arrived. Either way, you need some clothes. I think we should go now, don't you?"

I was ready to shop, apart from a quick touch-up to my face and hair in the bathroom. Polly went to change. While I waited for her, I looked at her bookcase, intrigued by her collection of books. Many of the English books were classics: Jane Austen, Charles Dickens. I was impressed. No doubt there was a copy of *Wuthering Heights* as well, if I could only find it. But I found a lot more in the bookcase of interest, particularly a framed photo tucked behind a few others. I wanted to know more about it, but I figured now would not be the right time to ask.

It was still hot when we left the apartment. Polly flagged down a taxi to take us up town. I had only been in a few shops so far on my trips to the city with Angus and I had found the saleswomen formidable. They followed you about like anxious puppies. Polly was no pushover, however. She knew the drill and deflected these over-zealous matrons with steely charm so that we were able to make some progress.

She took me to smart designer shops, where the price tags left me breathless. She had good taste. Her only flaw was in erring towards sexy creations, rather than the practical, as if she had already decided which way she wanted my social life to go. I bought a sleeveless summer dress in bright colours, and a soft knitted white wrap to go with it, a pair of blue linen summer trousers and a frothy sleeveless top. The swimming costume was trickier.

"I'm not having a bikini. I'm too white," I moaned, as she plucked things from racks and pushed me into a changing cubicle with one hand, while holding a saleswoman back with the other. I chose an eye-catching, 50s-style one-piece that Polly thought wasn't the least bit sexy.

"You have lovely curves, Bronte. Why do you want to smother them?" Whereas I was sure the cut of the swimsuit actually enhanced them, without showing too much flesh. Polly shattered all my illusions about prim, conservative Greek women. But what I knew about Greeks was so miniscule it would swim in a D-cup.

After the shopping trip, we stopped on the way home for a drink in a small bar in a side street. We drank ouzo and ate from a small plate of *meze*, appetisers, which was perfect after our big lunch.

"This has been such an interesting afternoon for me, Bronte. We must do it again." We clinked glasses. Despite the dramatic start to the day, and the tormenting story Orestes had told us, I was feeling more and more content with my Greek sojourn. And I definitely liked Polly. She was modern, warm and open, except for one tiny thing: the image I had seen in that photograph on her bookcase.

16

Happy as Hades

When I got out of the taxi at Villa Anemos that evening, I was just in time to see Myrto leading her donkey Zeus towards the farm. She stopped beside me on the road, rubbing my arm affectionately. "Ah, Bronte, where have you been these days?"

"Sightseeing," I lied. "Where have you been with Zeus?"

"I take some firewood to friends in the village. They are piling up the shed for winter."

"We're a long way from winter, surely?"

"Yes. But you'll see. Bladdy cold winds in autumn blow down from the Taygetos at night. Have to be prepared."

"I won't be here in autumn, Myrto."

She looked me up and down, as if she didn't comprehend what I was saying, as if the idea of having any kind of deadline was an outrage. That was a Greek aversion, I was sure, and charming in its way.

"What's happening with your piece of land, by the way? The sale?"

"Ach! Hector has an agent now and put it on the market. Nothing I can do. Soon I will lose my trees."

"That's terrible, Myrto," I said, shaking my head. But I could offer no other consolation.

"Come see me soon for a coffee. We talk." She waved me goodbye, pulling the donkey along the road.

Back at Villa Anemos, I found Angus sitting at the balcony table, drinking a beer. He had a Kalamata phone book on the table. He looked up and smiled. "So, how was the shopping?"

"Very good. I was thoroughly pampered – *and* there was time for ouzo and plenty of gossip."

"What gossip?"

"Never you mind," I said, eyeing up the telephone directory. "What are you doing?"

"Looking up all the people called Maneas. There's plenty of them."

"Are you going to call them all?"

He shrugged. "Well, I will if I have to, but I live in hope that something else will turn up."

"Polly's going to contact a few people herself. She'll probably have better luck than you."

"She's a treasure," he said, not looking at me, but flicking pages of the phone book, running his finger down columns of names.

"What a lovely apartment she has, so many books. And I also found an interesting photo on her bookcase, kind of hidden. You and Polly on a beach ..." I had his full attention now. "It's a nice picture. Must have been taken a few years ago, because you both looked younger. It's quite romantic, even a bit sexy."

"I know that photo. It was at someone's name day, a party at the Gorgona taverna, actually. I don't know if romantic or sexy is the right way to describe it," he said, pouting. "From memory, we're just standing side by side on the nearby beach."

That's not how I saw it, however. He had his arm around her back, pulling her in close, their bodies wedged together. She was turned slightly towards him, smiling, her head thrown back a little, as if someone had cracked a joke. It was more than just a friendly picture.

Or so it seemed to me. Polly looked lovely, her dark hair flowing round her shoulders. She was full of life and so was Angus, handsome as well, his hair darker and shorter, thick and wavy. There was an unmistakable intimacy about the shot.

"You and Polly have been more than just casual friends, and for a long while, haven't you?" I probed.

His eyes flickered towards the olive groves and back. "Well ... yes, we became good friends over the years, but that's all," he said evasively. "And perhaps there was a frisson of attraction there from time to time, but she was still married then."

I knew he was lying. Even before I saw the picture I had suspected something more intense. It was implied in their easy, bantering manner and their mutual affection. Polly had also lied in her way as well with the pretence of just being friends, but it seemed easier to overlook this failing in her, and in any case I didn't know her well enough to judge.

"Does Polly know you found the photograph?" he asked, not looking at me, his fingers running down more columns in the phone book.

"No. But if she did, would she be embarrassed?"

He shrugged. "No, I don't think so."

"Look. You don't have to panic over it. I like Polly a lot. I just wondered, that was all!"

"There's nothing to wonder about. And I hadn't seen Polly for months, as it happens," he said with a dismissive shrug. I knew he didn't want to discuss it. He probably thought it was none of my business. Except it was, because if they had been lovers, and for a long while, it was one reason why he didn't come back to Scotland and forgot all about Marcella. I adored my mother but knew that she was no match for Polly, who was not the kind of woman Angus would sit up with all night, conjugating verbs. I was steaming a bit over the photograph but decided to let it go for now. However, I wasn't about to let Angus off too lightly.

"By the way, I forgot to tell you that Leonidas has asked us out for a drive on Saturday, down the Mani, sightseeing and lunch," I said.

Angus pulled a massive face and girned. "Flippin' hell! Socialising with the landlord. Next he'll be moving in with us."

"Not into Villa Anemos, I imagine. Not quite his style," I said sarcastically.

"Aye, you're right there." His eyes strayed towards the phone book again. He was itching to get on with his research. "Look, I don't think I'll go. I've got no urge to play the tourist. I've been down the Mani. It's lovely, but it's you he's really inviting," he said, flicking his eyebrows at me suggestively.

"Don't start with that old chestnut again. I'm just trying to be polite."

"I've got other plans for Saturday. I want to get the four-wheel drive again and go back to Platanos to speak with Pavlos in the *pantopoleio* about Panayiotis and Dimitris."

"Drive up there on your own? What if you suddenly get chest pains, up a bloody mountainside? Be sensible! Go another day and I'll come as well."

He sat for a while, drumming his fingers on the table top, plotting. "Okay. Here's a good solution. How about we ask Leonidas to take us up to Platanos on Saturday, instead of touring the Mani. He gets the pleasure of our company, *yours* especially, and in return he will be very helpful to us."

"Now you're *really* acting like a bampot!" I said, raising my voice. "Dragging Leonidas up to the old village when he's offered to give us a nice day out? He will think we are totally mad – obsessed." Furthermore, I had just bought coastal outfits, not hiking gear.

He merely shrugged. I felt exasperated with him. "Look, I'll think about it, Angus, but it seems selfish – on our part."

He gave me a churlish look. "Oh, you've come round now. A while ago you thought Leonidas was a bit too haughty, I seem to recall. Now you're feeling sorry for him. You're not going soft on him? Which, incidentally, I suspected you would, right at the beginning, remember?"

I shook my head. "Now stop it right there. I'm just trying to be pleasant to these people in the village. He's generous with his time. He deserves a medal as a landlord for putting up with you, that's for sure," I said, raising my voice again, but stopping short of an argument.

"Och, don't get crabbit. And remember my heart," he said, in a simpering fashion.

"How could I forget your friggin' ticker!"

"That's enough! I'm going out for a drink! If you don't want to come with me on Saturday, it's fine. You can go on your tour with Leonidas. I don't care." He stormed off.

I was relieved when he left the house because I felt guilty, remembering that it had been a fairly emotional day hearing Orestes' story. I didn't want an argument but I was piqued over that photograph. Nothing was ever straightforward with Angus. Then I began to realise that applied to almost everyone I knew here. Nothing was ever simple. Lives were bound up in layers of protection and obfuscation. The aphorism Leonidas told me about Greek rural life – "the trees have ears", that everyone's life was being lugged into by others, up for grabs – wasn't the whole story. People here believed what they wanted to believe. They saw what they wanted to see. It was Freudian editing at its very best.

186

I awoke early the next morning after a surprisingly deep sleep. Angus was still in bed. I decided to go for a walk in the village before he got up, to stave off a morning stoushie with him. The road into the village was quiet. It was warm, with puffs of cloud scattered over a deep-blue sky. It promised to be another splendid day. I would perhaps talk Angus into a swim to douse our aggravations.

As I walked through the *plateia* towards the back steps, people waved: Elpida from the *kafeneio*, and Miltiades as he wiped tables outside his taverna. Myrto was in the square, talking with some women, and called 'good morning'. I walked up the steps and onto the Palios Dromos. A few women were sweeping the front of their houses and also wished me good morning, *kalimera,* as if I had been here for months.

I had not yet been to the famous bakery on this road, where the volcanic loaves were fashioned. The bakery was an old-style place with a large wood-fired oven commanding one wall. On the counter were baskets of loaves in different sizes. Thekla, the owner, looked as nippy as Angus had described her, with a gaunt face and a long bony nose, made slightly comical by over-large, black-framed glasses. I hovered about the counter, squeezing loaves in baskets.

"*Kalimera sas,*" she said, rattling off a few Greek sentences.

"Sorry, I don't speak much Greek. I want *horiatiko* bread, village bread," I told her, which was the volcanic stuff, for Angus. He had taught me the word, as well as giving me a well-thumbed phrase book to advance my ailing Greek.

"Village bread," she said, thumping a loaf down on the counter.

"Ah, you speak English?" I said, though I wasn't surprised. In a place with a contingent of expats with little Greek, but with a lot of dough of their own, it paid for a shopkeeper to have a smattering of English.

"*Horiatiko*, keeps all week," she said, pointing at the loaf. "Good. *Kalo*." I didn't doubt it would last a whole century.

"Fine, I'll take it. And can I have another loaf as well? Something a little more soft?"

She made a face like a suck on half a lemon, as if asking for a soft loaf was an insult. However, she turned and rummaged around on a wall shelf, searching the loaves.

"Here. This one soft," she said, slapping the loaf on the counter and squeezing it, by way of illustration, so energetically that the shape of her surprisingly big hand left a doughy imprint.

"Okay," I said, feeling the start of a nervous giggle bubbling up from my stomach. I coughed instead.

"You *kori* of Angus?"

"Yes."

She looked me up and down with laser-like eyes and then opened the back of a glass-sided display case and cut two slices of the famous honey cake. She put them in a small box, touching her heart at the same time. "From me to you," she said, smiling, showing a row of gappy teeth. It was as if the mere thought of her own honey cake had magically sweetened her temperament. She put everything in a plastic bag, including the soft loaf, which still had the hand print.

I left with a spring in my step, very pleased with my first shopping expedition in the village. I walked back to the *kafeneio* to check emails, as I had my laptop with me. I also had Angus's mobile because I wanted to call Polly to suggest we meet for coffee one day. Perhaps I could sound her out about her relationship with Angus. Surely one of them could be honest? It would either clear the air or end my friendship with her, which would be a pity. But I needed to know.

Just as I sat down in the *plateia*, the mobile rang. It was Leonidas.

"*Kalimera*, good morning. I am calling just to check if you and Angus are still free on Saturday for our drive?"

"Em ...yes." *That was quick*, I thought. We had only discussed it a few days earlier. "We'd love to go on a drive, Leo, thank you. It's just that ... Angus is set on going somewhere else and I can't change his mind. And I don't want him to go on his own."

I told him about the proposed trip to Platanos, without telling him all the details, or all of the story that Orestes had shared. While I was talking, I heard a dull sound like fingers drumming on a desktop.

"I understand," he said at last. "But you have already been there with your father, yes? And you want to go again? But there are so many other things to see in the Mani, and you have such little time left."

"I know, but it's just that we need your help with something, if you can spare the time. We've made a bit of progress about my grandfather and we need to track down a certain person. We'll explain when we see you."

"I see." The fingers drummed again.

"And it would be very helpful to have you there. Angus struggles with his Greek."

"I will try to help, Bronte, but I am afraid I don't keep up contact with the village. I rarely go there." He didn't sound keen at all, but he was impeccably polite. I admired that.

"You will understand when we explain our difficulties."

"If you have your heart set on Platanos, I am happy to help. Perhaps we will see the other places another time."

"Of course. I would like that. And thank you. It's very kind of you."

"Okay. I will be at your house, 10 in the morning on Saturday. Goodbye."

I had just opened my laptop and was tapping into my email account when I saw Cynthia, the expat, approaching.

"Can I sit with you a moment, Bronte?" she said, pulling out a chair and sitting down without waiting for a reply. She was wearing a voluminous kind of dress, with her hair in another odd up-do, the ends of it springing loose about her head. She looked like an exotic parrot.

"No, not at all. Would you like a coffee? I was just about to order one." I managed to get Elpida's attention as she cruised about the *plateia,* picking up empty cups and gossip. I ordered two instant coffees.

"I wondered if you'd heard the awful news about poor Myrto and the dreadful stepson Hector, trying to sell the land. What will she do?"

I quite liked Cynthia, she was genial and caring but I was in no mood to talk about village news. My mind was mulling over the trip to Platanos and whether I had done the right thing or not, or if it would have been so much nicer going around the Mani with Leonidas – smartly attired! I was warming to his generous nature.

Cynthia was prattling on about Myrto and I was half-listening. My eyes trailed down the emails and I saw one from Crayton.

"I have no idea what Myrto will do. The law is not on her side," I said.

Cynthia leaned in across the table. "I know, but …. Greek women, even in the recent past, have been so oppressed by men. I've heard terrible stories," she said, just as Elpida brought the coffees to the table, taking more than her usual amount of time to set the cups down and the plate of rivani cake. Cynthia waited until she had gone. "Well, it was worse when the dowry system was still legal, when women were often expected to hand over family property in marriage. But even now there are ways of coercing women into giving over their possessions to greedy husbands. What does Angus think about it all?"

"I don't know, Cynthia. I imagine he would say that we shouldn't interfere. The foreigners are just passing through. I think that's how he feels."

Her up-do quivered. "I'm not passing through, Bronte. I'm here for the long run."

But I knew exactly what Angus would have said to that. He would have got mad at her. *There's a crisis here, Cynthia. None of us is here for the long run. Even the Greeks.*

"The other expats and I were talking last night about Myrto, and we think that a group of villagers, including the expats, should try to stump up enough to buy her land, so she can continue to do her olive harvest, which is her main source of income. And it will stop the land from being developed for something probably out of character."

I gave her an incredulous look. "I don't think the Greeks will manage that in a crisis, do you?"

"They all have money stashed away, Bronte. They always have, for little emergencies. Not that I blame them, especially now. I'm sure some of them could help." Was poor Cynthia mad?

"Are the expats cashed-up enough to buy the land?" I asked.

She pursed her lips. "I'm not, that's for sure, but some of the other Brits here are, and some of them without much land are often saying they'd like to do the olive harvest. A few of them have agreed it might be possible to pool their funds."

I hope she didn't want Angus to contribute. He would blow a gasket over that. "Do ask Angus what he thinks of the idea," she said.

"Sure, I will, but maybe it will resolve itself. My guess is that Hector probably won't go through with it, or he won't get a good enough offer for the land."

When a few other expats walked through the *plateia*, Cynthia excused herself and fluttered away, no doubt to continue the discussion on how to save Myrto. I had never actually met these other expats properly, but they didn't look much like olive harvesters, at any rate.

I clicked on the email from Crayton, fearing he may have changed his mind about the extra three weeks, but it was a short note asking me to file the story ASAP with photos. I told him I would do my best but I still had people to interview.

The next email was from Sybil:

"Hello, Grecian Hen. How is life in the sun? Wish I was there. Wish I was anywhere – but here. Management is offering redundancies and tapping certain people on the shoulder, like two of the older sub-editors and a photographer. Jason Peregrine has lost his travel editor's gig and some young colt brought up from London has taken his place. Truly mingin'. I've thought of putting my name in for redundancy. What do you think of that? Ach, I can see it's going to be shite working here. All these little hammer blows to the editorial operation have an effect. Did I ever mention my uncle Harry in Australia? He keeps telling me to get over there. Plenty of work. I fancy something different, like wrangling on a sheep farm. Anything but journalism.

Love and hugs,

Sybil XX

When I got home I found Angus sitting in his usual place on the balcony. He looked tired, hung-over possibly from his randan the night before with village mates. He had his elbows on the table, staring out towards the gulf. When he turned and saw the bag from Thekla's bakery, his eyes lit up. Never have I seen a man look so delighted at the prospect of eating bread that tastes like it has been hewn straight out of rock. I produced the village bread, the soft loaf, still with the hand-print, and the honey cake.

"Peace offering for last night," I said. He smiled and shuffled off to the kitchen to make himself Greek coffee, returning with a tray loaded with crockery and the *briki* steaming with hot mud.

"Thanks, Bronte. Appreciate the thought."

"Leonidas called about Saturday. Against my better judgement, I told him we'd be delighted to go out with him, but to Platanos instead. I don't think he was all that keen, but he agreed to it."

"That's grand. See, I always said he was a good guy. Women think that just because a guy's gorgeous he's got to be arrogant. Not always true. Look at me, for example."

"Ha! Very droll. Well, he does improve on acquaintance, I admit, and so do you, I hope."

He wasn't listening, however, and was carving through his village loaf and spreading slices thickly with what looked like butter from a thick pat on a white plate.

"I haven't seen you eat butter before. This is new."

"Great, isn't it? Since I'm taking those cholesterol-busting tablets, I might as well live a little."

"I don't think it works that way, Angus. You're still supposed to be careful about – if I can use the dirty word – lipids."

"Shh. Don't tell a soul. Our lipids must be sealed," he said, touching his lips and cackling. I laughed as well and marvelled at the way he could make endless jokes about mortal fats. He was in a good mood, at least, with last night's wrangle now forgotten.

I told him about meeting Cynthia, about her suggestion that everyone should put the hat around for Myrto and buy her land. He nearly choked on his bread and butter.

"For God's sake! Why do expats always think they know what's best for Greek villagers?" he said, shaking his head.

"They mean well, I think."

"Oh sure, but they bumble into things they don't understand."

"If they're as insular and dim as you make them out to be, why do they live here, in this remote place, and not somewhere easier, like the Costas in Spain?"

"Because a local Greek developer sold them new holiday villas, after advertising them in a UK newspaper, during the property boom seven years ago, when the expats had heaps of spare dosh. I bet they all wish they hadn't done it now, with property prices tumbling here in the crisis. Honestly, I think expats leave their brains on the baggage carousel when they land in Greece."

I could possibly have said the same of Angus!

17

Platanos revisited

On the Saturday morning I looked longingly at the expensive outfits I had bought in Kalamata: the floral sundress, the strappy sandals, all inappropriate for that day's hike around Platanos, where light trousers and stout walking shoes would be more practical. At 10am, with impeccable timing, Leonidas was at the front door of Villa Anemos. He looked fresh and sporty in casual clothes, reflective sunglasses and a cotton jumper tied over his shoulders. There was no sense of rancour at having his touring plans for the day changed.

He had an expensive black four-wheel drive vehicle that looked fairly new. I saw Angus give the car an appraising look as we got in. I let him sit in the front, while I sat in the back. A woman should know her place in Greece!

It was an easier drive up through the mountains this time and Leonidas knew how to negotiate the road. The scree we had encountered weeks ago had dispersed somewhat, and even if it hadn't, the car would have floated over it. Greek music was playing on the radio when we set off, but after a while Leonidas switched it off. That was Angus's cue to recap for Leonidas the whole story from the beginning of how he had read online about two Scottish soldiers last seen heading from the coast up to the mountains after the Battle of Kalamata and then to explain what we had discovered from Orestes. Leonidas listened closely to the tale, never interrupting until Angus finished. His face in the rear-view mirror betrayed nothing, apart from a slight arching of his eyebrows over the reflective shades.

"We want to walk up to the cave first, if we can find it, just to see where the shooting occurred," said Angus.

"I know where the cave is. I used to go up to the village in the summers as a kid to see my uncle Tomas. I know the hillsides there. I know of the family of Maneas. I have seen them once or twice when I was young, when there used to be a lot of summer *yiortes* in the village and the family came back from America. Now, I don't think they do. I have not seen any of them for years, but then I don't come up here much any more."

"Perhaps we can go and talk to the man who runs the general store. He may know something about the son, Dimitris. It will be easier if you speak to him for us," said Angus.

"Okay, we can do that."

Driving past the Platanos signpost, we saw the two houses again, just a bit further on from the spring water outlet, and it all made Orestes' story come to life. The bigger house was first, slightly further back from the road, the smaller one further towards the village, but both were out of sight of Platanos. Leonidas told us the big house was very old and that Panayiotis's forebears had probably been *kleftes*, freedom fighters, against Turkish insurgents. They had built a house as a kind of lookout near the top of the *kalderimi* and the main road, both of which would have been no more than narrow dirt tracks back then. Both houses were crumbling now. Whoever had bought these houses last had left them to the ravages of the mountain climate.

Leonidas parked the car and we took the track up the ridge, or rather the one Leonidas imagined the Germans would have taken, which started just behind the spring outlet. After a while it became narrow and slightly over-grown, winding up between the fir trees. Leonidas asked Angus a few times as we ascended if he felt okay to climb.

"Of course. That's why I'm here today," he said, beginning to huff and puff before we'd gone too far up, so that we had to keep stopping.

"So, you think that this young soldier who was shot by the Germans could be your grandfather?" Leonidas asked Angus.

"I don't know, Leo. We have no proof of anything. It could have been anyone at all. I don't even know if Kieran came to this village. He could have gone further down the Mani to one of the other mountain villages."

Leonidas looked thoughtful. Poor man, this surely wasn't his idea of a jolly day out.

The path wasn't difficult to climb, worn flat over the centuries perhaps by families taking their flocks up the ridge, but no-one seemed to have used it lately. Near the top there were empty sections, where trees had been cut down for firewood, no doubt, and which provided small, secluded grazing areas. The ridge faced south-west, so that from the clearings near the top of it you could see the whole length of the Taygetos range rolling down to Cape Tainaron. It was much more impressive from this height than anything we'd seen below. The air was cooler and fresher and there was no sound, apart from the wind in the trees and occasional birdsong. Leonidas led the way and I followed, while Angus trudged along behind. Now and then Leonidas stopped to let him catch up.

"Are you all right, Angus?" he asked again.

"Ach, a bit out of breath, I admit."

"No chest pains?"

"No, nothing like that. Don't worry if I have a heart attack. I'm in the right company, eh?" he said, with a smirk.

"Yes, but I have left my defibrillator in Kalamata," Leonidas said, turning and winking at me when Angus wasn't looking. I laughed.

"What did you say?" asked Angus.

"Oh, nothing," Leonidas said.

At the top of the ridge, the land flattened out. The other side of the ridge looked north-east into a wooded ravine and more mountain peaks rose up beyond. Where we stood there was nothing apart from trees and a few rocky outcrops. Leonidas led the way to the cave. It was fringed at the front with low bushes. The mouth of it was high and inside it was roomy, sloping at the back to a damp seam of rock. It felt cold inside. There was nothing much to see here, apart from some discarded water bottles, the remains of a small fire, where probably a shepherd had sheltered, and the smell of animal dung. It wasn't hard to conjure up an image of how the soldier had spent agonising hours in here, wondering how he could avoid his inevitable capture.

Angus sat down on a raised edge along the rock wall, wiping his forehead with a handkerchief. He looked dispirited.

"Now that we've found this place," he said, "I'm definitely hoping it wasn't Kieran whose life ended here. It's ... dreich ... sad."

"You are right, my friend," said Leonidas, standing in the middle of the cave with his hands on his hips. "I have come here a few times as a child and I never liked it much. It has an atmosphere, I think."

The place was making me shiver. I walked to the mouth of the cave and Leonidas followed, bending close and whispering. "We'll let your father stay a few moments on his own. I think he needs that."

I was glad to be out in the light again. I kept thinking about the spot where Orestes said he found the body, close to the edge of the north-facing ravine. Leonidas explained there were a few smaller caves on the side of the ravine that only villagers would have known about. They were only reached by narrow, perilous tracks and perhaps it was one of these the soldier had been heading for when he heard troops on the hillside.

We walked through the trees at the top of the hill and I kept wondering where the body might have been buried, but there was no grave marker at all. I guessed that even after the war, no-one had thought to erect one, or perhaps the grave was a long way from here.

When we walked back to the cave, we found Angus leaning against a fir tree, looking pensive. "I tend to believe that whoever betrayed the soldier knew this area well. He obviously knew there were hiding places up here."

"Perhaps," Leonidas said, rubbing his chin between his fingers. I didn't doubt that the possibility of a local traitor would have made him feel deeply uncomfortable.

"Do you find it hard to believe a villager would betray a foreign soldier like that?" Angus asked.

Leonidas sighed. "In a way yes, but in war people can act out of character. But if it is any consolation, often the Germans shot those who betrayed others, perhaps to avoid paying out bounty money. There were many reprisals during that time on every side. I have even heard a story that a well-respected Kalamatan *papas* was shot by local Greeks for becoming too friendly with the Germans."

The mood on the ridge had turned gloomy. "Shall we go?" I suggested.

"I think we've seen all there is to see for now," said Angus.

We descended without talking, picking our way carefully down the path, letting Angus trail along slowly behind. When we returned to the car Leonidas agreed to take us to the *pantopoleio* to speak to Pavlos.

The *plateia* was deserted — just like the last time — though a small metal table and chairs were placed outside the shop, as if in the hope that someone, sometime, would pass this way. Luckily, the door was open.

"I will go inside and talk to Pavlos, but first what can I order for you both?" said Leonidas.

"I'll skip coffee and have an ouzo," said Angus boldly.

"Okay, and for you, Bronte?"

I didn't know if he was having a laugh. Surely he knew there was nothing on offer here, apart from Greek coffee and ouzo. "I'll have a cappuccino actually, no sugar," I said, feeling a bit minxy.

"Okay, that's fine," said Leonidas, with a straight face. He went inside the shop and while we sat outside warming ourselves in the sun, we could hear the two men talking, sometimes vibrantly. Angus cocked his head but complained that he missed much of the conversation. Finally, the pair came outside, with Pavlos carrying a tray with one Greek coffee and two miniature bottles of ouzo.

"There's an ouzo for you, Bronte. I think you might need one as well after our morning excursion. And anyway, Pavlos's cappuccino machine is regretfully out of order today," Leonidas said, with a sardonic grin, placing the small bottle in front of me. What the hell! I twisted the top off and poured the ouzo over the stack of ice cubes in a tall glass until it fizzed and popped, releasing its strong aniseed aroma. Angus gave me a sly look.

Leonidas sat down to drink his coffee and Pavlos joined us for a moment. He obviously recognised us from our previous visit and yet he didn't refer to it. I was intrigued to see he was wearing the same dated, oversized suit, and the same slightly lugubrious expression. I began to feel as if Platanos was like a mythical Brigadoon but with a darker underbelly and no singing. A village from another dimension that only appeared every now and then, when the stars were in some kind of whacky alignment. Pavlos lit a cigarette and inhaled deeply, blowing out a plume of smoke that drifted across the empty *plateia*.

"I have explained to Pavlos what you have discovered from Orestes," said Leonidas. "As I think he told you last time, he was born in the sixties and does not remember many stories from the war. He says he is sorry but he has not heard of soldiers hiding in Platanos or the shooting."

I hadn't expected Pavlos to be any more helpful than he was last time. Leonidas sipped his Greek coffee, absently licking the thin line of froth that clung to his top lip. He seemed thoughtful. Pavlos smoked his cigarette without looking at us and pushed the packet around on the table top. Angus was sitting quietly, sipping his ouzo.

"Pavlos has said if Panayiotis Maneas had hidden a soldier, it would not have surprised anyone in the village," Leonidas explained. "He was considered a very good man. The villagers always referred to him as '*Barba*', a term of respect."

Pavlos got up from the table and went back inside the shop, returning with a couple of photos that I imagined must have been pinned on the back wall we saw last time.

"This is Panayiotis," he said, holding up a dog-eared black and white photograph showing a group of village men in formal clothing, standing with a *papas* in this same *plateia*, under the plane tree, not far from where we were sitting. Pavlos pointed to a tall, thin man with high cheekbones and a long nose. He looked dignified, proud. The other photo was more recent: a group shot of many villagers sitting at a long table in what looked like the forecourt of the large church beyond the *plateia*.

201

Leonidas pointed to one of the figures in the group and explained, "This is Dimitris, the son, when he was in his fifties. This was taken in 1980. He had come back from America for a holiday and was here in the village for a summer *yiorti*."

Dimitris had a similar long face and nose and a head of thick, greying hair. He was holding a glass of wine, smiling for the camera, along with several other villagers. I could see a row of plates on the table, a wine carafe, a basket of bread about to be offered by a young boy with curly hair and laughing dark eyes. There was a joyous feel to the scene, which contrasted so dismally with the deserted backwater the place was today.

Leonidas leaned over the photo and pointed. "This young boy, serving the bread – is me!"

We crowded in to get a better look. "Of course," I told him. "The same smile, and the same hair, exactly. Very handsome. We should have known." Leonidas almost seemed to blush. It was quite curious. It was a lovely snapshot, but what made it especially interesting was that it fixed Leonidas in this village finally, even if he hadn't been born here and seemed to have little time for it now – at least we had proof he had been happy here sometimes.

Leonidas took the photo for a moment. "I was 10 years old. We used to come up here most summers for the village celebrations. It was fun, before everyone started to move away."

He handed it to me. "Pavlos says you can keep this picture, if you like."

"Thank you," I said. Pavlos shrugged nonchalantly.

"Pavlos has told me that he remembers talking to Dimitris a few times at these village gatherings, but he does not know him very well and does not have contact details for him in Athens, or America. Or if he did once he no longer has them. But he can ask around and see if anyone he knows from here has a number or address in either place, though it may take time.

"There is one small possibility, however. Every year in the village there is the feast day of Saint Dimitrios, in the main church named after this saint. It is one of the biggest feast days in Greece, and the name day for anyone called Dimitris, which is quite a common name here. As you know, the name day in Greece is like a birthday but more important. This photo was taken at the summer *yiorti* for Saint Dimitrios. In recent years few people are coming, and hardly any of the very old ones in their eighties and nineties. Pavlos seems to think that Dimitris comes to Greece every five or six years, to his Athens apartment, and when he does, he comes back to Platanos for this celebration.

"He remembers he saw him maybe five years ago. He is in his eighties now and a little frail. Pavlos doesn't know if he would still make that trip. It is a small thread of hope, and maybe quicker than trying to track down a contact, but he may come this October 26th for the feast day of Saint Dimitrios, and maybe this will be his last time. So, you will have to come too, my friends, and see."

Angus and I looked at each other. "That's great," he said. "That may be the only chance we'll get to find him, even though it's a long shot."

"Will you come?" I asked Leonidas, thinking we might need his help again. He hesitated for a moment. "I don't usually, because I have reason to celebrate it in other places, but this year I will so that I can help you with this. I am also intrigued by the story of your grandfather and I want you to find out what happened to him."

"Thank you," I said. "And for today."

"You are welcome, but I can't promise you will find what you are looking for."

Pavlos got up, stacked the tray and went inside. Leonidas followed him. We could hear them having a vigorous conversation inside. Angus cocked his head slightly.

"What are they saying?" I asked.

He held up his hand to silence me. His face was puckered with concentration. Then he bent forward and whispered, "I didn't get it all, but I think they're talking about the shooting up on the ridge. I just heard the words 'German', 'British soldier'. It all sounded a bit heated … it makes me think that …" Angus stopped mid-sentence when he heard footsteps at the door of the *pantopoleio*. It was Leonidas coming back. He had settled the bill and Angus thanked him and asked him casually what he and Pavlos had been discussing inside, as it had sounded quite animated.

"Oh, nothing, just about the village, how the population here has sadly diminished and how nice it is on the feast day of Ayios Dimitrios, when we see a few more people in the village."

"I see," said Angus.

"Do you want to see the church of Ayios Dimitrios while we're here?"

"Yes, why not," I said, feeling more optimistic about our mission now and the possibility of meeting Dimitris, the one person who could shed light on the identity of the soldier. If his family had hidden him for several weeks, then Dimitris had to know something.

Leonidas led us to the church on a pathway that cut through from the *plateia* to the edge of the large church with the blue dome that we had seen from the roadway on our first trip. Angus took my arm as we walked along. He whispered in my ear, "I don't think they were talking about the village population back there. It was about the war. We'll talk later …"

The church was set in its own grounds, with a low stone wall around it. I could see the area where the long table had been laid out in the photo Pavlos had given us. Around the periphery of the churchyard were tall trees, cypresses and an orange and pomegranate tree. On the other side of the church was a raised stone wall and spring water spout. The village was blessed with water spouts, it seemed. Behind the church was a graveyard. The graves were ornate, with marble and glass mounts filled with icons and photos.

We wandered around. Leonidas took us to one corner of the cemetery, where some of his own family were buried. The graveyard was neat and orderly but rather forlorn because the dead now outnumbered the whole living population of the village at any time.

"Is the church open?" I asked.

"I don't think so. It isn't used much now and the *papas* who keeps the key lives in Kalamata," said Leonidas.

On the drive back to Marathousa, Angus was in high spirits, chatting about this stroke of luck, but Leonidas was quiet, keeping his attention on the road perhaps. I kept going through things in my mind that Pavlos had said, and I wondered why he hadn't bothered to mention the feast day for Saint Dimitrios the first time we met him, suggesting that we might want to come as a way of making contact with the older villagers. Or did he think that as foreigners we would have no interest in trekking up to Platanos for a religious event? The upcoming gathering was opportune, but when I calculated how much time I had left of my holiday, something occurred to me.

"I won't be here on October 26," I said.

Angus half-turned in his seat. "Ach, Bronte, you're not serious?"

"I am. My boss gave me three more weeks, remember, but they run out just before the 26th."

Leonidas glanced at me in the rear-view mirror. "You will have to try to stay longer, Bronte. You cannot miss this event," he said.

"Jesus, yes! Tell that numpty boss you must have more time," said Angus.

"Do you know how lucky I was to get six weeks here. He won't agree to more time, I know him," I replied.

Angus grabbed his ponytail, as he did in times of delight or frustration, and gave it a twist.

"You can manage without me. Leonidas will help you," I said, watching his face in the mirror. He grimaced. Already things were going pear-shaped. "Okay. I will write to Crayton today and ask for more time, but it's not going to work, I tell you."

When we got back to the village, Leonidas suggested we might all like to go out for lunch down by the sea, as he was free for the day. Angus declined, saying he had to go into Kalamata. I gave him a searching look.

"I have something organised, Bronte," he said with a shrug from the front seat.

Leonidas had stopped the car outside his house and swivelled round in his seat.

"Would you like to accompany me for lunch, Bronte? I know some nice places by the sea."

It would have been churlish to decline lunch when we had already messed around with his touring plan. The idea had sudden appeal, anyway, because spending the afternoon with Leonidas would be better than spending it alone in the house.

"Okay, that would be nice, thanks. I'd like to get changed for lunch, if you don't mind, so I'll meet you back at the car in 20 minutes."

"Excellent. And we can swim later, if you like. Your father tells me you like to swim."

Angus cleared his throat and jumped quickly out of the car. Ah well, I had bought the new swimming costume for just such a baptism.

When Angus and I got in the front door, I rushed about, trying to get ready. I was hot and dusty after the trek and wanted to shower and change. I grabbed Angus before he disappeared.

"What's happening in Kalamata? A date with Polly?" I asked.

"Och, you don't want the ageing old dad hanging about. You'll have more fun on your own."

"You're winding me up again, aren't you? And you didn't answer my question," I said firmly.

"Is this how you carry on with difficult interviewees?"

"I do worse than that. I cut off their ponytails," I said, grabbing his hair, and tugging it. "Well?"

"What was the question again?"

"You know damn well!"

"Does it bother you if I see Polly?"

"No, it doesn't. It bothers me that you can't just admit you've got something going on."

"That's because we don't. I told you that. And by the way, you've just wasted five minutes blethering to me when you should be getting ready, right?"

I let it go. I showered and went to the bedroom to change for lunch, but not before I had retrieved the photo from my bag, the one of Leonidas at the *yiorti*. I leaned it against the picture of Kieran. The top of the chest of drawers was slowly gaining more characters. I got changed into the swimming costume, with the sundress fitting snugly over the top, and matched it with the strappy sandals. No point in wasting an expensive outfit, even if I looked a bit too clean and crisp. What the hell! I brushed my hair and applied some subtle make-up and wondered why I was suddenly faffing over lunch with a man I would probably never see again in less than three weeks' time.

Angus was standing in the sitting room when I left the bedroom and gave me an appraising look.

"You look nice!"

I held up my finger. "Don't!"

"I mean it. You look lovely, Bronte. Beautiful, actually." He couldn't resist a wink.

"One night, old man, I will sneak into your bedroom and cut it off. Just watch yourself." I laughed.

"I hope that was the ponytail you were referring to."

"What else!" I replied, as I quickly left the house.

18

That minx Medusa!

Despite having spent the whole morning with Leonidas, as we drove together to the sea I felt strangely on edge. I hadn't been on any kind of 'date', if you could even call it that, since Rory. Now I was lunching with a Greek god, blessed by the Hippocratic Oath, whereas most of the men I'd ever been out with had been showered with the Hypocritical version.

We went to a small fishing village called Kitries at the end of the sea road heading south, at the foot of a wooded cape which formed a natural barrier between here and the next few villages further down the coast. The name gave me a jolt. It was the village that Angus had once told me he thought Kieran and the other soldiers in the RASC had been heading for to find a boat. They would have set out on the same road from Kalamata, which hugged the coastline, though it was a rougher kind of road back then.

At the turn-off from Marathousa, when I looked back, I could see some of the distant peaks of the mountains to the east and the deep Rindomo gorge cleaving the land down to the sea. From here on the coast, it wasn't hard to imagine how a long, arduous trek would end up at the *kalderimi* Angus and I had checked out. For a moment, I felt I was stepping into Kieran's shoes, but the scenes of summer bathers on the long beach to the right, the busy cafes and tavernas, belied the terror of those war days.

Kitries had a small harbour crammed with boats and several tavernas at the waterside. We took a table in the Delfini taverna, with the crystal water of the gulf lapping gently just a foot in front of us. In the distance, the long Messinian peninsula shimmered in a blue-grey haze. It was quiet here, with only one large table of Greeks at a respectable distance. Leonidas ordered a selection of seafood and a bottle of white wine from Santorini.

"You look very lovely, Bronte. The colours of your outfit suit you, may I say." Well, the shopping trip with Polly hadn't been in vain then.

It was a leisurely lunch, and while we ate we talked about Platanos and about Leonidas's own family, who had lived there since the early 19th century. He told me that his forebears on his mother's side had come from further down the Mani and were fugitives to Platanos after fighting against the incursions of the Turks. On his father's side, the family had originally come from Sparta, hence his name, Leonidas.

"My grandfather also had land in Marathousa with olive trees, and built what is now Villa Anemos. He spent summers in Platanos and every winter he came down to Marathousa to harvest the olives, and to escape the harsh mountain winters, as many people did. All the family would move down and the children would go to different schools for winter. In the spring they all moved back up again. As my grandfather got older, this life became more arduous and one day he moved down to Marathousa for good. He was a hard worker and shrewd. When he had some money saved, he bought up small parcels of land in and around Marathousa, and then passed them to my father," said Leonidas.

"My father built the original house that is now mine. He also built some apartments near the beach to rent out to tourists and he made a good business out of that, and still does. Good enough to send me and my brother to universities in Athens. My brother is an accountant and lives in Kalamata now. My father lives in Kalamata too, but he still likes to harvest his own olives every year, with help, of course. He has about 700 trees. All the village people here are tough and resourceful. It's how they have survived the Turks, the Germans, and now the economic crisis. They never do just one thing," he added with a laugh.

"I understand now how difficult life must have been in the past, but I get a sense that it was also more satisfying, too," I said.

"Perhaps. You hear a lot of Greeks now who will say that they used to be happier, even before we joined the EU and things improved financially. We were happier people because we were more in charge of our lives and they were less complicated."

He took off his sunglasses and wiped them with a serviette. The sun was on his face. His eyes were remarkable, so dark they were almost impenetrable. Yet today there was something more about him, a thoughtfulness in his expression.

"Tell me, what do you think about Dimitris Maneas? Do you think he will show up this year?" I asked.

"Bronte, I just don't know. I am very sad about the story of the Germans shooting the soldier. More sad if it was actually your grandfather. How old was he?"

"Twenty-five."

"Too young. And he died after trying to defend us."

"I would be devastated to think of Kieran dying up in Platanos the way he did, if it really was him, but it would bring us all closure. My father doesn't talk about it much, but he has been haunted by his father's death. After he enlisted, I don't believe Kieran ever received his wife Lily's letter to say she was pregnant, so he never knew he had a son. Angus feels his loss deeply, I think."

He held my gaze long enough for me to feel a jolt of discomfort and then he reached over and squeezed the back of my hand. It reminded me of the day I interviewed him at his house. This time the gesture felt more than avuncular.

"Well, all the more reason, Bronte, why you must be here for the *yiorti* of Ayios Dimitrios."

I sighed. "I don't know if I can pull that off."

"You must."

"If only life were that easy."

"It can be. You are young. You are free. It depends how much you want something."

"Sadly, it's not up to me at all. I'm sure my boss on the paper will knock back my latest request to stay longer. He wasn't happy the last time." Leonidas looked uncomprehending. "It seems harsh, I know, when I'm here to help my father, but it's one of the things you will soon discover about working in Britain, if you go … too many rules and regulations, too much interference, and we have austerity too."

"Yes but perhaps we have gone to the other extreme in Greece, with a lack of organisation and everyone doing just what they want. And when we have new regulations now, often they make no sense at all. Crazy taxes come and go constantly, more new forms to fill, new anxieties. Life may be more straightforward in Britain. Phaedra always gives a good account of life there."

I stared at him, smiling. "I have a feeling you've made your mind up *finally* to go to England, yes?" *I've got you this time*, I thought.

He did that Greek thing then: the raising of the brows, eyes narrowed, the tiny tilt of the chin, the 'no-comment' thing. I actually laughed, more out of frustration. It was absolutely maddening, and so effective. It was meant to totally disarm the opponent. Or was it a warning shot across the bows. 'Go no further!' it seemed to say.

"I saw Myrto the other day, and was sad to learn that her stepson Hector has now put the land up for sale, with an agent," I said.

"Yes, I have heard this too," he said.

"Is there no-one in the village who could perhaps talk Hector out of selling the land? Or maybe someone in the village who could buy it from him?"

"No-one has money to buy land now. And Hector is obviously desperate for funds."

"But to lose the trees, her income!"

"Bronte, it is so very kind of you to be touched by our village and the people suffering in the crisis, but you can't become too involved. It will drive you mad and will spoil your time with your father. Angus needs you right now," he said, with a hint of paternalism.

"Yes, I do realise that," I said. It was nice he worried so much about Angus, but I wondered what he would have said if he knew the whole truth about my father leaving the family for his mid-life odyssey and that I was already putting my own life on hold to help him out.

Leonidas perhaps sensed that the mood of our lunch was turning. He quickly summoned the waiter for the bill. After he settled it, he gathered up his mobile and his keys.

"There are some lovely coves nearby. Shall we go for a swim?"

A few minutes' drive up the coast, he stopped the car at a cove with a pebbly beach, where the water was calm and enticing, protected by two rocky arms that seemed to hold it in a steady embrace. We fetched our beach bags from the car and clambered down a rocky path to the empty beach. We spread out our towels and got ready to swim. I wished I had been browner when I peeled off my sundress and saw pale Celtic legs barely air-kissed by the sun.

"I like your costume very much. It is very elegant. You look like ... a Hollywood starlet," he said, his eyes lingering over the halter top of the one-piece. I burst out laughing. No-one had ever put me and Hollywood together in one sentence.

"Did I say something wrong?"

"No. And thanks for the compliment."

The water felt cool and silky as we dived in. He was a good swimmer and did a fast freestyle away from the shore before turning and swimming back towards me.

"Thank you so much for suggesting this," I said, as the slightly serious conclusion to our lunch floated off. It was glorious to bob about in this secluded cove, with its backdrop of mountains and olive groves under an indelibly blue sky. I knew just how lucky I was at that moment and it felt good.

"I'll race you to that rock over there," he said, pointing to a protruding wedge of rock on one of the arms of the cove. We went into a fast freestyle but I knew I was no match for him. He was a powerful swimmer and he easily made it before me. He laughed as I got there and I clung onto the side of the rock to catch my breath, like a breathless limpet. We hovered around a while longer in the deep water, talking about nothing in particular. Occasionally, when a wave rippled through the cove, our arms and legs brushed against each other. Or so I imagined.

Then I felt a nip on my left arm. I let out a squeal. "Something stung me, I think."

He came closer and inspected my upper arm, holding it slightly out of the water.

"I can't see anything much. It was perhaps a small jellyfish. Nothing serious, I think. Come on, let's swim back to the beach."

We did an easy swim back to the shoreline. He examined my arm again. I felt rather silly making a fuss over such a small thing, a jellyfish, even though it was still stinging quite a bit.

"There's a small red mark. It will be fine in a moment, I think. This is the time of year, I am afraid, for jellyfish and perhaps a bigger one. We call it the *medusa* in Greek. It can give a very nasty sting."

"You've named a jellyfish after the mythical Greek character Medusa?"

"Yes, it's very expressive, is it not? They have long tentacles, like Medusa's hair snakes."

He picked up his towel and dried himself, rubbing his own hair quickly so that it looked slightly menacing. His thick curls, which had been weighed down by the seawater, started to spring back into life, twisting and turning in the sun, I fancied, like restless serpents intent on some minor felony. Unconsciously, I began rubbing the sting on my arm.

"Still sore?" he asked, pulling my hand very gently away so he could inspect it again. I gave in like a meek patient.

"It is definitely not life-threatening, I assure you," he said, with a playful hint of sarcasm. He kept his hand on my upper arm for a moment, but instead of letting it go he moved his hand to the back of my neck and pulled me gently towards him, kissing me lightly on the mouth. It was a whisper of a kiss, nothing more, and yet I felt my stomach lurch. I let him kiss me again, stronger this time.

How attractive this man was! Even as a boy in that old village photo he radiated beauty and vitality. I would be lying if I said I hadn't secretly imagined this moment. It was better in reality, so much so that a daft gremlin in my head took hold of my reason, trying to convince me that a summer romance wasn't such a bad idea really. He kept on kissing me, hotly this time, our bodies leaning into each other as we stood on the sand. I could sense he was very aroused and my urge to resist was – in equal and opposite measure – flagging.

When his hand started to edge towards my right breast, I had all but surrendered. Then, suddenly, from nearby came the sound of a dog barking, followed by an angry Greek tirade. The perfect moment was shattered. We both turned to see an old man in a baggy suit and black hat with a small white dog on a lead. We hadn't heard him approaching – of course. He was shouting something and brandishing a walking stick, as if he might give us a good thrashing.

Leonidas, his face flushed, unhooked himself from our embrace and turned, trying to placate the interloper. After a short exchange, the old guy looked at me, smirked, a little salaciously, and left with a big windmill wave of his arm, dragging the dog with him.

Leonidas shook his head. "I am sorry, Bronte. That was unexpected."

"What, the man or the other thing?"

"Both. I am sorry."

"What did he say?"

"He's a crazy old guy. He said he couldn't walk the dog any more without seeing people having 'sex' on the beach."

"But we weren't …"

"Well, his old mind was getting ahead of things." So had mine.

"What did you tell him?"

"Ha. Well, that will have to be my secret. I think," he said, looking coy.

"Intriguing!" I said, wondering with what piece of male blagging he'd fobbed off the old guy. Whatever he'd said, the incident had the effect of a bucket of cold water dropped from a great height. We lay down on our towels, side by side, staring at the sky, not talking for a while.

Then he levered himself up on his elbow and stroked the red welt on my arm.

"*Me sighoreis*. I apologise, Bronte, for the lack of control. It is the fault of the jellyfish, of course."

"Is this how you routinely treat jellyfish stings in Greece?"

He laughed. "If it works, why not. I expect your arm feels much better. Am I right?"

"Yes, much better. I doubt I'll require further treatment," I said in mock snippiness.

He was still leaning on his elbow and I struggled not to turn and look into those dark eyes because, if I did, I'd want to kiss him again. I got up and walked to the water's edge, paddling about. I couldn't think what was going to be worse now, dealing with the fact we had lost our heads for a moment and it would be hard to go back to the 'friendship' we had, or wondering forever what it would have been like making love to Leonidas on the beach, if the old man and his yappy dog hadn't come along. I unconsciously ran my tongue over my top lip. I could still taste the sweetness of his lips. The tang of regret was all mine.

He walked down to the water's edge and dived in, uttering something in Greek I couldn't understand, though it was spirited. He did a few easy strokes in the water and got out, standing beside me at the shoreline, his hair dripping wet again, the snakes for the moment becalmed.

"Leo, it was as well we were interrupted. I mean, I have to leave in a few weeks. You have Phaedra in the UK."

His face was unsmiling. "Yes, you are right."

"When I said at lunch that it seemed you were leaning more towards England now, you never said anything. I've noticed you're always rather evasive about the subject, if you don't mind my saying. But I think you've definitely decided to go, and very soon probably. Am I right?"

He ruffled his hair with his hand and pouted. I feared he was going to pull out another 'no comment', but finally he said: "Yes, you're right. On both points."

"Okay. Now we understand each other. So, what happened just now was pleasant, but it would be madness for us to get involved, wouldn't it?"

"Only pleasant?" he said, looking wounded.

I said nothing. Best not to.

"Look, I didn't mean to kiss you ... not like that, Bronte. I like you very much. But what happened was a thing of the moment perhaps. A lovely lunch, wine, the swim. The way you look. Fantastic," he said, his eyes flickering again over the 'Hollywood' costume. "I am sorry."

But I wasn't sorry. I was more than that. I was mortified he'd called it just a 'thing of the moment': a caprice, nothing of any importance. To me, it seemed he had been moving towards this since lunch: the warm squeeze of my hand, the frisson of interest he gave out. How easy it might have been, after all, to have a holiday affair with a handsome Greek doctor. There would have been no complications really, no guilt, no heartbreak. Easy. Maybe that was all the invitation for lunch had been leading to anyway. Perhaps he had been more predatory than I imagined.

We stayed a while longer, drying off in the sun. The chatter changed to easy subjects, but the magic of the day had evaporated. Time to go. We packed up our beach bags and strolled to the car. I admired him for his good grace in trying to maintain the friendship, at least, if that were possible. When we got back to the village, he stopped the car in the driveway of his house.

"Thank you for a wonderful day, Bronte. You are very good company. I hope you are not angry with me," he said.

"Thank you too. And no harm done," I said, not looking at him. I slipped quickly out of the car. I didn't want Angus, or any of the village gossips, to see us having a cosy chat in the parked car. I waved him goodbye.

19

What Greek men want

Angus was sitting outside in his usual spot, his 'office', on the back balcony, with books and notebooks spread around him. He looked up when he heard me approaching.

"So, how was lunch?"

"Fine. We went to a taverna in Kitries."

"Oh! I meant to take you to Kitries. It's one of the places where the allies hoped to find escape boats." Then he talked on about the Battle of Kalamata, but I wasn't really listening. I had a view of Leonidas's back terrace. I wondered if he would stay at the villa tonight, or return to Kalamata.

"Did you hear me, Bronte? I asked if you'd been swimming. You've got a nice glow about you."

"Yes, after lunch. A small cove nearby. Lovely!"

"Good," he said, tapping a pen on his front teeth, watching me.

I was dreading his usual impish wind-up when it came to Leonidas, but his eyes merely trailed to his notebooks. He seemed eager to get back to whatever it was he was doing and I left him and went downstairs. I had a long cool shower. It didn't take long to rinse the salt away, but no matter what I did, I could still feel and taste those kisses. I still had the sensation of his body pressed against mine. No amount of water would erase that.

Afterwards, I slipped easily into a siesta. It was deep and restful, but when I awoke I had thoughts chasing around in my head. I replayed the incident on the beach. Despite Leonidas blethering about it being a 'thing of the moment', it surprised me, the ease with which he might have been unfaithful to Phaedra. While he'd seemed a bit haughty when I first met him, he had never struck me as the insincere, philandering type. Perhaps the truth was that, although he believed he and Phaedra were well matched, he didn't really love her. That was why he had dithered so long over going to England, and why he still didn't sound absolutely certain. That idea sat quite well with me, yet it was messy. I would forget it. It would be easy now to leave when the time came. One rickety heart in the family was quite enough, without mine being broken as well.

I got up in the early evening and dressed. I was going to the *kafeneio* to send yet another pleading email to Crayton, even if it was Saturday. I knew he sometimes checked his work emails from home. Sad bastard! I found Angus sitting at the kitchen table this time, drinking beer.

"Do you want to come to the *kafeneio?* I need to use the wi-fi."

"What did you say, Bronte?" I noticed the notebooks around him again.

"Didn't you have a siesta?"

He shook his head. "I tried to sleep, but my head was buzzing."

"What with?"

"Just thinking about Kieran and this Dimitris guy. Wondering what I can do if he doesn't turn up. Also, it's curious, isn't it, that you find that wee icon in your bag of Saint Dimitrios, and our best lead turns out to be a guy called Dimitris, and a plan to meet him at the feast day of the same saint. Spooky or what?"

Funny how that had escaped my mind until then because I had heard it was a common name, but now Angus mentioned it, it was kind of interesting.

"I told you in the beginning, remember, that you'd probably still be here for the saint's day. And we saw it all in the coffee cup reading: the mountain, the cross. And Saint Dimitrios, I should add, was known for a few miraculous acts in his lifetime," he explained.

"Good, because it might take a miracle to get Crayton to give me another holiday extension. I have a feeling this time he'll have a proper strop. And by the way, what are you doing with all those notebooks? Research?"

"Just getting a few ideas down."

"For what?"

He gave me a 'no comment' gesture, with the eyebrows flicking up.

"Did you see Polly today?"

"No, I didn't go out in the end."

It was just what I thought, an excuse not to bother going out with Leonidas and me to lunch. It would probably have been better if he had.

"I thought we should meet up with Polly when we go to Kalamata for the cardio's appointment next week. I think I'll call her," I said.

"If you like," he said, sipping his beer with a vague expression on his face, as if his mind had been hijacked by aliens.

I set out for the *kafeneio*. As I passed Leonidas's house I noticed his car was still in the driveway. All the shutters in the house were closed. Probably sleeping still.

Walking to the village in the hour just before sunset had become one of my favourite activities for its sense of wound-down magic. The sun, descending behind the Messinian peninsula opposite, had turned the sky pink and purple, and the sea glimmered a dark burgundy. It was still warm enough, with a jacket on, to sit outside in the *plateia*. There were a few tables with Greek families eating outside the taverna, the usual collection of expats chattering away over carafes of wine, and a table with an old Greek man dressed in black and the village *papas,* in his black robe and stovepipe hat. How normal it seemed for a priest to be engaging with a villager over a glass of wine and a few small plates of food. It was oddly comforting. I would need some comfort when I came to deal with Crayton.

I took a table outside the *kafeneio* and Elpida came to sit with me and remarked on how good I looked.

"You have colours now, Bronte," she said, scrutinising my face closely, as only a Greek woman can, looking me up and down, all but taking my temperature. "Greece suits you."

I laughed. "You think so?" *Like father, like daughter*, I thought.

"You a bit plump too, from good Greek food and olive oil, eh?"

"Plump?" I didn't feel plump but, for a picky eater, I was eating a lot more than I would normally. Too many cakes. I looked down and noticed I now had a bit of a tummy.

I asked her what was happening about Myrto, as I hadn't seen her for a few days.

"Ach, Myrto, *kaimeni!* Poor woman! People coming to look at the land now. I hear someone is interested in buying it." She lowered her voice and darted a look around the *plateia*. "You never guess ... It's a German, looking for a place to build nice holiday house."

In God's name, how could she know that already? But I didn't doubt the veracity of her sources.

"We are already under the German boot with the austerity, the crisis, and now they want to buy up our village land too," she said, with a lemony expression.

I didn't know why she was making such a fuss when there were already a few Germans in the village with holiday homes, unless it was an excuse to vent the national dislike of Germany. Naturally it had been sired during the devastating occupation of the Second World War, but stoked up again and growing every day because of the punishing role that Germany had taken in the economic demands foisted on Greece in return for bailout funds.

It must have felt to the Greeks that their country was being occupied by Germany all over again. Many Greeks now believed the severity of the austerity measures was little more than the German payback for the Greek resistance during the war years. It was unfinished business and the antagonism had increased even more just the previous week, when Germany's Chancellor Angela Merkel came to Athens, on a goodwill mission ostensibly. But to locals it felt like she was flexing her muscles at the same time the Greek government was debating a new austerity package. So the idea of a German buying Myrto's land would be anathema to many villagers, I supposed.

"Poor Myrto. How will she cope with all this?" I asked,

With her arms crossed tightly over her chest, Elpida shrugged, her shoulders up to her ears. "Not so good. I hear that the German is being difficult. There are arguments with Hector. The German wants to cut down the price too. Everyone in the village is talking about it. She should have stayed in Australia. Should not have come back."

Elpida left for a short while and returned with a carafe of wine and a little plate of appetisers, which would suffice for dinner. I poured a measure of wine into the squat wine glass and drank it, firing up my laptop. I glanced towards the road and noticed Leonidas's car was now parked near the church. Then I saw him walking towards the *plateia*. He looked in my direction and for a moment I thought he was about to come over. I glanced at the wine carafe. I would offer him a drink. Nothing wrong with that, to show there were no bad feelings between us from lunchtime.

I glanced up again just as he was heading towards the back steps of the *plateia*. He waved in my direction and disappeared. Well, that was that! Had I really expected him to drop by after the embarrassment of the beach incident?

I tapped into my message list and hit the reply button on the last email I'd had from Crayton and started typing. I drank wine and chewed the edge of my thumb. What lies could I tell now? Did I really want to jeopardise my job by asking for even more time off? Had I had too much Greek sun? I bit my thumb again. I had to go to the *yiorti* for Saint Dimitrios. Had to!

Dear Crayton,

This is just to let you know that I'm still researching that feature for you, working as fast as I can. I've got some fantastic material. It will be a cracker. You can't imagine what the situation is like here, what Greek people are going through. However, I have to ask you a huge favour again. It's to do with my father. We have had another appointment with the cardiologist and my father must now go to Athens straight away for a heart scan. They have no such equipment in Kalamata. Can you believe that – the capital of the southern Peloponnese? I will need to go with him. It means that I have to stay here until the end of October, at least. He will certainly need treatment. God forbid he should require something like a heart bypass. I am very worried about him, so please let me know soonest if you can clear an extension with the editorial manager, and once again I apologise for leaning on the company's generosity over this family problem, but it has become more serious than I thought.

Kindest regards,

Bronte

I needed another drink after writing that piece of bogshite. That lie about the possible bypass! Good God, I now had Angus practically at death's door! I hoped I wasn't tempting fate. I sat and chewed my thumb a bit more and poured more wine into the glass. I downed that and poured another.

Just as I was skulling it, I looked over the glass and caught sight of Leonidas again, walking back across the *plateia,* carrying what looked like a bakery bag. Volcanic loaves? His head was turned in my direction, a curious look on his face, his dark eyebrows mincing together. He didn't wave this time but went straight to his car and roared off down the main road towards the sea, back to Kalamata, no doubt. I didn't blame him. What a pathetic figure I must have cut: the prim woman who thinks a holiday romance is a punishable offence but is happy to sit alone with her computer on a Saturday night and get blootered on cheap village wine. Oh, what the hell! I poured another glass.

I read Sybil's email next.

Dear Grecian Hen,

Well that's it! Sent out yesterday to do a news piece about neds putting traffic cones on Sir Walter Scott's feckin head at the Princes St monument. Did you know it's begun to rival the Wellington statue in Glasgow for number of cone misdemeanours? Who friggin cares, hen! I was doing this kind of shite 10 years ago. Writing to my Aussie uncle straight away. I've had it with the Alba. How's it going in Greece? It must have been a hard decision eh? Giving up Edinburgh for all that sun and retsina. LOL. How's it going with the Greek doc? If you haven't made a move yet, you're a bloody disgrace.

Sybil XX

I swiftly tapped out a reply.

Sybil,

Cones an utter disgrace! LOL. Australia's a good idea. Go for it. I have just asked for an extension (again!) on the trip here

& no, nothing to do with the doctor. If my 'association' with the doc were a news feature I'd say it hasn't grown arms and legs yet! Not many, anyway. Much to tell you soonest.

Grecian Hen

I felt tipsy when I set off back to the house. The sight of Leonidas's villa in darkness and the prospect of a night alone with Angus in Villa Anemos didn't inspire me exactly. It was strangely quiet as well in the village. The next day would change that entirely.

It was gunfire that woke me in the morning. It wasn't the usual gunfire of the village hunters looking for songbirds to shoot and later pickle; a local delicacy. This was louder, nearer, like Myrto's yard, and there was a screaming session in Greek; her and a male voice. Angus knocked on my door and poked his head inside the room.

"Did you hear that racket?" he said, shaking his head. "Do you mind if I look out your window a minute. It's closer to the commotion." He opened the window and peered down over Myrto's farm. I jumped out of bed and looked over his shoulder. We could see Myrto between the olive trees, with a rifle in her hand.

"What the fuck!" said Angus. "Looks like she's really gone doo-lally this time. I think that's Hector down there."

"What shall we do?"

"I'll get dressed and see if I can suss out what's going on."

I got dressed as well. I threw on a pair of shorts and a T-shirt, wondering if we should call the police — or was that a funny idea in a Greek village? Angus had already slipped out of the house, though I didn't think it was a very wise move. Hector probably had a gun as well. I hung around on the bedroom balcony to see if I could

227

get the measure of things and call for back-up if needed. I could hear more voices now, another man shouting in Greek. I could see Angus between the trees. Things went quiet for a while, until the sound of a truck revving up, spitting gravel as it tore down the road. I waited for five minutes and decided to go down. When I opened the front door, Myrto and Angus were standing outside, with Angus holding a rifle. He rushed in and propped it behind the door.

Myrto looked flustered, her eyes slightly wild. She was wearing a thick shirt, dark trousers and boots. She rushed up to me and squeezed my arm.

"Bronte, I am so sorry for noise and craziness."

I looked at Angus. He rolled his eyes.

"I think I'll call Leonidas. We need advice," Angus said, picking up his mobile. I smiled at the fact that in every crisis we called Leonidas, as if he were a magician with the power to solve all our problems.

Myrto and I sat at the dining table.

"What happened this morning?" I asked her.

"Ach! I take a gun to that *malakas* at last."

"Hector?"

"Yes."

Angus had no luck raising Leonidas. Perhaps he was at church, as it was Sunday morning. Angus took up the story. "Hector turned up this morning to tell Myrto that the German buyer has now put in an offer for the land and he wants to get things moving along quickly. Hector's dropped the price quite a bit, so he's keen as well. I understand, though, there is a dispute over the land boundaries. It's a typical story with these village properties; the original survey is old and hand-drawn, probably by Myrto's grandfather, and the German says it doesn't match the current boundaries, or what he thinks they are and what the neighbour on the other side thinks they are. It could take a while to sort and Hector is getting angsty. He came around this morning to tell Myrto to remove some of her goat troughs and other rural junk from the land, as if he hasn't got enough of his own there. She just lost it with him and fired a shot."

"Whose was the other voice I heard?"

"One of the men from the village happened to be passing and managed to talk Hector into leaving, which was lucky. That was Hector roaring off in his pick-up truck."

"Too bad I miss Hector. I learn to shoot in Aussieland with hunting rifle. Shoot a kangaroo once. I give Hector a good scare though."

She was scaring me too. I always thought Myrto was quite maverick. I could well see her in Australia, shooting at kangaroos, but I didn't think she'd go mental in this village.

"I lose my land soon. No trees to harvest. No income," she said, her eyes imploring us. I could see tears glistening there.

"I'm going to try Leonidas again," said Angus.

"Pah! He won't care. He is tired of Myrto," she lamented.

Angus went onto the balcony to call Leonidas again. I could hear him talking finally, but briefly, and he returned. "He can't do anything today. We have to call him if Hector keeps coming around or becomes threatening. He will talk to the police."

"Pah! What good are police. They not interested in villagers."

"I don't think he was pleased, though, at the prospect of the land going to a German," said Angus, his eyes flitting in my direction.

"I wish we had the money to buy the land," I said, more out of an idle wish to help Myrto.

Angus laughed derisively. "I certainly don't. Do you?"

"Of course not."

"Mind you. I heard Hector was asking 40,000 euros for the plot now, which is very low. Is that true, Myrto?"

She nodded, twisting her hands around on her knees.

"You know, I always thought Leonidas might have put in a bid for the land. He's pretty loaded," said Angus.

"He's going to England. What does he want with more village land?" I said.

"Is he really going? I thought it was a bit of a fantasy," Angus said, looking puzzled, scratching his chin.

"No, that's what he said."

"He could have told me. I'm his tenant, after all. I hope I don't have to find another place." *Who else would want this old house*, I thought.

Myrto sprang to her feet. "I go now. And I take my gun too, in case Hector comes back. I keep my gates locked now, all the time. He will like to push me out of my house too, if he can. Thanks be to God I don' do something very stupid like sign over everything. Fotis, he push for that too. *Gamoto!* But I say 'no'."

She left hurriedly, taking her rifle with her.

20

The Spartan's strategy

Despite the threat of rain, Polly and I met at an outdoor café in the elegant 23rd of March Square, in Kalamata's old sector. It had a surfeit of atmosphere, having been the place where freedom fighters like Theodoros Kolokotronis took on the Ottoman Turks in 1821, but it had another claim to fame as well. In one of the old buildings overlooking the square, famous English writer Lawrence Durrell had set up a school of English studies in September 1940. Six months later he had to abandon the project and escape from the Peloponnese to Crete by boat – just weeks before the German invasion of Greece.

The weather had turned cooler now, with clouds banking up to the east of the city from the direction of the Ionian Sea. Angus had said that things would perk up later in October and we'd definitely have the Indian summer, the Little Summer of Saint Dimitrios. I don't know why he was so sure, unless his coffee-cup divinations had told him so. But for now, a storm was brewing.

We had come to Kalamata so that Angus could keep his appointment with the cardiologist and also his accountant, or so he said, because sometimes he seemed to just disappear on various errands that I wasn't privy to, unless they were just boozing sessions with old mates. In the meantime, I met up with Polly. I had wanted to somehow engage her in a chat about Angus and where their relationship was heading, but not for any kind of mischief because I liked Polly a lot. However, there were too many other things to discuss. She was keen to hear about our expedition to Platanos and delighted that it had yielded a possible breakthrough, with the chance perhaps of meeting up with Dimitris Maneas on the feast day of Saint Dimitrios at the end of October. She was also pleased that Leonidas had been so helpful to us. I mentioned our lunch, vaguely.

Then something peculiar happened. Just as we were discussing Leonidas, it was as if our words had acted like a vibrant lure, and he suddenly appeared on the far side of the square. We stopped talking. He was holding hands with a tall woman with long straight hair, dressed in tight white jeans and an elegant jacket. They were talking and laughing with great ease.

Polly and I looked at each other. "Well, my dear. That is so incredible. Just as we are talking about Leonidas..." she said quietly, her eyes engaging in a long, analytical stare towards the couple.

"I hope he hasn't seen us," I said, trying to wriggle down in my seat.

"Don't worry, he only has eyes for Phaedra, it seems."

So! The famous Phaedra. I strained my eyes towards her. This was no bespectacled swot with a power drill. This was goddess material.

"She must be back for her father's name day this month. He is a Dimitris as well. I know the family slightly."

"But there is still 10 days to go until those celebrations," I said.

"Perhaps she has come earlier to spend time with her family. They have a large holiday home near the town of Koroni and they will celebrate there."

We watched them walk slowly through the square on the opposite side, past shops, not looking at anything in particular, mostly each other. I didn't doubt now he'd be booking a flight to England soon.

"So, there you see, Bronte. He invites you to lunch one day, and a few days later he's in the arms of Phaedra. You can forget any fantasy you might have had about him," she said with a motherly squeeze of my arm.

"I didn't have a fantasy, Polly," I said, taking umbrage at her comment. "I was just being polite over the lunch invitation."

"Don't be silly, my dear. Every Kalamatan woman I know has a fantasy about Leonidas."

"Really?"

"Don't be surprised at his behaviour, Bronte. There is no mystery about Greek men. They are driven by their own sense of entitlement. They do exactly what suits them. That's what I too have learnt, the hard way." Her dark eyes followed the pair as they trailed slowly to the far end of the *plateia*. At one point, Leonidas put his arm around Phaedra's waist and pulled her close. She inclined her head towards him. They looked more and more like a loving couple. I felt a tide of anger in my stomach because this made his behaviour on the beach a bit sleazy. I had thought better of him. Then they were gone, out of sight.

The rain came later, in big gusts, driven over the gulf, followed by thunder and lightning. We went back to Polly's apartment so I could wait for Angus to get a lift home, wherever he was. We passed the time watching the storm from her side balcony that had a view of the sea. Great forks of lighting were zigzagging down over the gulf and the thunder boomed like gunfire. Angus rang to say he had been held up and he would collect me when the storm died down, if it did.

Polly suggested we have a bite to eat, as I might be staying a while, and warmed up a spinach pie with a golden

233

pastry top, and made a Greek salad. We chatted while we ate and drank a few glasses of red wine. Despite everything, the afternoon was so pleasant that I would have been happy to stay, instead of returning to Marathousa.

After the meal, her mobile rang. She got up and went into the bedroom to answer it. She was a while, and out of curiosity I looked again at her photo collection, especially the one with her and Angus on the beach. Perhaps I subconsciously set myself up to be caught, and that's what happened when she left the bedroom soundlessly. Polly came and stood beside me. "Oh, we were so much better looking then, weren't we?" she said, with a nervous catch in her voice.

"Not that different, really. How long ago was this taken?"

"Hm … six, seven years ago."

"I'm sorry. I hope you don't think I was prying. I couldn't help noticing all your lovely photos."

"It's okay. I like people to see them," she replied, ignoring the fact that this particular photo had been hidden in the back row. I replaced the photo and we sat either side of the coffee table.

I didn't want to cause any upset after such a lovely afternoon but I couldn't help asking if she and Angus had been an item. *Hell, not an item, more like a whole damned shopping list!* I thought.

"Did Angus tell you that?" she asked.

"No, he won't talk about it, and I know it's a very personal issue. But I can see the attraction between you is strong." I shrugged, trying to seem casual.

She leaned back into the sofa, her expression wary. "We don't have a relationship now, Bronte, but we did. I won't lie about it. We were lovers for a while, even before I divorced, but that was not the cause of my marriage break-up. That had started a long time ago.

Angus gave me English lessons and we just became good friends and later more. We got on so well and he helped me a lot. He was a support to me in difficult times. He is a wonderful man."

I ignored that last comment. The jury was still out on that one. "I'm not surprised that Angus was drawn to you, Polly. You're very attractive and good company."

"Thank you. And so is Angus – attractive – though a daughter doesn't always see that perhaps."

"He used to be but he's gone slightly wild in Greece – the long hair and so forth," I smiled.

"You are not angry then – about us?"

"No, I'm not angry, not with you at least. You've been honest. I get angry with him for stubbornly refusing to talk about it, just like he refuses to talk about anything personal."

"He is ashamed because he left the family. Perhaps he thinks that you blame me, blame us, for the fact he stayed so long here," she said, twisting her rings around on her fingers.

"I suppose it didn't help. Once he met you he fell even more out of love with my mother, Marcella."

"Perhaps. And I shouldn't say this but he never told me a lot about Marcella and you and your sister. Or rather he did not imply that it was a problem for him living his own free life in Greece. I just accepted that. It's not uncommon, Bronte, to find people who have escaped to Greece to live another life. Perhaps I should have asked him more about your family, but I didn't. In any case, after I divorced, we stopped seeing each other. I needed time to think about my life, where it was going. I also wanted to spend more time with my daughter in Athens. By then, Angus had become more preoccupied with Kieran. Until you came, we had not seen each other for many months."

"Look, Polly, I'm not blaming you. We have to move on, right? It might surprise you, but I think that if you like each other still you should get back together again. What difference does it make now? My mother's remarried anyway."

She smiled, out of relief, perhaps. "That is generous of you to say, but I do not think it will happen. We are better to have our own lives and just be friends, I think."

"Well, that's up to you, of course, but thanks for talking about it."

"I am kind of relieved actually, that we have now. It was worrying me."

I was relieved myself that we had got things out in the open.

"Would you mind if I use your wi-fi? I need to look at my emails. I've got my laptop with me."

"Sure, Bronte, whatever you want." She got up to tidy the kitchen and left me alone for a moment.

I sat on the sofa and checked my messages. Crayton's was at the top of the list, sent that morning. He told me he was astonished I could ask for more time off, notwithstanding my father's health issue. Didn't I know the company was in a state of upheaval? He then summarised the recent changes, that I knew too well already. Then:

My sympathies for your father's illness, but it's like this, Bronte. While I and the company value your excellent work to date, I am afraid the managing editor is not prepared to offer more time out, given that your father does not appear to be in a critical condition yet, it seems. Might it not be better for him to return to Scotland for the tests, given the state of the crisis in Greece? We have been patient with you throughout but we feel that either you return as planned, which is the beginning of next week, or I will be forced to put your name forward for redundancy, and I am fairly certain you will get it, as we're looking to cut back on our feature writers as well, unfortunately. Perhaps this is the best option for you now. Please let me know soonest. And by the way,

I'd still like that piece on the Greek crisis. We had an agreement.
Can you send it ASAP!"

Regards,
Crayton

Could this day get any worse? I chewed away at my thumb.

"Everything okay there, Bronte?" asked Polly. She must have been watching me from the kitchen.

"More or less," I said. Damn Crayton! That was the thanks I got for years of slavish loyalty. I quickly dashed off my response, telling him where to shove his job. I'd take the redundancy, and the feature wasn't ready yet. I would need more time. No need to rush. Polly came out of the kitchen.

"I am hearing a lot of furious typing, Bronte."

"Ach" I said, slamming the lid down on the laptop and leaning back on the sofa. "My boss at the paper is not giving me any more time off. He wants me to return straight away, or else he'll put me forward for redundancy."

She looked shocked. "Oh, Bronte! This is terrible news."

"Well, yes and no. I've decided to take the redundancy. I love my job but it's under threat now anyway."

"But you have come here to help your father, and look what has happened. Has your newspaper no sense of decency?"

"No, Polly. But it's the whole industry that's in turmoil."

"You are taking it very well."

"Not really, but the timing is perfect. Now I can go to the *yiorti* for Saint Dimitrios, as planned. And let's hope we find something out. If we don't, all this will probably have been for nothing."

She tipped her head to one side in a gesture of sympathy and pouted sweetly. "I am so sorry for you."

When Angus eventually rang the buzzer below, ready to pick me up, I told her not to say anything about the redundancy. I would tell him later, after the *yiorti*.

"Okay, Bronte," she said, stroking my hair in a motherly fashion. "You're a very good daughter to Angus. I'm so glad we've met. Now that I know you, I feel so sad Angus turned his back on you all these years. I don't know how he could have done that."

"Neither do I, Polly, but maybe it's not just *Greek* men who have a sense of entitlement?"

She nodded and I saw tears hovering in her dark eyes.

When I saw Angus downstairs I felt less inclined to go back to Marathousa with him, not helped by the fact that he smelt of alcohol, even though he didn't seem particularly tipsy. He drove slowly at least and while the rain had eased off, the sky was the dirty grey colour of wet newspaper. We didn't talk much on the way, only about the cardiologist.

"The doc says the cholesterol has come down a bit, but not enough. The blood pressure is still a bit high and so on. Not much change, really. He told me I need to live like a monk on Mount Athos," he chortled. I found the idea ridiculous as well. When we got back to the house, I offered to make him some coffee but I was dismayed to find he only wanted to drink beer.

"That was some storm, wasn't it? Glad it's blown over now. It will get hot again now. I have high hopes it will be fine for the feast day of Saint Dimitrios next Friday." He rubbed his hands together, almost in anticipation.

"Did you hear back from the paper about staying here longer?"

"Yes, I cleared it with the features editor," I lied. "He's not well pleased, but never mind that."

"Fantastic, Bronte. So we're all set then. Did you have a nice day with Polly?"

"Yes, we had a great time. We had a good chat."

I had one of those moments in life when you know instinctively you shouldn't venture into a certain conversation but walk away. You're too crabbit and emotional. But I couldn't let it go. Something raked at my mind and wouldn't be still.

"We were looking at that picture of the two of you on the beach. Remember?" He gave me a squinty look over the top of his beer mug as he took a gulp. "I know the truth now. You did have a serious relationship for a few years with Polly. She told me."

"Oh, did she?"

"Yes. No reason to deny it now."

"Okay," he said with a deep sigh. "I suppose you're going to blame us for ruining everyone else's lives."

"Not at all. These things happen. She's attractive. She thinks you're attractive."

"Yeah?" he said, with a satisfied grin.

"Don't be cute!"

"Listen. We didn't set out to have an affair. It happened. She was unhappy. I guess I was lonely. We were discreet. She used to come to my house when I lived down on the coast. We never went out much in Kalamata. Even in a laid-back place like Kalamata, you can't be too careful. After her divorce we just decided to cool things."

"Are you still in love with her?"

He started picking fluff off the legs of his trousers. He pouted. "Yes, I suppose I am, really. It's been nice seeing her these past few weeks. It makes me realise what a good rapport we had. Did she say how she feels about me now?"

"No." I didn't want to be a go-between. He frowned.

"She likes you, Bronte. I had hoped you'd be friends."

"We are. I don't have a problem with her. It's you I've got the problem with. The way you kept this relationship quiet all these years. Made us imagine you were here

239

searching for yourself. You never had the guts to fess up and tell us the real reason you weren't coming back. You never told poor Mum that the marriage was over because you were here shagging someone else." I hadn't meant to be offensive, but I'd suddenly lost my edit button. The day had soured me completely.

He whistled softly. "You journos don't mince your words, do you?"

"Why bother!"

"Well, it wasn't like that, Bronte, and you know it. Polly's way beyond that. She's a classy and very intelligent woman. Don't insult her!"

"I'm not. I agree she's lovely. Like I said, it's you I'm skunnered with. And all the illusions you seem to have had. All the lies you've told, including the one that got me over here, about the urgency of your health problem. Does the Greek sun make people want to tell porkies?"

He sipped his beer casually, but I could tell from the set of his mouth that he was straining to hold his temper. "I don't blame you for being angry. For thinking I'm a miserable toe-rag. Look, even if I hadn't met Polly I don't think I would have come back to Scotland. I've told you all that before. There was nothing for me there. I was jaded with teaching, everything. Marcella and I had grown apart. Now Marcella's remarried. It didn't take that long. I was surprised, actually."

We all were, because Marcella had been the reserved one, happy with her teaching and making her upside-down cakes. But then she met someone special.

I should have tapped on the brakes there, but something was still fizzing inside me. This was the conversation we should have had already, but the timing was never right. Now we were way beyond that.

"What about Shona and me? Didn't you ever think about coming back to Scotland, for us. To spend time with the grandchildren you've hardly ever seen? I mean, face it. Your time here was nothing more than a selfish bid for mid-life hedonism; sun, sex and an alcoholic randan, by the sounds of it."

"Oh, don't start, Bronte!" he said, shaking his head. "Look, okay, I lay on the beach a lot to start with and drank too much and enjoyed this wonderful freedom for the first time in my life and …"

I cut across him. "Then the good life ran out, didn't it? After a dalliance with teaching and olive harvesting, you had the love affair with Polly and then she decided to cool the romance. So what did you do then? You decided to have one last stab at finding poor Kieran; redeem your miserable, pointless life." I was on a roll now, like a big dipper about to crash off the rails.

"Don't bring Kieran into this."

"Why not? I'm starting to suspect that Kieran may be just an excuse to spend another 10 years in Greece. I mean, even Odysseus went home in the *end*," I said, raising my voice until it sounded ragged.

He glared at me, tried to stand up, holding his beer mug, and sat down again.

"I'd be lucky to get another 10 years, wouldn't I?" he snapped.

"And here's another thing. After you cooled things with Polly, before you turned your attention to Kieran, why didn't you think of coming back then? That would have been sensible, sorting out your health problem in Scotland. Much less trouble for all of us, instead of hanging on like all the other rootless expats."

"I don't mix with them, I told you. That's not my scene… I …."

He looked queasy but I kept going. "What makes you any different? I can't see it, apart from you speaking Greek."

He didn't reply. I ranted on a bit more in the same vein, buoyed up by a flood of frustration and anger that seemed endless, and ramped up more by the thought that because of Angus and his crazy mid-life missions, I had lost my job on the Alba, such as it was now, with nothing to fall back on. That's when I noticed he'd put his hand on his chest. I realised I'd gone too far.

"Are you okay?" I said in a small voice.

"Yeah, just a bit tired."

"Are you sure you're okay? You don't look it. Have you got chest pains?" This was what I had feared – a heart attack. Now I was pushing him towards it.

"No, not at all, but I just get a bit tight in the chest sometimes. My heart gets a bit racy. I've got drugs to take for that."

"You're to tell me if you get chest pains. Leonidas has told me that if you do, I'm to take you straight to Kalamata Hospital."

My anger had died completely now. I felt calmer. I pinched my lower lip with my teeth. "You know, Angus, maybe we should just book a flight back to Scotland straight away and get you sorted. We can always come back here again and finish the business over Kieran."

He looked horrified. "What, and miss out on the feast day of Saint Dimitrios? Our best hope so far? No way!"

I shook my head. Mission Kieran suddenly seemed like madness, getting ready to hare up a mountainside to hopefully talk to someone we'd never met about a relative who might have been murdered over 70 years ago but no-one can now remember in much detail. I rubbed my eyes as if I could make the last few weeks disappear, or even the last 10 minutes. I got up, went to the kitchen and poured a glass of water. I knew Angus kept his drugs in a kitchen drawer in a zip-up bag. I brought them back to the table.

"Here, at least have some water and take something for the tight chest."

"Thanks. Look, I've not had actual pain, honestly. Even if I did, the cardio guy gave me this angina spray. Christ, I'm out the door with drugs now." He managed a smile. "That will get me by."

He pulled a blister pack from the bag and took one of the tablets, to calm his heart, he told me. I fetched a glass of water for myself, gulped a few mouthfuls and sat beside him. I let the negative stuff go, it was all I could do. I couldn't change the past, or fix it, and in a way, I didn't *want* to care about it any more.

"Look, Angus, I'm sorry. I shouldn't have brought up the subject of Polly the way I did. It was out of line, but ... you know how things just *fester*."

"No, you were right to be angry, pet. Now we've said all there is to say. Let's just concentrate on the job in hand."

"Should I call Leonidas? See if he thinks you need to go to the hospital?"

"God, no! He'll definitely tell me to go. I told you, I'm fine."

"Okay, but don't you think you should at least contact the cardio guy again and tell him you want to make a definite appointment for a private clinic in Athens, straight after the *yiorti* at Platanos? It's got to be done some time. Everyone keeps telling you the same thing."

"Okay, I'll call him. I'll make the appointment. It's no bother."

"Okay, good."

He looked more composed now, less pale, but slightly broken. He sat back in his chair, staring at the table. I felt sorry for him.

"You didn't mean that about Kieran, did you? That I was making him an excuse to stay longer here? That was unfair, Bronte. I would never do that to Kieran."

"I know you wouldn't. I said it in anger. I'm sorry. I do worry about the mission though. Wonder if it isn't all too much for you, for all of us, really."

He hunched in his chair and nodded. I was also worried about the feast day celebration at Platanos, and what would happen. I may have been nettled over the image of Leonidas and Phaedra today but I was sure glad he would be coming with us. We couldn't have a better chaperone. If he could swing a defibrillator as well, that would be even better.

"You're smiling, Bronte."

"Not smiling, no. Feeling doo-lally!"

He laughed. "Don't go crazy on me, Bronte. Everything will be fine," he said, patting my knee. I felt my eyes begin to prickle. I had the childish urge to cry, out of pure helplessness, and disgust as well that I let my temper get the better of me. I got up and started tidying the kitchen.

"By the way, Polly said she will come with us to Platanos on the 26th," I said, with my back to him, trying to sound a more chipper note.

"Ah, that's grand. I'm pleased."

"I didn't tell you. Polly and I saw Leonidas in the old square in Kalamata with the girlfriend, Phaedra. She's quite something. Sex on legs," I said, trying to lighten the mood.

"Really?" he said, making a small derisory noise in the back of his throat. "I didn't think it would come to that. But I'd say he'll definitely be shipping out of here one day soon then. All the best Greeks will be leaving soon. Shame, really. Poor old mother Greece with her blood-soaked roots. And then finally abandoned. Not my words by the way, some Greek writer said that in another tormenting period of local history."

"But not abandoned by you at least, Angus, not yet."

"Aye, you're right, Bronte, and there's the irony. We expats are digging in our heels here and the Greeks are all shipping out."

The idea of this population swap horrified me but there was no more discussion on it. He got up, saying he wanted to rest downstairs for a while. I went out to the back balcony to watch the last gasp of the storm and the clouds scudding fast over the dark sky. A stiff breeze was blowing up from the gulf, ruffling the heads of the olive trees. The air was cold and tangy, with a salty nip.

I sat at the table, enjoying the solitude, grateful that a health drama with Angus had been averted, for now. I wasn't proud of the incident, and not surprised either. Everything in my life felt messy at that point, and yet there was something about Greece, its preternatural beauty and simplicity that undercut all the other crises. I liked Greece more and more the longer I stayed. I thought a lot about Kieran and the fact that, because of him, I was becoming inextricably linked to this place. To find the conclusion to Kieran's story would make all our lives seem more meaningful and would certainly calibrate mine. I began to need this mission to be a success as much as Angus did.

In the days before the Platanos *yiorti*, the weather became hot enough again, like Angus had predicted, for us to continue swimming in secluded coves. We had reached a calm plateau for now, keeping off difficult subjects, enjoying some nights out at the taverna.

I finished my feature on the crisis and while my redundancy was going through, I decided I would send it to Crayton, but a watered-down version with a few pictures. I would keep back some of the best quotes and pictures for another piece I was going to write for one of the London papers, which would pay me a lot more money and perhaps kickstart a freelance career for now. The Greek crisis was becoming big news everywhere in the world as the spectre of bankruptcy hovered over the country.

I had coffee with Myrto a few times, though she had a funereal glumness about her that no amount of cajoling would fix. But I got regular updates on how the German's boundary problem was proceeding: very slowly, by all accounts. Angus seemed optimistic at least, saying everything was fitting into place with Mission Kieran. Most of all, he was relieved I had scored the extra time off.

"What did I tell you, Bronte, when you found the saint in your handbag? That you'd probably still be here in October. The old bam daddy was right!" he said.

All the omens were good and the planets in their right positions. But there is a Greek saying: "When a man makes plans, God laughs." I had a feeling the Greeks didn't say it for no reason.

21

Saint Dimitrios

On the way up to Platanos on the feast day of Saint Dimitrios, we looked like we were ready for a funeral rather than a celebration – and not because of our smart dark outfits. We were all rather subdued, perhaps due to the early start. Leonidas had told us we needed to be at the church by 8.30 for the last hour of the service. He had knocked at our door at 7.15, dressed in a black suit with a white shirt, his curls bouncing with rude health. I was ready to go, armed with my camera and notebook and also the old photo of Kieran in case Dimitris did turn up at the celebration.

We all fitted comfortably into Leonidas's roomy four-wheel drive. Angus, in the front passenger seat, had scrubbed up well, dressed in an old but respectable charcoal suit, his ponytail brushed and shiny. I took his ponytail now as a barometer of his moods. Curiously, when it looked neat, he was generally in a good place. Polly and I sat on the back seat. Hardly a word was exchanged between any of us until the car turned onto the mountain road after Ayios Yiorgos.

Polly broke the ice, twiddling an expensive set of pearls around in her well-manicured fingers. "I see that Phaedra has come back to Kalamata," she said to Leonidas, speaking in English, to include us all in the conversation. But I could tell how her mind was working when she nudged my leg gently.

"Yes, she has come back for a holiday with the family and to celebrate her father's name day in Koroni. She does that every year."

"How is she liking England?" probed Polly.

"She is very happy there. I don't think she will want to come back to Greece for a long time." *If ever*, I thought.

"And what about you? How are your plans for England going?"

He didn't answer but I saw his face in the rear-view mirror and it looked strained. I couldn't understand his reticence, as I was sure the news about him leaving for England would have circulated by now. Perhaps Phaedra would be nudging the story along in Kalamata.

Polly seemed to be enjoying her little wind-up. Angus turned slightly in his seat and gave me an impish look. I smiled. Then, surprisingly, Leonidas switched to Greek and he and Polly had a rapid conversation. Perhaps he was rebuking her for being nosey. When their little chat finished I saw him in the mirror tugging on his bottom lip with his top teeth. It made me think of the day on the Kitries beach and how his lips had felt when we kissed. It seemed a long time ago now.

As the road climbed higher and higher we were approaching the point where the scree had challenged us when Angus and I first drove up to Platanos. As we neared it, a herd of goats suddenly appeared on top of a bank of rocks by the roadside and danced down it, bringing more scree from the rockface in their wake. Leonidas had to brake sharply to avoid them.

"*Gamoto!*" he said, with a wave of his hand.

The goat herd streamed across the road in front of the car, with the lusty noise of goat bells filling the quiet morning air. A shepherd in old baggy clothes appeared, holding a long stick, a big black dog at his heels. It was a timeless image that seemed to divide the world we'd left and the one we were about to enter, which was how I always felt when I came up here, as if on some level this place didn't really exist.

The village had a more festive air than we'd encountered last time. A dozen cars and a small people-carrier were parked along the main road near the church of Saint Dimitrios, whose grounds bordered the road. Coloured bunting, and small Greek flags, were slung between the church and the nearby trees. Two rows of tables and chairs had been set to the side of the church in the shade. Inside, there were some 40 people or so.

Most of the congregation were middle-aged or older, women to the left, men to the right. The *papas* was also old, with a grey beard and dressed in a gold and red embroidered robe. At the door, an icon of Saint Dimitrios was placed on a carved wooden stand, surrounded by a thick garland of flowers.

Leonidas led the way, dropping not a coin into the wooden donations box near the entrance but a folded banknote, as would befit his status here. He lit a candle and kissed the icon. Angus followed him and they sat to the right with the other men. When it was my turn to (air-kiss) the icon, I noticed it was similar to my own icon from the taxi, but bigger: a jaunty character perched on his horse; a caped crusader with an inscrutable expression, part stoical, part mischievous.

Polly and I sat on the women's side and I scanned the men's side, looking for Dimitris Maneas. I was expecting to see someone grey-haired and tall, slightly distinguished-looking, from the photo we had been given by Pavlos. I could see no-one who came close. These men were either much older or smaller, or fatter. As I studied the men, I caught Leonidas's eye. There was a faint flicker of his eyebrows, as if he might have been thinking the same thing.

The service was a sombre affair, as I'd expected. Now and then the *papas* turned towards the congregation and swung his censer. Great billowing clouds of sweet-smelling incense filled the air and rose to the vaulted ceiling. The service ended with a queue down the centre aisle for the consecrated bread. As I waited for my turn, behind Angus, I glanced around the men's section again and noticed a tall, thin man, who had previously been obscured by a stout column. He was stepping down from one of the high-backed wooden chairs against the wall. Beside him was a younger man. Angus was also watching and he gave me a meaningful look.

It was not until we were all outside that Leonidas told us he would go and talk to him. There was a buzz of activity at the front of the forecourt near a van parked on the road. Two men in aprons were standing before a trestle table carving into a hunk of roasted meat on a wooden platter, placing slices on paper plates. Women from the congregation were ferrying the plates over to the tables set up outside the church, where bowls of salad and baskets of bread were also being distributed.

"Where did all this food come from?" I asked Angus, wondering how a village with so few people could have organised such a feast.

"Vans go around on these kinds of feast days with spit-roasted pork. They go from village to village. It's a big thing in the Mani and this is one of the biggest feast days of the year."

I marvelled at the way Greeks could mobilise events quickly, especially for the feast days. It was all strangely reassuring. The congregation rushed to each of the tables to claim one for their family group, and Polly did likewise, though with slightly more grace in her sprint than the others. She picked a table under an orange tree, where only two other churchgoers had so far settled. In the distance, at the edge of the forecourt, I could see Leonidas talking with the tall man. After a few minutes, he steered the man to our table.

"I'd like you all to meet Dimitris Maneas and his friend Yiannis, who has brought him here from Kalamata this morning," said Leonidas. Dimitris gave a tentative smile.

I felt a wave of relief wash over me that all this effort had yielded something. Angus looked happier than I'd seen him look for weeks. We all shook hands and Leonidas invited the pair to join us at our table. Dimitris was 85, but looked good for his age, with a fresh complexion and thick grey hair. He also spoke near-perfect English, with an American accent from his years living there, whereas his friend seemed to speak no English at all. Dimitris didn't say much to begin with and looked at Angus and me with a curious expression. I wondered what Leonidas had already told him. The poor guy thought he was coming for a pleasant Greek celebration, and here we were planning to plunder his past.

Polly helped to serve the food and poured everyone a drink from the wine carafes. When I looked around at the diners I noticed the shopkeeper Pavlos. He gave me a muted wave and returned to his lunch. He was sharing a table near the church door with the two chanters and the *papas*, who was now wearing his everyday black robe, and holding court. Several people had sauntered past our table and stopped to wish Dimitris 'many years' on his name day. While he was distracted, Leonidas whispered to Angus and me, "I only had time to tell Dimitris that you were both interested to know about life in the village when he was a boy. I didn't say why, and that perhaps he could make time for you after the lunch is over. So let us just enjoy a nice meal for now."

"Thanks, Leo, for your tact in all of this," said Angus.

Leonidas shrugged lightly. "It is nothing, but I hope this is what you want. Dimitris might have a story to tell that none of us will want to hear." Leonidas caught my eye. His look gave nothing away. I wondered what he meant exactly. How could any of us have known then that this would be a day that would change our lives immeasurably?

Conversation over lunch was light and we decided we would all speak in English to make things easier. Dimitris seemed more comfortable talking English, in any case, because of his time in America. He was affable and chatted about his life in Chicago and his work, running his own real estate business. We also learnt that he still had the apartment in Athens that his father had bought in 1952, just three years before the family migrated to America. He told us he still liked to return to Greece roughly every five years – just as Pavlos had said – sometimes alone, as his wife had now passed away, and other times with one of his children. This year he had come alone and he confessed that each time the trip became more tiring.

"I can't deny that the economic crisis has made my time in Greece more upsetting. I see the demonstrations in Athens and it takes my mind back to other eras of Greek history I'd rather forget," he said, with a mournful expression in his light brown eyes. Angus and I exchanged quick looks. Here we were, about to take him back to the difficult era of the war.

"But I can't come back to Greece and not make the journey to Platanos, at least to honour the rest of my family who have gone now. It's a kind of pilgrimage, but I am thinking this year will probably be my last, or else I'll need to be dropped here by helicopter by the time I'm 90," he said, laughing lightly, showing good strong teeth despite his years, courtesy of American dentistry, no doubt.

"You can't imagine how much this *yiorti* has diminished over the years. Once when there were many people in the village, this whole area here would be crammed with tables and the festivities would last for hours. Few of us make this trip now, and the village itself is practically empty, especially in winter. If this place was in America it would be a kind of museum, with someone charging admission." He laughed again, though the mirth never quite reached his eyes.

Angus didn't say much through the meal and he drank a lot of wine. Polly was in good spirits and I was glad to have her along. She had the subtle gift of being able to take control of a difficult situation without it seeming that way. Despite her dig at Leonidas in the car, she got on well with him, and it was rather amusing the way she seemed to flirt with him as well, just slightly. I wondered if she had ever entertained her own fantasies about Leonidas, like the Kalamatan women she had alluded to the day we sat in the square. When Leonidas left the table for a moment, I asked her what their Greek conversation in the car had been about.

She smiled. "About him going to England. He is being very coy about the whole thing, my dear. He says he doesn't talk about it too much because he fears people will condemn him as a traitor."

"What do you mean?"

"You know, leaving Greece in crisis, when everyone is suffering. I've seen this a lot. Many Greeks don't want to say they are leaving until they are practically on the plane. But in his case, I think it is probably more complicated," she said, with a meaningful look.

The lunch seemed to wind up as quickly as it had begun, with some of the congregation folding up the tables and stacking them with the chairs in a small outhouse at the back of the church. Most people were in a hurry to get back down the hillside and, one by one, the cars departed. We adjourned to the *pantopoleio*. We huddled around two metal tables outside that we pushed together, while Pavlos went off to make Greek coffee. Angus was the only one wanting ouzo, however. Leonidas must have offered to drive Dimitris back to Kalamata because the young man he came with bade him farewell.

While we waited for the drinks, Leonidas explained to Dimitris the real intention of our visit that day, and our recent meeting with Orestes, when he spoke about the shooting of the British soldier. Dimitris smiled at the mention of his boyhood friend, whom he had not seen for many years, but I imagined that the reminiscences we were seeking would give him no joy. He rubbed a hand over his eyes, as if to collect his thoughts. I had no doubt he didn't want to talk about the war today.

He turned to Angus and me. "My friends, I am sorry to hear that the poor young soldier who was shot may have been a relative of yours, and if he was, then I am very honoured to meet you both. We kept him hidden in our house for about three weeks, and during that time he was like one of our family. I don't know if I can tell you anything useful about who he really was. It's a long time ago and some of it I have put out of my mind on purpose and have never talked about, beyond our close family. Some of it is difficult ..." He stopped for a moment, looking pained, as if he felt this was all too much of an imposition, on his name day, of all things.

Then he added, "But you know what? I think maybe it's time I did talk about it properly. I'm old. I may not get another chance."

I could hear Angus beside me exhaling with a deep sense of relief. And so Dimitris began to tell us his own remarkable story...

22

Road map to the past

"I was the one who originally found the young soldier, hiding in a cave on the ridge behind our house," Dimitris told us. "He was with another soldier then. It was the beginning of May. They looked real scared and hungry. I remember that so well, and how young they seemed. They told me they were *Inglesi*, English, one of the few Greek words they knew. I figured that naturally they had just escaped from Kalamata after the Germans occupied the city, but why they came so far up the mountains to Platanos, I couldn't imagine. I went home and told my father, and at dusk we went back up to the cave and brought them to the house.

"To Greeks, the allied soldiers were heroes. They started out as liberators, even though the Germans overran them in the end. Many Greeks felt that supporting the allies, and even hiding them, was a huge act of defiance against the German occupation.

"We hid them in the basement of our house, where we kept our donkey and some of the small goats at night behind a wooden partition. It was a cold, stuffy space and the boys had to sleep on the hard earthen floor on blankets. That was all we had for them. We were poor farming people and the house was old with few comforts, no electricity in those days and water came only from the spring nearby. The other boy left after a few days. We didn't know why. We couldn't communicate with them

255

properly, of course. We had no other languages, apart from Greek, but somehow, with a lot of effort and hand signs, we got some kind of message across. The other soldier, I think, changed his mind about the mountains. He seemed uneasy and wanted to go back down the coast to look for a boat. The one who remained wanted to stay a while and then make his way through the mountains to the southern part of the peninsula. Or so we imagined.

"He spent most of his time in the beginning in the house. We had heard the Germans were searching the Mani for fugitive soldiers and many had already been rounded up and taken prisoner. The soldier ate with us and sat with us round the fire at night. He retreated to the basement if anyone came to the house. After a while he became restless and begged us to let him out during the day to roam on the hillside above as long as he was careful. What could we say? He was young and energetic and seemed unafraid; he liked being outside. Although we were at the remote end of the village and you only came near our house if you were using the *kalderimi*, the track down the mountainside, we prayed that no-one else would see him.

"The villagers in the Mani were mainly sympathetic to the allies, as I said, but sometimes villagers would let slip certain things to the small number of other Greeks who may not have been as trustworthy. The Germans put out regular edicts after the Battle of Kalamata, saying that no Greek could associate with or help an allied soldier – or they would be shot. Anyone hiding a soldier would be shot and their house burnt. So, of course, we didn't want anyone to know the soldier was with us. Also the Germans had put a bounty on the heads of allied soldiers. There were plenty of villagers in the region desperate for money for food who would happily betray them. These were terrible times, my friends," said

Dimitris, squeezing together his large wrinkled hands and stopping to gather his thoughts.

Angus took advantage of his brief lapse in concentration. "The soldiers said they were English, but did they ever tell you where they came from? Or rather, did they ever tell you they were Scottish rather than English?" I knew Angus had latched onto that issue the moment he'd heard the word *Inglesi*.

"Well, we assumed they were both English. I don't think we even knew where Scotland was then. I am sorry. It was all the same to us then," he said, smiling bashfully.

"Do you remember his name?" I asked, rushing to the question that must have been on everyone's lips.

"He had an English name, of course, but we couldn't pronounce it, and I certainly don't remember it now." I could hear Angus sigh with disappointment. "But we gave him a Greek one," Dimitris added. "It was easier, safer too, and I do remember it. Kostas."

Angus gasped. "My father was called Kieran, so that's one small co-incidence, a Greek name starting with a 'K'. Does Kieran sound familiar perhaps?"

Dimitris shook his head. "I wish I could say it did, but I'm afraid not."

"Please continue, Dimitris. We are very grateful for anything you can remember," I said, gently urging him on, but I did feel a glimmer of optimism with that one piece of information.

"We didn't know a whole heap about the soldiers because they had nothing much with them when I found them in the cave, apart from their army clothes, a small rucksack each, a rifle, some ammunition, and not much else. If they had identification with them, I don't remember seeing it. After the other boy left, I spent a lot of time with Kostas and took him around the hillside at the back, sometimes a bit further on. He was a swell kind of guy.

We felt for his predicament and wanted to keep him safe. We gave him some of our clothes so he'd look like everyone else: old baggy trousers and a jacket, and an old woollen shepherd's bag. We thought from a distance, with his dark hair especially, he might almost pass as a Greek." Dimitris beamed at this recollection, one of the few times he smiled throughout his narrative.

Angus shot me a look at the mention of 'dark hair'. I could tell he was getting more buoyed-up. His hand trembled slightly and the ice cubes in his ouzo glass tinkled like chimes every time he took a sip. That's when I remembered the photo in my bag. I reached in and pulled it out and showed it to Dimitris and said quietly, "Is this the Kostas you remember? It's a picture taken in Scotland of my grandfather a few years before the war."

Dimitris held it in his hand, staring at the image of Kieran sitting on a rock on the edge of a loch. Everyone around us was eerily silent, watching him. Dimitris sighed and finally looked up at me, and then Angus. His eyes glimmered with the start of what looked like tears.

"Gee! This guy here is damned handsome, just as Kostas was, and the dark thick hair, too. He could be Kostas … but I have to be honest, it's been decades and I knew him for just a short time. I just couldn't say for sure. I wish I could bring back to mind that exact image of the Kostas we knew. But, folks, I can't." He gave me a sorrowful look as he handed back the photo. I left it on the table in front of him, hoping it might jog his memory later.

"It's okay, Dimitri. It was a long time ago, you're right. Not a part of your life you wanted to remember, I imagine," said Angus.

"No, and not when I tell you the rest of my story." He stopped to gather his thoughts again, and then continued. "More and more, my father let Kostas roam about the hill but told me to keep an eye on him. He spent time also in the cave Orestes mentioned. Only the villagers knew about this place. It was quiet, out of sight. I wondered how he could spend so much time there. It was a cold, lonely spot, yet he was the kind of young man … how can I explain … who seemed happy with his own company, who liked to be with nature. He had a small notebook, I remember that, and he liked to draw …"

Angus cut across him, gripped by renewed optimism. "That's incredible, Dimitri! My father loved the outdoors. He loved to walk the Scottish hills and he also loved to draw. My mother told me that."

"Angus, let's hear the rest, shall we," I said, tapping his arm lightly. I felt we were merely clutching at straws as long as we didn't have a positive identification. Angus frowned and fell silent again.

Dimitris continued. "Kostas liked to sit on the hill in a certain clearing, where you can see the whole Taygetos range. I sat with him there a few times while he was drawing in the notebook. He wrote notes in it too, like a diary, though I never read them, of course. English was as foreign to me then as Chinese. We told him as best we could that if he ever suspected the Germans were nearby to hide his notebook somewhere and also to go down the ravine on the other side of the ridge because there were smaller caves there, where he could hide. I had shown him one or two. But, as you know from Orestes' story, Kostas didn't get that far on the day the Germans came to our village.

"I remember that day very well because it started off with rain and a howling wind from the north, even for a spring day at the end of May. After the rain stopped it was dark, cloudy, the kind of day you know will depress you whatever you do. There was no light that day, in every sense.

"The Germans had arrived in a foot patrol of around eight soldiers, fully armed. They came up the *kalderimi* from the village below, Ayios Yiorgos, which was no small trip up that steep stone path. It was always perilous and slippery with the rain or snow, and sadly for us they managed it. They came to our house first. Only my mother was there. My father and I had gone to the town of Kambos on the plain the day before to see my father's uncle and to buy farm supplies. My brother Alexandros, who was 16, was in the village with our grandfather. We had stayed overnight in Kambos and came back late in the afternoon after the Germans had left.

"We found my mother in a helluva state and the house a real mess, everything pulled apart. The Germans had ransacked the place, looking for a British soldier, they said. Luckily, they didn't find any trace of him and that's the way we organised it. Nothing belonging to Kostas was ever left lying about. The few small possessions he had he took out with him in his shepherd's bag and left his sleeping blanket upstairs in the house. Then the Germans did exactly the same at Orestes' house, pulled it apart, and his father was beaten up. Four soldiers stayed below while the others went straight up the ridge at the back of the houses. It was as if they knew exactly where they were going and what they were looking for. Kostas was found not far from the mouth of the cave, as if he had been trying to make a run for it. He was shot dead, one bullet in his back, one in the forehead to finish him off," he said, his voice trembling.

He stopped momentarily, visibly upset at the recollection, and drank some water from a tall glass that had come with the Greek coffees. I looked around at the others. Polly seemed downcast. Leonidas, who had previously been surreptitiously checking his mobile for messages, was now listening quietly, his head cocked to one side. Angus was slumped in his chair with his arms over his chest, and Pavlos was glumly smoking, half turned towards the *plateia,* with one elbow on the back of his chair. He probably hadn't understood a word, yet he picked up on the sombre mood.

"It would appear," said Dimitris, with a little more composure, "that someone had seen Kostas one day up on the ridge. It must have been someone who knew the village well enough to know this was a stranger, even with the shepherd's outfit. We will never know, but this person must have informed on Kostas for sure because of the way the Germans behaved. The path up the wooded hill was not obvious to the casual visitor if you didn't know it was there.

"After they shot Kostas, the Germans came back down and the patrol marched into the village and continued ransacking houses, ordering people out onto the *plateia.* One old guy called Babis made trouble, refusing to line up in the *plateia* with the other residents, and he was shot in the head. Mercifully, he was the only one killed. It could have been much worse for all of us if the Germans had found any shred of evidence that any one of us had hidden Kostas. Or maybe they didn't want to discourage any more useful informers by butchering the lot of us.

"When my father and I got back to the village in the afternoon from Kambos and poor Orestes came to our house to tell my father what he'd seen, my father was real cut up about it. I think he felt he had let Kostas down and had gone off the day before and left him to his own devices. Straight away, he sent for my brother and we went up the hill to find Kostas and bury him and cover up the grave as much as we could. It was the safest thing to do before the other villagers heard anything about him and started asking awkward questions.

"My father and Alexandros did most of the work. I was taken along as a lookout. They dug a grave near the top of the hill, where the land wasn't so rocky, but it was hard labour with old farm shovels. They wanted to bury him with his notebook, but it wasn't with him, so I was sent up to the cave to look for it. I searched about and had a moment of panic when I couldn't find it. What if the Germans had discovered it first? They would be back in the village again. But I did find it in the end, wedged into a crevice in the rocks at the back of the cave. It was stained at the edge from water seepage. I wanted to keep it, to remember Kostas, but my father said 'no' and that it would be better if the notebook was placed with the body for everyone's safety while there was an informer in the village.

"At the grave, my father said a prayer for him. It was one of the saddest days of my young life. I didn't think it would end this way, you know. Kostas had such energy and life in him. I was sure he would escape one day and find his way to Crete – and live … "

Dimitris stopped to compose himself. His eyes were red-rimmed. I felt my lower lip tremble. I glanced at Angus and saw him rub a hand over his eyes.

Dimitris picked up the story again. "My father wanted to do the right thing for Kostas and promised at the graveside that after the war he would exhume the body and give him a proper burial and he would have a blessing from a *papas*. We never spoke to anyone about Kostas. We tried to get on with our lives, such as they were because Greece was a living hell during the war. After that came the terrible conflict of the Greek Civil War. These were dark days, folks. In the 1950s, my father was tired of conflict and the mountain life. That's when we sold up and left, as I've told you."

"Tell us, Dimitri, if you believe that Kostas was betrayed by someone in the village, do you have any idea who it was?" asked Polly.

I sensed the tension around us. Dimitris squeezed his big hands together and said, "It seems clear he was a villager seeking the bounty money and he must have told the Germans where the boy could occasionally be found. Fortunately for everyone else, Kostas wasn't in the house when the Germans arrived. Also, the informer hadn't sussed out that we had anything to do with it, or if he had, he decided to leave that part out so as not to incite reprisals from villagers if we were shot. Well, that's what I'm guessing."

"And you don't know who the informer was?" asked Angus.

Dimitris shook his head. "We never found out exactly. It could have been one of a number of people. We couldn't start asking a lot of questions after Kostas died, stirring things up."

We all lapsed into a dismal silence. I know Angus was thinking, as I was, that it was the end of the story. No identification. We were no further forward in knowing who poor Kostas really was.

Leonidas had said nothing throughout Dimitris's narrative but he suddenly roused himself. "Dimitri, did your father exhume the body of the soldier in the end?" he asked.

How fitting that Leonidas would ask this, as a doctor, after the rest of us had forgotten it. It would turn out to be the most significant question of the day.

"Yes, of course. In 1949, after the civil war, my father carried out his promise. Kostas's body was exhumed and the remains prepared in line with our village custom. For those who don't know perhaps," Dimitris said, looking at Angus and me, "my mother and one of her sisters came to help prepare the bones after exhumation, washing them in wine, as we have always done in Greece. The local *papas* was called and he said the traditional prayers for the dead because, though Kostas wasn't Orthodox, in our eyes he was one of us. Then we stored his bones in a reliquary box in the ossuary. That was the way we did things."

"What's an ossuary?" I asked Dimitris.

"It's the small building that you see beside the graveyard of certain churches. We have one at the church of Saint Dimitrios, too. In the past in Greece there was little room in a village graveyard for everyone, so you would bury someone in the family plot and after a set number of years, usually three, the body would be exhumed to make space for another and the bones would be placed in a wooden or metal box, which usually has the deceased's name on the outside, and stored in the ossuary. It is a macabre practice to some, and not so common now. As you see, there is almost no-one left in our village to bury," he said, with an apologetic smile.

This was something I knew nothing about. And if Angus had even scant knowledge of this grisly custom, he was as dazed as I was.

"Dimitri, are you saying Kostas's remains are actually in that building behind the church?" asked Angus.

"Yes, they must be. That's where my father put them in 1949. I hope the box is still there, but so many years have passed and there have been some small changes to the building in that time. Every time I come here for the summer *yiorti*, I light candles for all my deceased family, and for Kostas too, but I very rarely go inside the ossuary. I've become quite American about matters of death, I'm afraid."

Angus and I stared at each other with a mix of shock and hope.

"Let's go look in the ossuary, Dimitri. At least it will be open today," said Leonidas, and we all rose, ready to hurry to the church. But Polly, always the more measured of us, said quietly, "Let us go by all means, but we should remember that even if we find the right box, it may not give us any more clues to the identity of Kostas."

"The notebook, Dimitri. Did your father salvage it from the grave in 1949? What became of it?" asked Angus.

We had all momentarily forgotten the most important piece of information that might identify the dead soldier. Dimitris rubbed his hands over his face. He seemed to be deep in thought, rummaging through the backblocks of his memory.

"I'm not really sure, folks. I wasn't in the village in 1949. I had been fighting with the Greek army during the civil war and was wounded. I was in a hospital in Athens for a few months. When I came back to Platanos, I found out that my father had only recently given Kostas the exhumation. As far as I remember, my father said he put the notebook in the reliquary with Kostas's remains. I asked my father if I could see it, or if I could keep it as a memento of Kostas. He said the notebook had been badly damaged after years in the ground, and it was best to leave it where it was," Dimitris said, with a weary shrug. "So I guess it must still be there."

"If the notebook is in the reliquary, even if it's damaged, we might glean something of the soldier's identity. Or we can hope that he was still wearing his army identification discs when he was buried, and if they were salvaged we can identify him that way. Let's go straight to the ossuary and see," said Angus, visibly excited at this new lead.

We all set off briskly towards the church. Angus was walking ahead, huffing and puffing, with Polly, Dimitris and me behind. Leonidas was last, still fiddling with his mobile phone. I suspected he had been speed-dialling Phaedra all day. I glanced round at him and he caught me up, taking my arm.

"Bronte, you say you have never seen an ossuary. You might find it distressing. If you don't want to see it, Angus and I will go in."

"No, I must. If these remains could possibly be Kieran's, I want to see them," I said, with a determined lift of my chin. But who was I fooling? This wasn't at all what I imagined we'd find. I didn't expect a box of bones.

The ossuary was a rectangular building with a metal door that had bars at the top over a frosted glass window. We tried the handle and found it was unlocked. Inside was a long room with a window at the far end. The air was warm and musty. There was deep shelving on the two facing walls, stacked with boxes, as if it were a left-luggage department. Each box was about one-and-a-half feet square, mostly made of wood, inscribed with a name and date of death. Some were padlocked, some were not. Some had photos of the deceased or framed icons nearby. There was a stand for lighted candles and a small table at the front with a chair.

At the far end of the room was a concrete sink and a flat surface like a draining board. Dimitris told us it was where the women washed the bones of the deceased. It made me shudder. I caught Angus's eye and he gave me a wan smile. I noticed that Polly had sidled up to Angus and gave his arm a squeeze. Only Leonidas remained impassive in this charnel house.

Dimitris told us he had no idea where the box would be, so we had to check the names on them all. Leonidas walked along one side of the room with Angus, while Dimitris and Polly went along the other, with me trailing absently behind. The lower shelves were easy to check but the ones at the very top seemed to be reserved for odd-shaped boxes, or old wrecks covered in dust. At one point, I spied a large cardboard box, used once for transporting tins of corned beef with a trade name on the side. A Greek name had been scrawled underneath it and I tried to imagine what kind of person had earned this wretched resting place. At least it didn't appear to be Kostas.

Once we reached the back of the ossuary, near the sink, there were only two boxes left to check on the top shelf. They were dusty, hunched together, with no names visible.

"We will need a ladder," said Leonidas, and he went outside to look for one, returning five minutes later with a rickety wooden ladder he had found propped up against a pear tree. "This will have to do. I hope it will hold my weight." No one argued with his willingness to climb. He seemed the most able among us. Angus held it steady for him. Leonidas managed to edge the first box out and turned it slowly. It had Petros Psareas written on the side. The other was a bit smaller, also made of wood but thinner and less substantial, and tied up with thick twine. Leonidas edged it out and slowly turned it around, so he could see each side. On the third side we could all clearly see the word 'Kostas' written in a large neat hand and the word *'filellinas'*, which Polly told me meant 'Friend of Greece', and the date: May 1941. We all gasped. The story began to seem shockingly real. Leonidas handed the box carefully to Angus and climbed down the ladder.

"Are you okay, Angus? You look pale," said Leonidas.

"I've never felt paler," he replied, with a thin smile.

Leonidas took the box from him and turned to Dimitris, who was standing back a short way from the rest of us, his head slightly bowed. "Well, there can be no doubt that this is the box you were talking about," said Leonidas, and Dimitris nodded.

Leonidas carefully carried it to the table near the door and set it down. There was forensic care and delicacy in the way he took charge of it, insisting we all stood in front of the table while he opened the box at the other side. Angus produced a Swiss army knife from his pocket and the twine was quickly cut. Leonidas gingerly pulled the lid up at one side. It made a grating sound. Angus linked his arm through mine. I was glad of it. I felt as if I might faint. Even Polly was losing her usual composure. There seemed to be no air in the room and I began to wish we'd done this outside.

Dimitris stood against one of the shelves, his hands crossed in front of him. He had obviously seen much worse things in his long life than the rest of us, but he must have been suffering terribly from the memory of how this had all come to be. I could understand why he had avoided the ossuary in the past. Leonidas kept the lid at an angle, with the intention of obscuring our view – and our feelings, no doubt – then he replaced the lid.

"There are bones inside. But, really, I think it is best if you all wait outside and I will check everything properly. It might be upsetting for some of you," he said, looking straight at me. I felt a mix of relief and shame.

"Is the notebook there, or anything else?" asked Angus excitedly.

"I can't tell yet."

Polly ushered us towards the door. "Leonidas is quite right. He is the doctor. He should examine the remains first."

I didn't need any encouragement to follow Polly out the door, leaving Leonidas with his grisly task. There were some wooden benches outside and we sat quietly. We could hear Leonidas inside, carrying out his investigation, and a hollow rattling sound as he shifted the contents of the box about.

"This is terrible, isn't it?" said Angus, dabbing his forehead with a handkerchief.

"I am sorry for your anxiety, my friends," said Dimitris.

"Oh, not at all, Dimitris. Your story has been invaluable. You may yet be our saviour," said Angus.

"You mustn't speak too soon," Dimitris replied, glumly.

We could hear Leonidas walking through the ossuary and then the sound of running water, as if he were perhaps washing his hands by the big concrete sink. Finally he came out, looking rather grave.

"It is the remains of a young male, I would say, and there is a fracture to the front of the skull consistent with a bullet wound, though I can't tell now if he was also struck in the back. But it ties in with what Dimitris has told us."

"The notebook?" said Angus, in a trembling voice.

Leonidas shook his head. "I'm afraid not. Only the bones."

"Oh, no!" said Polly.

"Oh my! So my recollections were wrong," Dimitris said, biting his lower lip.

"Were his army ID discs there?" asked Angus.

"No, Angus, nothing. I am sorry," replied Leonidas.

Angus looked inconsolable. "Without the notebook or the discs, we don't know anything. This could be any poor soldier."

So we'd come this far and we were no closer to solving the mystery. All this mental anguish for nothing. Even Leonidas looked tired, raking his hand through his hair, and it struck me how much he had done for us lately in this quest, and today of all days. I would always admire him for that.

Dimitris seemed agitated. He stood up suddenly. "I'm sorry, folks. I know my brain's not what it used to be, but I'm sure my father said he put the notebook in that box. If not that, then he must have hidden it some place and forgot to tell anyone, and it was left behind after we sold up and moved to Athens."

"If he hid the book, we'll have to turn the village upside down to find it," said Angus.

"Something isn't quite right about this … Maybe it's been stolen for some fool reason. I'm going to find the *papas*. He may be able to help us," said Dimitris, striding off towards the church.

"Poor Dimitris. He's taking all this very hard," said Angus.

We all nodded, and while we waited silently I wondered how the *papas* could possibly help, and how we could begin to search for this notebook unless we started with Dimitris's old house and pulled it apart. We waited for about 20 minutes. I had butterflies in my stomach. Polly had gone off to pick oranges. Leonidas was nervously flicking through messages on his phone. We were about to go looking for Dimitris when we saw him rounding the corner of the church with the old *papas* in tow, one hand tucked into the side of his robe, the other tugging at his long grey beard. He looked faintly biblical. Angus and I were sitting on the wooden bench and Polly rejoined us.

Dimitris's face was long and drawn, as if set for bad news, but then it suddenly brightened and he burst into his most American drawl of the day. "Well, I'll be damned!" he said. "The notebook *was* inside the box when it was placed in the ossuary. Just as well I had a hunch to find Papa Theodoros. He has just told me that a few years ago the church elders decided to make an extra shelf on each wall to store the boxes, as many of them had been lying on the floor crammed together. Some had spilled over. Everything was taken out and Papa Theodoros supervised the return of all the boxes. He was intrigued by one old box with a single name 'Kostas', which was most irregular in our way of doing things. And the date, from the war years. He was curious and decided to open it and see what was inside. Lying on top of the remains was a linen pouch with a notebook inside. He opened it and guessing it was written in English, a language he doesn't speak, he decided to keep it in the church, in a safe place, in case someone came one day to claim it."

There was a collective cry of excitement. I could sense Angus's mood soar like an eagle.

"Where is it?" asked Leonidas.

"Right here, folks!" said Dimitris, with a wide smile.

The *papas* produced the pouch from where he was hiding it in the fold of his robe, as if he wanted to surprise us. Angus leapt to his feet and took it from him, thanking him in Greek. The pouch was yellow with age and embroidered with flowers and a 'K' on the flap. Dimitris explained that his mother must have made it specially. Angus opened it and pulled out a notebook about six inches square with a black leather cover, a bit scuffed with age but otherwise not in bad condition, which didn't square with Panayiotis's comment that the notebook had been ruined. Perhaps Dimitris's memory of his father's exact words had let him down.

Angus stood back a little way from us, as if to seize a private space in which to open the book, which he did slowly, with trembling hands. I don't think I had ever felt such a sense of taut expectation before. I felt almost physically sick, and afraid. Angus didn't say anything. He was staring at the title page, as if in a trance.

"What is it, Angus?" said Polly softly.

Angus looked up. He had tears in his eyes. "It has an inscription on the first page: Kieran McKnight, Royal Army Service Corps, 1940."

"Oh, my God!" said Polly, putting her palms on her cheeks.

I felt my legs tremble. I couldn't speak. None of us did. We just stood and watched as Angus glanced quickly through the notebook. His eyes were still wet with tears, but there was a smile of joy too.

"It's amazing! It's got notes, drawings. Better than we could ever have hoped for," he said.

He came over to me and put the notebook in my hands. "Bronte, my love, we found him, at last!" Then he hugged me as everyone looked on. I fought with a trembling lower lip. I glanced at Polly and saw her eyes fill with tears. I looked away. If I cried now, I might never stop.

I sat down on a wooden bench, with Angus beside me, and everyone crowded around us as I opened the notebook. The pages were marked and water-stained at the edges, probably from being hidden in the cave. But they were perfectly legible for something that had been buried underground for nearly 10 years. I flipped through the pages quickly, wishing I were alone somewhere and could pore over them, but there would be time enough to read it properly and come to terms with the enormity of this special day. The sight of Kieran's writings, his sketches, meant that for the first time he wasn't just a ghost in our lives. He was right here!

The *papas* approached and said something to Angus and me. He looked rather serious. Polly translated for us. "Papa Theodoros says he apologises that when he found the book he never thought to show it to someone then, someone who knew English. Perhaps the owner's family could have been traced sooner."

"Polly, please tell the *papas* not to feel bad," I told her. "We are here now. Tell him that fate brought us to Platanos in the end, and we are very grateful for his help."

"Well said, Bronte," said Leonidas.

"Aye, and more than just fate, Bronte. Thank you too for believing in a daft old man and his crazy ideas, and thanks to the rest of you, my friends. This day wouldn't have happened without you all," said Angus. Everyone was beaming with satisfaction. It was a feast day for Saint Dimitrios that no-one would forget in a hurry.

But it fell to Leonidas to remind us of something less cheerful. "Angus, Bronte. Do you want to see Kieran's remains before we go? Or would you rather wait?"

We decided it was probably the right time and so, after much joy and excitement, we followed Leonidas into the ossuary and I engaged in one of the strangest and saddest rituals of my life. Having heard Dimitris's account of Kieran's short time in Platanos, and the shooting, gazing at this jumble of pale bones made it seem bewilderingly real. The skull sat on top, almost pristine and fresh, apart from the smashed forehead from the bullet. None of it seemed to have any link to the dark-haired young man whose picture I'd kept on my chest of drawers in Marathousa. The rest of the bones were concertinaed into the small space below, the sum total of Kieran's life. It was enough. I couldn't look any more. I believed I was up to this, but now I knew I was not. And a dozen other anxieties came rushing up, like a flock of birds scared into sudden flight.

I ran outside, heading to the back of church and around the corner, where there was a quiet garden and a raised stone wall at the perimeter, with a small spring outlet dripping into a marble bowl, similar to the others in the village. A few tall trees overhung it. It was out of sight of the ossuary at least. A narrow banquette had been created on one side of the spring outlet and I sat down and gave vent to the tears that had been building up – for a long time. This anguish was not how I had envisaged closure to be, but also what I didn't expect was the sudden redemption that came with it for everything negative that had swirled around the whole of my family for decades.

I don't know how long I sat there sobbing, but eventually I saw Leonidas striding towards me. I felt comforted by the sight of him but I was embarrassed by my red-eyed, dishevelled appearance. He sat beside me and put a hand lightly on my shoulder.

"Are you all right, Bronte? I did warn you it would be a difficult experience."

I couldn't speak. I blew my nose and wiped my puffy eyes on my handkerchief. He said something in Greek and though I didn't understand it, I felt a little better, as if I'd gleaned something soothing by osmosis. Finally I got a grip. "You were right. It was difficult. An odd day: pain and joy, all mixed up. Too much!" I squeaked.

"Quite an experience for all of us, and for me as well, for many reasons," he said, shaking his head, but I didn't think to ask what he meant. "The *papas* has said a prayer for Kieran in the ossuary and we will leave the box there for now, until you both decide what to do with it. The others have gone back to the *pantopoleio* in the *plateia*. I think we should leave soon. Angus has had a very stressful day. I worry about him."

And I did too. I wiped at my tears and took a deep breath. I felt much calmer now. Leonidas had taken off his jacket and his white shirt sleeves were rolled up. He looked more like a doctor now than at any other time I'd seen him. I was suddenly glad of it. We stood up to go.

"Thank you, Leonidas, for being here today. For all your help. We owe you a great deal," I said, with a gush of gratitude. I put my arms around him, hugged him and kissed him on the cheek. How safe I felt then! Yet, I couldn't stop my mind from trailing back to that day on the Kitries beach, that small flash of near-lovemaking that tormented me, even now. I kept my arms around him and caught the lemony aroma of his aftershave, the smell of his hair. He responded after a moment with an avuncular rub of my back.

He put his hand on my arm firmly. "Come with me," he said, pulling me away from the banquette. My mind soared stupidly and illogically with possibilities, until he led me over to the water tap. He turned it on and retrieved a crisp white handkerchief from his pocket. He wet it under the tap. With one hand on my shoulder, he wiped my face gently with the other, around my eyes and over my cheeks, gathering up the mascara smudges. I felt slightly ridiculous, and yet there was a pleasing kind of intimacy in it, the sweep of his hand over my face, the attention his eyes gave to the task, his warm breath on my skin. Then it was over and he popped the handkerchief back in his pocket.

"That's better," he said, giving my forehead a quick, light kiss, as if I were a troubled child, which is how I felt.

Despite all the things I wanted to say about why he should terminate his exit plan with Phaedra and not let his head rule his heart, nothing came out. And it was all too late, anyway.

When we got to the *plateia* we found the others sitting at the metal tables again, but this time drinking ouzo with Dimitris, the guest of honour, celebrating his name day properly. It seemed like an impromptu party. Pavlos was there as well, drinking and smoking. When he saw us, he got up to fetch more ouzos. Leonidas declined, but I didn't. I definitely needed a drink. Angus was still clutching the notebook, wrapped in its pouch again. He patted the empty chair beside him and when I sat down he leaned over and whispered in my ear, "The last bit was too much for you, eh? Too much for me as well. My ticker's still doing a cha-cha."

Everyone wanted to chatter about the day, but Leonidas seemed pensive, as he had been all day. I caught his eye and he smiled, then looked away. Dimitris had also been thoughtful. I sensed that something was bothering him. Finally, after he'd drunk all his ouzo, he told us what it was.

"You know, folks, I was looking at the notebook earlier and it's hard to explain the feeling. The last time I saw it in 1941, I couldn't understand a word. Now that I can, it's heart-breaking to discover what torment poor Kostas, or Kieran rather, went through while he was hiding out. But one thing about the notebook doesn't seem quite right. It's in pretty neat condition, which makes me think my father couldn't possibly have buried it on the hillside with Kieran like he said. And I have to say, I didn't see that part of the burial where he placed the body in the grave. I was the lookout, after all. So I reckon my father must have hidden the book in a safe place for years, without telling us, and then put it in the reliquary later on. But why did he do that?"

We all looked at him blankly.

"I mean, why didn't he just hang on to it and give it to me when I came back from the civil war? He knew I always wanted it keep it. Why did he say he put it in the reliquary because it was in such a deteriorated state? It doesn't make sense and it raises a whole heap of issues here, but most of all, if we had kept hold of the notebook, we could have traced Kieran one day to his British regiment – and Angus and Bronte would have known the whole story years ago. Their lives would have been very different, I imagine," he said.

No-one spoke at first. We hadn't even considered this fact. It had been too tormenting a day.

"I see what you mean. Yes it's odd," said Angus. "But your father must have had his reasons, Dimitri. And don't forget he risked his life to help Kieran. So it's not for us to question what he did or didn't do."

"Well, I guess you're right," said Dimitris, not looking very convinced.

"The thing is, the notebook survived. And we've found it. The story had a good ending," said Angus, patting him on the arm.

"Yeah, sure did, folks! And the timing was right in the end because I don't think I'll make it back to Platanos again, not in this life," Dimitris said, with a wan smile.

We made light of his fears, wishing him 'many years'. I took a photo at that point of everyone sitting outside the *pantopoleio*. I knew it would become one of the most memorable of my life and would take its place beside the other pictures I'd accumulated on this Greek trip.

After a short while, however, our party seemed to run out of steam. We had all grown weary from the day's excitement. I caught Leonidas's eye and he seemed lost in thought. I guessed he was keen to get going. Even the *papas* was leaving now. We saw his black form swishing through the *plateia*, having locked the church. He waved as he went towards the road, where his car was parked. I fancied as he passed that a strong slipstream of air followed him, with a crackling undercurrent, like hundreds of autumn leaves whipped up in the wind. Or perhaps it was the aftermath of Saint Dimitrios, galloping homeward on his russet-coloured horse. I fancied I could see his curly hair and blue cape billowing out behind. Was this one of his more miraculous days?

After our morning of excitement and revelation in the mountains, Marathousa seemed to crouch in front of us, earth-bound and stolid, not its usual place of bright vistas and wind-raked olive groves. As soon as the car stopped outside Villa Anemos, we all dispersed, back to normality.

Polly was to drive Dimitris back to his Kalamata hotel. Leonidas said a quick farewell to everyone. But Polly, even now, seemed determined not to let him go without some probing. She asked if he was going to Koroni now to spend time with his girlfriend and her family.

"No, I am leaving for Athens this afternoon. I have an old friend there, also called Dimitris, celebrating today and I will visit him. And I want to see Apollo, my son, who I have not seen for a while."

Polly's eyebrows flickered slightly with interest, in my direction.

23

Hearts of fire

Later that afternoon, Angus and I had a light meal. I had planned a siesta as I was exhausted, but Angus said he probably wouldn't be able to sleep. He wanted to read the notebook properly on his own before giving it to me. I lay on my bed a while, my head buzzing from the day's events. I finally fell into a restless sleep and was woken a few hours later by Angus shaking me by the shoulder.

"Bronte, wake up, love!"

"What is it?" I said, trying to rouse myself.

"I'm not feeling well," he said, touching his heart.

"Oh, no!"

"I read the notebook and then lay down, thinking I might get some shut-eye. But I've had some pain in my chest. I've used my angina spray. It took a few doses to shift the pains, but I'm still not feeling great."

I wasn't surprised, after the day we'd had. He looked pale and sweaty.

"You shouldn't have read the notebook so soon."

"It didn't take long to read, but I admit it upset me a bit. Och, it's tormenting how he died alone up on that ridge. You'll see when you read it."

"Right," I said, jumping out of bed. "This time we're going straight to the hospital."

I considered calling Leonidas for advice, but there wasn't time. Then I remembered he would be in Athens.

"Go and get ready. I'll drive," I said.

His eyes widened with horror. "You've never driven here. It takes a while to get used to it … not to mention the roads."

"So, I'll get some practice in, won't I?"

Angus looked paler still. "That will really bring on a coronary."

I shrugged. "Pack a bag in case they keep you in."

He went downstairs to get ready. I got dressed quickly. My stomach felt queasy. I was filled with apprehension. This was not meant to happen. I rushed into the kitchen, to the drawer where Angus kept his pills, and dumped a load of them in my bag. We needed to move fast. I started to worry about the drive to the hospital. What was I thinking? I found Angus in the sitting room with a small bag at his feet, chewing the end of his thumb.

"Where are your car keys?" I asked.

"You won't need them now. I've got another driver for the hospital."

"How did you swing that?" I said, with great relief.

"I just rang Miltiades in the taverna. He said he would drive us down. He always told me to call him if ever I had a problem."

"That's nice. I was happy to drive though," I said, lying.

"No, Bronte. Trust me. You wouldn't want to do that."

Minutes later I heard Miltiades' car pull up in front of the house. We dived into it, Angus in front, me behind, with nothing as sensible as a working seatbelt, of course. Miltiades tore off down the road like a racehorse at the starters' gate and pretty much kept the pace all the way down the hillside, screaming around hairpin bends, accelerating more on the straight bits, shouting at other drivers.

As we got into the city, I called Polly. Her phone rang for a while before she answered it, sounding sleepy, as if she'd just woken from a siesta. She promised to be at the hospital as soon as she could. I felt better knowing she'd be there.

At the hospital, Miltiades ushered us quickly into A&E. Nothing seemed to faze him and at the reception desk he took charge, gabbling on with the young girl manning the counter, who wrote out a few details about Angus and his condition before asking us to sit in the crowded waiting room.

"I hope Angus gets seen pretty soon," I said to Miltiades.

He clamped a big, strong hand on my arm. "You don't worry now, Bronte. I told them it's the heart. *Kirios* Angoose has pains. He needs attention right away. They will call him soon. You will see, Bronte *mou*." My Bronte.

Not long after we arrived, Polly turned up, rushing into the waiting room, her dark hair tied back. She looked out of breath. "Oh, Angus! How are you, my dear?" she said, kissing him on the cheek.

"I'm fine at the moment, Polly. Chest pains earlier. Best to get it checked."

She gave me a concerned look and went to reception to seemingly have the same conversation as Miltiades had, trying to hurry things along, or maybe handing over an envelope with a few banknotes stuffed inside. I had heard of such things. Bribes were still being paid in hospitals for speedier treatment, even though Angus had told me that it had been outlawed. I had a sneaking suspicion that in Greece nothing was really ever illegal.

Perhaps it was Polly's influence, but we were soon called into a large treatment room by a young doctor, who ushered Angus into a cubicle and closed the curtains. We huddled around the bed. The doctor's English was good and he asked Angus a lot of questions and performed a few rudimentary checks before arranging to transfer him to the cardiology department. Despite reports of medical cutbacks in the crisis, the hospital seemed clean and orderly, the doctors and staff were pleasant and efficient.

In cardiology, Angus was put in a small room on his own and seen by another young doctor, who ordered blood tests and a cardiogram, all of which would determine whether Angus had had a heart attack or not, or whether it was stress related or something else. Miltiades stood with us, but he was looking twitchy, and I knew his good nature was prevailing over the urge to return to the village to prepare the evening meals at the taverna. We told him to leave because we had no idea how long Angus would be kept in hospital.

"You call me, Bronte, if you need me again. Any time day or the night, okay? If Angoose stays here tonight, tell me and I will bring him some food later. He is a good man, okay?" He bear-hugged me, and then Angus on his hospital bed, and left.

"Bring food?" I asked.

"Hospitals in Greece don't provide nursing and the food is very basic, unlike your hospitals in Britain," Polly explained. "Families must bring food and help out. That's why if you went into one of the wards you would see many people sitting around each bed." I could see why Angus thought he might need help with his health problem and why he wasn't keen to go to Athens.

He was taken into a treatment room down the corridor for his tests, while Polly and I sat in a waiting room, where a Greek family were huddled in one corner, looking anxious. Out in the corridor people walked back and forth, patients talking loudly to doctors in old-fashioned white coats with stethoscopes round their necks.

Time seemed to drag on. After all the anxiety of the past hour and the effort to get here, I suddenly had too much time to think. I felt frightened. Angus and I had shared such an extraordinary experience that day it had brought us closer together in a way we hadn't been since I was young. The idea that I could possibly lose him now, and in a foreign country, where I didn't know what was going on most of the time, made me feel wretched. I tormented myself as well, wondering if all the time I'd been in Greece he had kept quiet about other chest pains, dousing himself with his medications. And then we'd had that argument over Polly. I'd helped to push him over the precipice.

Polly picked up on my mood. "Don't worry, Bronte. If Angus has had a heart attack already they will treat him here first and then send him straight to an Athens hospital. We are not living in the Dark Ages here," she said, patting my hand.

She was right but still, the outskirts of Athens were a three-hour drive from Kalamata.

"You look exhausted, Bronte. Did you sleep this afternoon?"

"I had a small siesta, but it hasn't helped. My mind is racing from everything that has happened today. It feels like a day that will never end."

"I know what you mean. But this morning when the notebook was found was just so wonderful. Such a good outcome. But too much for Angus."

"At least now that I'm not pressured to go back to Scotland for a while, I can try to get his health sorted out."

We waited for over an hour until the doctor reappeared. Angus was back in the small room lying on the bed, his hair still tied back, but ruffled. He opened his eyes when we approached. "I'm still alive," he said, with a sardonic grin.

The doctor told me the tests showed Angus had not had a heart attack. "Ah, that's such good news. Thank you," I said, feeling grateful that we had avoided the worst scenario. And yet the doctor wasn't quite as chipper.

"For now it is okay, yes. But now I come to the rest of the diagnosis. Your father has had angina pains, caused most probably by some narrowing in the arteries. Your father needs to have an angiogram, where a small tube is inserted into an artery, like here," he said, pointing to his wrist, "and dye is put inside to show up the coronary artery system. We have not the equipment to do this here and he will have to visit a hospital in Athens. It is not urgent for today, but it must be organised as soon as you can do it. All right?"

Angus nodded. He seemed resigned to it now, even though it was the one thing he hadn't wanted.

"For now, he must continue to take all his drugs, to keep everything stabilised, and I will be sending a letter to his cardiologist in Kalamata to inform him what we have found. He will be able to organise the appointment in Athens for your father. In the meantime, if the pains return, and the drugs are not helping, you must return to the hospital immediately. Your father tells me he has had some stress today, and this is the likely cause of the angina pains. So, you see, even in Greece, when the sun is shining, we all have anxieties." It was the first and only time he laughed, showing some boyish good humour. Angus rolled his eyes.

I hoped he hadn't told the doctor the whole story of Platanos. The doctor would probably have thought we were all crazy people, slogging around a mountain village and tormenting ourselves with the grisly contents of an ossuary box, but I think Angus had not gone into details.

"Your father needs rest and, most of all, the next test," he said, holding up his finger, as if pointing to the almighty.

When we finally left the hospital, it was early evening. Polly offered to drive us back to the village, but Angus wouldn't hear of it. He wanted to take one of the taxis parked outside the hospital. But Polly had a better idea. "I think you should both come back to my apartment. We will have some dinner and you can both stay tonight, or for the next few days. You both look exhausted. What do you think?"

Angus and I looked at each other, then he said, "That's incredibly thoughtful, Polly, but you've probably seen enough of us today."

"Not at all. I think you have both had a traumatic day. I am sure that Bronte doesn't have the energy to worry about cooking and looking after her patient in that old village house," she said, with a wink.

Angus didn't object to her suggestion, but I felt differently.

"I've got another idea, Polly. You take Angus back to your apartment. That way, if he has any problems, he's closer to the hospital than we are in the village. It makes sense. But if you don't mind, I would like to go back home. I have some emails to send and some calls to make."

"Oh, are you sure? I've got two spare bedrooms. Enough room for everyone."

"I'm very sure," I said, feeling rather pleased with my brainwave. I rather hoped that Angus's stay might present an opportunity for them to talk about the future of their relationship. All that day I had seen nothing but the great affection and respect they had for each other and wondered why they couldn't start afresh.

They walked me to the taxi rank. Polly waved goodnight and went off to fetch her car. Angus approached the first taxi in the line-up and spoke to the driver, then turned to say goodnight. He put his hands firmly on my shoulders, as if he wanted my complete attention.

"Thank you, Bronte, for an amazing day. For being with me. We've got a lot to talk about now. Read the notebook. It's on my desk."

"Yes, I will. And by the way, stay till Sunday if you want. You and Polly have things to talk about, I think."

He gave me a curious look and kissed me on the cheek. "Sleep well, love," he said, looking at me in a way I hadn't seen for years. It was a familiar, comforting look.

He opened the taxi door for me and I dived into the back seat before he could notice my eyes were prickling with tears. I waved goodbye as the cab sped off. I almost felt the need of an entourage of kindly saints again along the dashboard, but all I could see was an air freshener above the radio dial and a set of worry beads swinging from the rear-view mirror.

When we got to the road that split, with one way towards the city, the other towards the village, I looked towards the gulf in the distance, shimmering under a full moon. How beautiful, how serene it looked that night. I tried to imagine what it would have been like here on those nights in 1941, with desperate allied troops hiding in the olive groves near the sea as the Nazis stormed into Kalamata. Along Navarino Street at the head of the gulf were modern apartments, cafes and bars. A social hub of the city. But underneath all of that, the land was steeped in fear, violence and bloodshed.

From then on, whenever I looked at the Kalamata seafront, I would think of those war days – especially after reading Kieran's notebook.

24

A friend of Greece

"Kieran McKnight, Royal Army Service Corps, 1940" was written on the top of the title page, as Angus had said. Underneath was a pen and ink self-portrait: a handsome young man in army uniform without his cap, showing thick wavy hair, alert eyes, a mischievous smile, ready for the adventure of his life. I saw a bit of Angus in his expression. I have no doubt the resemblance would have tugged at his heart.

Kieran's writing was neat and slightly slanted. There were dates and brief notes from his arrival in Alexandria, Egypt, and his first weeks in Greece in the spring of 1941, but more sketches than notes, as if there was little time for words. The diary started in earnest in late April. He didn't write much initially but by the end the entries were longer and more personal, as if he were slowly discovering his writer's voice.

When he arrived in Greece, he was billeted to a racecourse in Phaleron, outside Athens, which served as one of the allied camps. He had been assigned mainly as a driver for one of the officers and tasked with bringing petrol in from local suppliers. Before the German invasion started in April 1941, there had been some downtime and excursions into Athens with other RASC soldiers to see the ancient sites or hang around the bars and tavernas in the Plaka district, sometimes getting 'guttered', drunk, and sometimes fantasising over local women.

By the middle of April, however, everything changed when the Germans advanced quicker than expected from the north to the outskirts of Athens, with heavy Luftwaffe raids, mostly at the port of Piraeus, on the allied ships carrying ammunition. The allied forces then began their retreat south, ending up in Kalamata, where thousands of troops were waiting to be picked up by Royal Navy ships sent from Souda Bay, Crete.

April 26

Driving a one-tonner truck for three days now, carrying tins of meat, rum, cigarettes and a few troops as well. No driving at night with headlights because of possible pounding from the Luftwaffe. The Jerries are throwing everything at us. Plenty of our lads killed. Roads bad, a few trucks gone off the edge full of troops. We had to stop on the way and push the truck into olive groves when we got caught up in bad Stuka fire. Back tyres blown out. Lost a day over that. Looks like we're set to have a right old rammy in Kalamata with the Jerries. They've been moving in behind us the last few days. Parachute troops have arrived at Corinth Canal. Won't be long for them to get down to Kalamata.

April 27

We've arrived in Kalamata, and by the looks of things so have hundreds of others. The place is hoaching with soldiers. We're under constant air attack from the Luftwaffe. A group of RASC lads have taken cover in olive groves half way up a hillside overlooking the city. We've been instructed to smash up all our trucks, supplies, equipment, everything. Och, it fair kills you to do that but we don't want the Jerries to get their mitts on it. Nothing to do here now but wait for evacuation on the beach below. We've heard Navy destroyers should be in the gulf tonight to pick up troops. Hundreds picked up last night. We're the late ones and I don't like our chances. It will be fighting forces first. The RASC will be at the back of the queue and more arriving all the time. Will we be lucky?

April 28

Och, we didn't make it out last night. Slept in the olive groves. We've got to bloody embark tonight. May be our last chance. Jerries came at us from dawn, up to 50 planes bombing and machine-gunning everywhere. Dropped mines at the entrance to harbour. Destroyed quays, sunk small fishing boats. Part of the city on fire.

It's evening now and we're still waiting for the signal to get down to the beach. Told destroyers and cruisers on their way to the port but maybe holding back with this stramash goin on and there's fear over the mines in harbour. Jerry soldiers arrived in Kalamata in force at the port. Fierce fighting. We heard those gallus NZ lads gave the Jerries a right hammering up there. Plenty of casualties and Jerries taken prisoner. We've been told to wait in the olive groves again til we get a signal to move down to the beach for embarkation. I cannae wait to get going.

April 29

Daybreak and we're skunnered, the lot of us! We've just lost our last chance to be picked up. Hid in olive groves for hours waiting for a signal. After midnight told to get to the beach. Felt wretched at the sight of thousands of troops lined up along beach waiting. Fighting forces, signal men at the top of the queue. Waiting our turn – RASC lads. Four destroyers came at 2am. Queue was orderly, moved slowly but tide was strong and there was a right struggle with landing craft. Some poor lads waded out and were pulled under, drowned. Panic, confusion. Fear over mines, and Stukas. Few hundred maybe fighting forces embarked, and then navy retreated. Thousands left on the beach including us RASC lads. No more ships tonight. No more planned for tomorrow. Brigadier Parrington surrendered this morning. Told us to make our own escape. What a muckle mess this is!

April 30

Scores of us left Kalamata yesterday just as the Jerries were pegging swastikas along the beach. A group of RASC boys heading south along the coast road. Joined by Aussies, Kiwis and a Greek Cypriot lad. Plan is to find a boat. Get to Crete. We've trauchled for miles down here searching for boats. Everywhere there's dozens of us doin the same. Greeks running about in a panic as well. Some villages empty. At night we've found caves. Locals bring food and water as supplies are low. Can't fault these people. Risking their lives too. I've got a pal at least. Raymond MacArthur from Aberdeen, and RASC. We have a right blether. Passes time. He speaks his doo-lally Doric, the way they do up there. Calls me a skinnymalink cause I'm thin. And he's always stammygastered, shocked, at everything. The other boys think he's a foreigner. I do as well sometimes. That's a right laugh. All the laugh we're goin to get.

May 2

We've come to a long beach. You can see the mountains now and a deep gorge. We've met a local man who's helpful. Told us about a fishing boat in a cove. When we got there, found it smashed up by Stuka fire. We've heard Jerries are moving this way. Sooner or later we'll be rounded up if not machine gunned first from the air. Some of the lads are all for moving further south, even though shortest route means a steep hike over a clifftop. We're all still hoping to find any kind of boat to get into the gulf and find a navy ship, but every day there's less ships. Some lads have made it, some gunned down on the way. The Greek we met told us to head to the mountains. Villages there are hidden from sight. Raymond and I are all for that. We don't have faith in finding a boat. The Greek, with the help of the Cypriot lad for translator told us about a village called Platanos. I hope I got that right. Wrote it down straight away. No road to it, only a mule track. Well hidden. We told the other lads we were setting off for the mountains. They thought we were doo-lally.

May 4

A trauchle for two days through olive groves, dirt road and then up a stone path. Bloody long trek. All a zigzag with about 80 turns on it. Lost count. Murder on feet. Half dead at the top. Still wearing our great coats. Too scared to ditch them. Last tin of corned beef, biscuits, gone. Water low. Felt mingin. Found outskirts Platanos. Waited. Didn't know how welcoming the locals are. Maybe a Jerry here after all. Stayed on northern edge and climbed a hill in the dark past a couple of farm houses. Found big cave to sleep in. No food now and bloody freezing. Passed the night reminiscing about Scotland and Raymond made me laugh with more of his doo-lally Aberdeen words. He's invited me there after the war to meet his family. I hope we make it even though won't understand a word of their Doric.

(There was a long gap here in the entries but a few sketches done from the hilltop looking down along the length of the Taygetos mountains).

May 16

Writing in the notebook by candlelight tonight in the basement of a house. I've got time on my hands now. This is a dark dreich space divided by a wooden barrier. A donkey sleeps in there. Couthie wee beast, and company at least. After two days in the cave a young lad, Dimitris, found us and we were taken down the hill to his family house at bottom. They have been good to us. A father and two sons, an older one to the lad who found us and the mother. She doesn't speak to us much. Suppose it isn't the thing for Greek women to talk to strange men in her house. The family only speak Greek so it's hard to explain things but they know we've escaped from Kalamata and seem mighty proud of us. Raymond has gone now. I was right sad about that. Miss all his blethering. I tried to talk him out of going but he thought we'd made a mistake. He felt trapped here. Wanted me to come with him to coast, try again for boat. Not me. I'd rather take my chances here.

The father Panayotis is a rare fellow. He explained, with plenty of hand signs, I must keep out of sight, even from other villagers. Maybe the Jerries will come up here. I don't know how long I can stay here. Will need to make my way along mountain tracks, south. It should be quieter, and fewer Jerries. Panayotis showed me maps of places I can head for. The days are getting longer, warmer. Finally managed somehow to persuade the father to let me go up the hill during the day. It's dreich inside when the sun's shining and braw to be out in fresh mountain air.

I have darker thoughts as well when I'm stuck here, though the family give me plenty to eat and sometimes a bit of wine they make themselves. I can spend time with them upstairs when there's no one about. That's braw, but up on the hill, I feel better. I take my notebook and scribble and draw. The family gave me clothes so I'd look Greek. I think I look more like a highland teuchter. They say my army kit has been well hidden, and I've ditched my ID discs down a ravine. Now nobody will know who I am. They're right taken with my hair. I've let it grow, and I've a wee scruffy beard. They can't say my name so they've given me a Greek one, Kostas. I like it. Kostas McKnight. I might even keep it when this flamin war is over.

May 20

Stayed the last three days in the house. I've not been out at all. The father said Jerries have been close by in villages below. I guess they might come up here some time looking for escapees, even though they'd be as skunnered with that mule track as we were. Or maybe they won't find it. At night can't sleep much. The basement floor is hard. I can light a candle though and scribble. The sound of the donkey snuffling nearby is right comforting. I miss Raymond's company, even his mad bam talk. I wonder if he found a boat. Begin to wonder if I should have gone with him after all.

I think about the old folks on the farm and Lily most of all. What I wouldn't give to be back home. Wish I could get a letter to her. Tell her how much I love her and miss her bonnie face, her douce wee smile. I worry I'll never see her again. It fires me up to move on. Can't stay here forever. Panayotis' map shows paths down through the gorge, up the other side and down the peninsula avoiding the coast road. Have to go. Can't risk the lives of this family. They've been good to me. Like my own. The son Dimitris is a braw laddie, like a brother to me. If the Jerries find me here, they're as doomed as me. That's why I go up to the cave when I can. Keep out of their way, plan my next move.

May 26

I'm up in the cave. I've been coming up here a lot in the past few days. It's quiet. No sign of Jerries. Panayotis and his sons are away today so I'm free to stay out all day if I want. I'm beginning to know every crack in this foosty old place. Here's a wee sketch to prove it. (Kieran had included a small sketch of the cave underneath the entry. The inside of the cave and himself, sitting on the ground, his notebook on his knees.) *It's been dreich the day, rain first thing in the morning, not the soft smirring rain of Scotland. It was a proper load o rain, just dingin doon for ages. When it rains here, it rains. I poked my head out the cave just now and walked a bit to where you can look down the length of the mountains. My favourite spot. Deep grey sky but the sun broke through the clouds a minute. What a bonnie sight the mountains were, misty and lit up in places. Light and shade. I've just done a wee sketch of that as well.*

I've finally decided I'll set off in two days' time. I think the father understands what I'm wanting but he's got another idea. Thinks he can smuggle me down the zigzag track on a mule, looking like a local and drop me at the town of Kambos to some of his family where I can hide a bit before I move further south. I don't like that idea. If he gets caught with me, he's finished. Even writing this notebook is a risk. If the Jerries found it, and just supposing they read English, they'll know everything. I've got a secret place to hide it in the rocks, high up if I hear anyone coming. If I go ahead with my plan I know the father can give me supplies to take and addresses of some Greek folk on the way to help me. It will keep my mind busy. I need to do this. I have this feeling if I stay, something bad will happen. Och, there are some moments when I've never felt more feart and more alone in my whole life and I am

The text stopped abruptly. It chilled me that he hadn't finished the sentence. It must have been then that he heard the Germans approaching, got up and hid his notebook, then tried to make his escape. Too late! As I held the notebook, my eyes filled with tears. I felt desperately sad for this wonderful grandfather I had never met who, just a few weeks ago, had been a phantom in my life, but now seemed achingly real, so full of promise and longing and who, despite his fears, still thought of others.

I put the notebook on the chest of drawers beside the icon of Saint Dimitrios. It seemed appropriate. In my mind, these were two brave souls, sired by the same life force many centuries apart. Both had aimed to be liberators but became martyrs. One has a cathedral named after him in Thessaloniki and his life is celebrated every October in a blaze of glory. The other had been stored away in a church ossuary on a Greek mountainside, never to be discovered – until now.

I thought again about what Dimitris had pondered: why Panayiotis had put the notebook in the reliquary, as if to bury it forever more. I couldn't figure it either, unless maybe Panayiotis wanted to bury the horrors of their past life in the war, before they embarked on a new one. Perhaps he wanted his younger son, in particular, to make a clean break with Platanos and the memory of what would have been one of the saddest experiences of his young life. Perhaps that was more important than hanging onto the notebook.

I accepted that the Maneas family were simple farming people with no education and not much idea about the world. They'd had their own cataclysms, and Dimitris especially, fighting in the civil war. Once in America, as the years passed, they would have given little thought perhaps to the young soldier they had once known and to his clandestine 'scribblings', apart from lighting a candle in the village to his memory every so often.

I didn't really feel remorse for Panayiotis's oversight. In the end, helped by fate, and good timing, I now held the notebook in my hands; my first real contact with my grandfather's life, even if I bitterly regretted that he never got to flee through the mountains and onward to Crete; to make it home to his beloved Lily. How different our lives might have been if he had. But right at that moment, it didn't matter very much. We had the note-book. We had brought Kieran 'home'.

25

Myrto's landing

On Sunday morning there was a loud knocking on the door. I looked at the clock: it was 10am. I had slept in after sitting up late poring over Kieran's notebook. I reached for my dressing gown and went to the front door. Myrto was outside, dressed in her farm clothes. She looked me up and down.

"Did I wake you, Bronte? You sleep late. You sick?"

"No, no, come in."

She bustled into the sitting room, gazing about her. "Where is Angus?"

"Ah, you haven't heard. He went to the hospital last night. Chest pains. I feared he was having a heart attack, but he's okay. He's staying with … a friend in Kalamata."

"*Po, po, po*! I am sorry to hear this."

"Sit down, Myrto. I'll fix some coffee." She sat down at the dining table.

"I know you prefer Greek coffee, but I can't get the hang of it."

"It's okay. I drink all the coffees. I am woman of the world," she said, patting her chest.

She sipped quickly, her eyes gleaming over the top of her mug. She seemed enervated.

"I feel as if you have something to tell me, Myrto."

"I have news," she beamed. "My land is bought finally. Guess who buys it?"

"Not the German?"

"No, thanks be to God." She crossed herself and waited a moment to ramp up my interest.

"I don't have a clue."

"LEONIDAS!" she shrieked. I was speechless. "You see. You react like Myrto. What the hell going on, eh? He calls me last night from Athens to tell me. He puts in better offer than German. And he doesn't worry about boundaries and all that. He knows what he is buying. He says he wants it for a particular reason and that I can still do trees." She smiled vibrantly.

"So ... he has done you a great favour," I said, feeling pleased that Leonidas had apparently acted with honour despite Myrto's antipathy towards him.

She blew air through her lips, puffing them out. "I just don' know, Bronte. Leonidas is a cunning man. He gets one piece and later he will want the other bit with house too. He will push me out."

"No, Myrto, you judge him too harshly. He's got other things in his life to worry about than doing a massive land-grab in the village. And he's going to England soon."

She flipped her eyebrows up. No comment on that.

"What does he have planned for the land? Did he say?"

"He says he will tell me soon. But I still lost a piece of my land."

"But that's not the fault of Leonidas, is it? And he's got Hector out of your hair finally. Think positively!"

"Okay. I try to think great bonza things like they say in Aussieland," she said, skulling her coffee and bouncing out the door as if she'd just shrugged a great weight off her shoulders. I thought about her news and marvelled that Leonidas, yet again, had proved to be so contrary. I was now eager to learn what his plans were for the land. As it happened, I didn't have to wait long.

An hour or so later, there was another knock at the door. "*Kalimera*, Bronte," said Leonidas, standing on the doorstep and wishing me good morning, dressed in a smart suit. He must have been to church.

"I heard about Angus and I have come to see him. Is he okay?"

"He's not here. He's in Kalamata, staying with a friend."

"With Polly?" Of course, he was shrewd enough to have sussed that out. I nodded.

I invited him in. The place was untidy, though he didn't seem to notice. We sat at the dining table. He refused any refreshments, apart from a glass of water. He couldn't stay long.

"Why didn't you call me about Angus?" he asked.

"I would have, but I knew you were in Athens."

"You could have left a message on my mobile," he said, tipping his head slightly to the side, in a quizzical fashion.

"I know, but I was in a panic."

"Is he all right?"

I updated him on what the hospital doctor had said.

"Well, I am not very surprised, but I am glad he didn't have a heart attack. If he had, it might have been fatal. And he must make that appointment for the angiogram. It's very important now."

"I'll remind him when he gets back today. You can call back and see him later, if you like."

"I may not have time. Phaedra is flying back to London this afternoon and I will take her to the airport."

Well, that wasn't bad news at least.

"Myrto told me this morning that you have bought her land. That's amazing news."

He smiled, with that little twitch of his bottom lip. "Not for her perhaps."

"I know you two don't seem to get on, but this is much better for her, far better than the German buying it. And she says she can still harvest the trees."

"Myrto has always imagined I am against her, and I am not. She can be paranoid, I am afraid, about male intentions. Her husband was a ... " For once he was lost for a word.

"*Malakas*," I said, filling in the gap. 'Wanker'.

He laughed. "You are learning all the worst Greek, I see. But you are right. And Myrto has some strange rural ideas. There are divisions in these villages, and Platanos, as you have discovered. Jealousy, resentment, anger. It's all there. I try not to get involved in these things. Sometimes Myrto thinks I am *malakas* as well." He shrugged majestically.

"No! Not quite. But in any case, she is so happy about the olive trees."

"Good. But my main motive in buying was not to help Myrto, though I'm happy it does. My brother's son, Angelos, who is 25, is drifting, like so many young people now. He had a job in Athens and then lost it when the company went out of business because of the crisis. He decided to come back to Kalamata, where my brother lives, but still he is drifting. My brother worries about him. Then Angelos decided he wanted to be a farmer for a while. Many young people are going back to their family's roots, especially in the Mani, for security.

"So I thought this was a good opportunity to buy Myrto's land and do something to help my family. My brother also put some money in and we got it for a good price. Hector just wanted quick money. I haven't discussed all of it yet with Myrto, but she is an expert at olive harvesting. Her problem is that she can't do it all herself. There are about 600 trees. She never does all of them and many of them are in a wild state. My nephew will learn how to prune the trees, harvest the olives. It's a big job but I think something could be made of it. They can sell the oil and divide the profits," he said, smiling broadly.

"It's a great plan, Leo, for everyone. It's just a pity you won't get many opportunities to see how the olive venture is doing while you are in England." *Slogging it out in some dingy, over-subscribed health centre*, I thought.

He looked away and fiddled with his silver watch strap.

"Well, actually, I'm not going to England now," he said casually.

"Really?" I didn't have time to hide my surprise.

"I've never been sure about it, to tell you the truth, but lately, less sure," he said, pushing an errant curl away from his forehead.

"Why is that?"

"It may sound strange to you, but the experience in Platanos, that incredible outcome with Kieran. It caused me to think a lot. About my life here. Things I am not really able to explain to you. But I would miss Greece, I know that, and my son in Athens, too, whom I saw yesterday. Too many things. And I see how people like you and Angus, foreigners, love my country, and yet I was in a great hurry to desert it."

I didn't think I'd ever said I was in love with Greece, but maybe some little infatuation was beginning to show.

"I think you're doing the right thing, Leo. Greece needs good doctors like never before. I am happy for you." Except I wasn't. "What about Phaedra?" I asked. "Will she return to Greece then?"

He shut his eyes briefly, as if he were pained. "No! She likes life in England. We have decided to end things. It cannot work. Neither of us feels we can make enough commitment to be in the same place together."

"I'm sorry to hear that," I said, forcing a grieved expression. I wasn't sorry at all.

"I am relieved, actually. Now I have made a decision and I will have the satisfaction of keeping my eyes on Angelos and Myrto. It will be a nice project, I think."

"A perfect plan," I said.

"Almost, perhaps. But may I say my one regret will be that you will be leaving soon for Scotland. How nice if you were staying longer and I could finally show you around the region."

I don't know why I didn't fess up about my redundancy and that I'd be staying a bit longer. Maybe I just needed time to digest everything I'd heard that morning. The break with Phaedra had changed things. The incident on the beach now had a less negative spin on it than before, but for now it was safer to make him think I was leaving soon.

"Maybe we still have time for sightseeing before you go?" he said.

"Perhaps."

He got up to leave and took my hand, squeezing it lightly. He was about to say something when we heard keys rattling in the front door. Then it opened, with Angus and Polly breezing in. They looked surprised when they saw us.

"Leonidas called around to see how you are, Angus. Now you can tell him yourself," I said, moving off to the kitchen with Polly, while Leonidas sat on the sofa with Angus to talk about the health scare.

"So, you've been busy, Bronte?" she whispered, her eyes flickering back towards the sitting room. There was a charming, minxy side to Polly that was coming to the fore the more I got to know her. But today there was something else in her look that I couldn't quite place.

"It's not what you think," I said. "He came over to find out about Angus."

"Oh, really? Well, it's good that he did because your father wants to discuss something with him about Kieran. He wants to have an interment of Kieran's remains in the graveyard in Marathousa. He will have to talk to the *papas* and will need permission from the church since Kieran was not Orthodox, and from the village council. It will be good if Leonidas can help him with all the red tape, as you say in English." Leonidas continued to be the go-to man for every eventuality and I wondered how we would ever have got anything done without him.

He left not long afterwards and Angus went on chattering about the arrangements. He seemed to have had a sudden gust of energy since the hospital visit and was wasting no time in sorting out the fate of Kieran's remains. We agreed the burial in Marathousa was a good plan and better than Kieran spending an eternity in a mountain ossuary so close to where he had spent his final tormenting hours.

"We will have some closure at last, Bronte, and other people can come here in time and pay their respects if they want," said Angus.

Closure. It was a word I never thought I'd hear. Now the arrangements were coming upon us so quickly. I told Angus and Polly about Leonidas buying Myrto's land. They listened with increasing amazement.

"I did think all along he was the most logical buyer, to be honest," said Angus. "I just didn't think he'd do it in the end."

"Is he still going to England?" asked Polly.

"No. He's staying here. And he and Phaedra have called things off."

"Well, I never!" said Angus, exchanging a look with Polly. She got up and went over to the kitchen to pour some cold drinks. Angus leaned towards me, whispering, "I heard some even better news yesterday. Polly let slip about your redundancy. You should have told me before, Bronte. But no harm done. Best news I've heard for weeks. Now you can stay as long as you like."

"A little while, yes."

"She didn't mean to tell me. An innocent slip." But I wondered about that. I imagined Polly would have wanted Angus to know what I'd just given up to have this adventure in Greece.

"No harm done," I said.

"Well everything's slotting into place now," said Angus, rubbing his hands together.

Early in the evening, we decided to go out to the Kali Parea taverna to thank Miltiades for helping us and to celebrate our good fortune on several fronts. We were all in high spirits, especially Angus and Polly. I sensed they had talked a lot about their relationship over the weekend and maybe it was back on track.

Miltiades made sure our carafes of wine were over-flowing, but it was Angus and I who drank more than our fair share, as Polly was driving back to Kalamata later. It was one of the best evenings I'd spent in the village. I felt wonderfully happy and carefree – just as well because the feeling wasn't about to last.

When we got home, Angus claimed he was suddenly dog tired, as if the excitement and drama of the past few days had finally caught up with him. We urged him to go to bed early and rest. Polly and I sat on the sofa to talk about the day's developments.

"It's good news about Leonidas. I mean him not going to England," she said. "I never thought it would last with Phaedra. He likes you. I could tell that day in Platanos. He was being incredibly attentive. I feel sure he will want to see more of you now."

"He doesn't know about the redundancy yet and that I'm staying longer."

"Oh, that's good."

I gave her a searching look. It was an odd thing to say; contradictory to her previous comments.

"I know you have feelings for him. That was always clear to me," she said, with a knowing smile.

"I like him, sure, but it's not as serious as you think." I don't know why I decided to be cautious and not confide in her the fact that I had begun to feel something much deeper for Leonidas since the trip to Platanos. Later, I would be glad I was guarded.

"I am so relieved to hear you say that, Bronte, because I have something to tell you that could change everything."

"What?" I felt a rising sense of panic.

"I wasn't going to say anything, but now I feel I must. So … on the way back to Kalamata on Friday, Dimitris and I had a long talk about the day. He told me he was so happy to have helped you and Angus, but there was one thing he hadn't been able to mention before. You remember when we asked him who the villager was who betrayed your grandfather, and he said he didn't know? He did know, but didn't want to say it in front of everyone."

"Why ever not?"

"Because that man who betrayed your grandfather was a relative of Leo's."

"No! You're kidding!"

"I wish I was, but no. It's quite true. And how ironic too … of all people."

"But that's surely not so strange in a remote village, is it? Probably everyone was related in some way."

"Well, not quite. There were a few dozen different families living in the village at that time. This man was one of the brothers of Leonidas's grandmother. His name was Nikos Pantazis. That side of the family originally came from the deep Mani. They were a quarrelsome family, tough Maniots, but Leo's grandmother was a very decent woman, or so Dimitris Maneas says. Nikos was not a nice character and was not liked in the village. Dimitris said that the day after the Germans shot Kieran, Nikos's body was found not far from the bottom of the *kalderimi*, hidden in bushes. It was what happened often to those Greeks who took money to betray someone. The Germans shot them to avoid paying the bounty money, or perhaps, with their twisted logic they didn't like traitors.

"When the villagers found Nikos's body, they just assumed he had got on the wrong side of the Germans, somehow. They wouldn't have known the exact reason at that time because they didn't know about Kieran. It was kept quiet, remember. But Panayiotis knew why Nikos was shot. Dimitris said that his father had once seen Nikos sneaking around the ridge behind the house, claiming he was hunting birds, even though he lived in the centre of the village. That's why Panayiotis warned Kieran to be careful not to be seen. Leonidas's family would have suspected at the very least that Nikos had been up to no good, for him to be shot by the Germans. He was a natural troublemaker and they would have been ashamed of him. More so if or when they discovered he betrayed a British soldier. It may be why the whole incident seems to have been hushed-up."

She stopped talking to see how I was taking it. I was shocked. What a mess things were. I thought about Leonidas, how withdrawn he had seemed on Friday, and now I understood why. It wasn't something he wanted us to know, or anyone to know. Now I understood when he confessed that the day had been traumatic for him as well.

"How strange. Of all the people this Nikos should be related to, it had to be Leonidas," I said, looking at Polly and feeling a bit faint.

"Yes, but I suppose we mustn't think badly of Leo, or his family. These things happened during that war, and then the civil war afterwards. People betrayed their neighbours, brothers killed brothers. All manner of horrible things. You don't mind me telling you all this, do you, my dear? But I felt you should know."

"Of course I don't mind. Why would I? It makes no difference to me," I said, with an airy tone of nonchalance. But my stomach was twisting.

She rubbed the back of my hand, like a consoling mother. "Are you sure, because if you really *did* like him a lot, you know … if things progressed … it could be a problem. Okay, it's in the past, but it would still be there, like a little thorn in the foot. It could create mistrust. It would be a dark shadow over things."

"Yes, possibly it would. But I almost feel sorry for him. What a terrible thing to come out at this time."

"Well, I think we must make sure that it stays between us. And I don't think we should tell Angus, not yet. It might upset him."

"It would. He admires Leonidas, especially after all the help he gave us in Platanos."

After Polly left, I went to bed with the windows and shutters open slightly. It was nice to have the room bathed in moonlight and hear an evening breeze toying with the olive trees and the sound of an owl nearby. It cheered me a little as I lay in bed agonising over Polly's news. When Leonidas told me he wasn't going to England after all, it put our 'friendship', and that day at Kitries, on a different level. It made me believe the passion we shared was more than just a 'thing of the moment' after all. But this news had scuppered everything. My grandfather, the handsome young man who had written that notebook, had been brutally killed moments after his last entry because of the actions of one of Leonidas's family. If I really fell in love with him, it would, as Polly said, nag at me forever. How could it not? And why hadn't he told me about this Nikos Pantazis by now. He had plenty of opportunity when he came to the house today.

I decided that night that when Kieran's burial was over and Angus had sorted out his health, I would return to Scotland without too much delay. It was time.

26

Destiny goes large

I had a restless night and awoke to the sound of gentle knocking at my bedroom door. I had become strangely used to this routine now. I saw Angus's head poke through the gap. Because I feared the worst, I roused myself quickly.

"Are you okay?" I said.

"Yes, love. Sorry to wake you. I've made you some coffee."

He came in, holding a mug, and set it down on the bedside table. He sat on the bed. I elbowed myself into a sitting position and plumped up my pillow.

"We've hardly had time together since Friday to talk about the notebook. Well? What did you think about it?" he asked.

"Ach! It's amazing, and sad. I can't believe our luck in finding Dimitris, and then finding the notebook. We've been blessed in that regard." *If not in others,* I thought.

"I know, Bronte. I can't believe it either. I don't mind telling you now I had no great hopes of finding out anything when we started."

"Me neither."

"I can't stop looking at it. It makes me proud. What a brave lad Kieran was. But that last bit of the text, where he doesn't finish the sentence, it just blew me away. I cried, Bronte, I don't mind telling you. I felt gutted."

"No wonder you had chest pains ... but I know how you felt. I cried as well. I kept thinking what bad luck he had in the end. A few more days and he'd have left the village. Maybe he'd have made it to the coast and escaped. But I guess his Aberdeen pal Raymond didn't make it either. I'm sure he would have tried to contact our family after the war if he had survived."

"Aye, you're right," said Angus. "Poor Raymond. We'll never know. Or maybe I could try to trace his family in Aberdeen one day."

We sat quietly a moment, each with our own thoughts.

"I've been thinking. I definitely want to write about the Battle of Kalamata and Kieran as soon as I've got my health sorted," he said.

"A book?"

"Why not?"

"Well you always said you wanted to write one."

"Aye, so I did. There's plenty to write about now and it's a good yarn."

I nodded. He played with his ponytail. "Now that you're out of a job — and a good bloody thing too, since the newspaper industry in Scotland is going down the pan – you might like to help me with the book, I mean co-write it. What do you say?"

"Sounds like a great idea. We'll talk about it later," I said, thinking there was time enough to tell him I was returning to Scotland after we'd sorted his health problem.

"I've got to go out soon to make those plans for Kieran's burial with the *papas*. I've called Leonidas and he said he would be there too. He has some free time this morning. I'm thinking we should have the burial this Friday."

I flinched a bit when he said 'Leonidas'. I wondered how he could still involve himself in our lives without telling us the truth.

"Can the burial be sorted so quickly?"

He laughed. "The Greeks may be slow with their fiscal spreadsheets but they can mobilise themselves in a heartbeat for a wedding or a funeral."

"Don't overdo things. And remember to call the cardiologist today and sort an appointment for Athens for next week."

"Yes, yes, of course," he said, but I could see that idea had flown in and out of his head like a dizzy bird. I would need to nag him about it.

"By the way, don't mention anything to Leonidas about my redundancy. I haven't told other people yet."

"Oh, okay, if you want," he said, with a puzzled look.

"Have you talked to Polly, you know, about the two of you getting back together – maybe?"

He shrugged. "We've talked but I don't think we're rushing into anything. We're great friends. Why push it?"

"At your great age. Yes, I kind of agree."

"I'm not completely past it yet. I didn't mean that. I can't think that far ahead. I need to be Greek at the moment."

"Whatever!" I said, with a shrug and a windmill arm.

Not long afterwards, I heard Angus leave the house. I got up and had breakfast on my own balcony, at the single table with my view of Myrto's farm and the gulf beyond. Clouds were scudding across the sky and the sea was rippled with waves, each topped with a curl of froth. I loved to watch the gulf, the way it mirrored the winds and their different directions, and how it changed from hour to hour, from glassy to white-capped, and back again. There were so many winds in Greece, all tinged with romance and daring: the *tramountanas*, *levantes*, *bonentes*, even the mad one, *sirokos*. They were a template for the national character.

In the early afternoon I walked to the *kafeneio* to check my emails, and passed Angus on his way home, just before I reached the village. He had spent some time with Leonidas and the *papas*, organising the details for Friday. He looked happy. I was glad, but I wondered what he would have said if he knew Leonidas's dark secret.

When I got to the Zefiros, Elpida came rushing over to see me. I knew the whole village would somehow know about Angus's hospital visit and the upcoming burial. Angus had probably already enlightened her, but I offered her a few more details. She kept shaking her head in disbelief about Kieran.

"*Leventis*, just like Angus. Marathousa will be proud of them both, Bronte," she said, her dark eyes glistening with emotion.

"Tell me something, Elpida. Did you ever hear any stories from your family about British soldiers hiding up in Platanos during the war?" I was just testing. She rolled her eyes around a bit, as if racking her memory.

"No, Bronte. My poor old head never strays higher than the hills around Marathousa. It's another world up there. Even I can't be worrying about what the mountain folks do," she said, with a massive shrug. I laughed. If there was ever an Olympic sport for shoulder-shrugging, Elpida would take the gold.

While I was working at my laptop, I heard the sound of a chair scraping over the terrace. I looked up to see Leonidas, sitting opposite. Despite everything I knew about him now and his family, I could still feel my stomach turn over at the sight of him, with lust, and definitely not revulsion. But I needed to hold my nerve.

"Always working, Bronte. I'm impressed."

"Just emails. Angus tells me you've helped him to organise the burial for Kieran. That was kind, thank you."

"It was no trouble. Everyone is happy to help. In the eyes of the villagers, Kieran is a hero and he should be honoured. The *papas* said he will also offer a small service in the church beforehand as well. It will be an important event for the village."

Elpida arrived to take his order, but he didn't want anything. Her eyes swept over us several times, like a mine detector. After she left, he continued to go over details of the burial service and how the villagers had reacted to the news of Kieran. I wasn't really listening properly. My mind was being stalked by so many opposing thoughts, I almost felt dizzy. When he stopped talking, he looked at me, his head tipped slightly to the side.

"You are thoughtful today, Bronte."

"Yes, a little." I closed my laptop and placed it in my shoulder bag. "Actually, there's something I need to talk to you about, but not here," I said, looking towards Elpida, who was standing by the door of the *kafeneio,* her hands on her hips, watching us.

"Okay. We can go back to my house," he said.

"Let's go for a walk instead," I suggested.

I led the way up the steps to the Palios Dromos to a place I had discovered recently. It was beyond the end of the old road, where a dirt track continued through the fields to the hills. But first, it branched off to an olive orchard, where a small white chapel was set amid the trees. You couldn't see it from the village, but it had a clear view over the orchards below and down to the gulf and Kalamata. It was one of the smallest churches in the village, named after Saint Konstantina. It was always open. But its main attraction was the narrow terrace in front and a wooden bench, where you could sit and enjoy endless solitude.

"I'm glad you like this place, Bronte. It was always one of my favourites too when I lived in the village."

We sat side by side. I didn't waste any time. I told him everything Polly had told me about his relative, the traitor. He listened and slumped sullenly back against the bench.

"Were you never going to tell me about Nikos Pantazis, about what he did? Assuming you knew, of course."

He turned his dark eyes on me. In the sunlight, they were lustrous and his errant curls were springing as usual over his forehead. It was a pity I had to have this conversation today when he looked so appealing, and the dental queen was now well extracted.

"Of course I knew the terrible story about how Nikos betrayed a foreign soldier in Platanos, but I have always kept it to myself. It is not something to boast about. But imagine my shock to discover on Friday the awful truth that the soldier was not just any soldier but *your* grandfather. It was devastating. And I am so sorry, and ashamed for that. But once I knew, when Angus read Kieran's name in the notebook, there was no time to explain properly, and I had to leave for Athens."

"Couldn't you have told me yesterday when you came to the house?"

"Yes, I should have. I put it off. I imagined what you would think of my family, especially when the sight of your grandfather's remains in the ossuary was still fresh in your mind. My father years ago told us about what Nikos had done. Nikos had even bragged about his deed to others in the family and then he was shot himself. That was his punishment. But it disgraced the family and they preferred we didn't talk about this to others. And that is how it has always been. When you and Angus told me weeks ago that you were trying to find out about your lost grandfather, I did not imagine then it would be the man Nikos betrayed. Why would I think that? During the war some soldiers were hidden in the lower villages and sometimes in the mountains further down the Mani. It wasn't such a rare thing."

"But you haven't answered my question. Were you never going to tell us the truth?" I said, more sharply.

"Bronte, of course I would have told you. I was waiting for the right time. I did not realise that Dimitris would confess it to Polly, at least without talking to me first. I am surprised but perhaps he bears a grudge. The Maneas family liked Kieran. They were honourable people." I reflected on the day of the *yiorti* at Platanos. After Leonidas introduced Dimitris to us at the table, I couldn't remember the two men talking to each other again, as if there was some bad blood there.

"I wanted to tell you yesterday, but then your father asked me to help organise the burial. How could I tell you all then? It would have been horrible. It would have spoilt things for you."

"It has spoilt them anyway, Leonidas," I said, with a bitter edge to my voice.

I saw him flinch. His eyes had a tormented blackness to them I had never seen before as they flickered towards me and then back towards the gulf. When he spoke, he sounded weary and defeated. "I am so very sorry, Bronte, it has all come out like this. It's not what I wanted."

We sat in glum silence, staring at the broad stretch of scintillating water in the distance, as if it held the key to everything.

"You know the best thing about this church, about sitting here?" he said at last. I shook my head, assuming he was trying to change the subject. "All you see is Kalamata and the gulf. It's peaceful. You can't see Platanos. It's out of the frame. Even though I was not born there and didn't suffer the hardships there, I had no pull towards it. In some ways, it has shadowed me throughout my life."

"But you've allowed it to do that by not being honest, surely. From the beginning you tried to discourage Angus and me from digging around in Platanos. You wanted to hush up the truth. And Pavlos from the *pantopoleio*. He knew something of the story, didn't he? At least that an allied soldier had been shot there, even if he didn't know all the details. But he told us he knew nothing."

"I can't speak for Pavlos. Perhaps he did not want to open up a difficult subject and with foreigners he did not know. The villagers are loyal and they are reserved. I think I told you that. But I was wrong to try to influence you. I have been wrong about many things, Bronte. I have been guilty of feeling too proud. My grandparents were too old to talk about such things, but I, and my father, should have been honest, you're right. We should have confessed the whole story of the betrayal because it was bound to come out in the end. Nothing is secret forever in Greek villages, as you know. I think Myrto has always known the truth, somehow. And perhaps it's why she dislikes me and my family."

If that was really true, it maddened me that even Myrto had pretended to know nothing about soldiers being hidden in Platanos when I asked her one day. But I knew so little about Greek feelings of honour and shame. I knew so little about any of this. How could I judge anyone?

"I understand what you say, Leonidas, I do. I just wish you'd told me before Polly did."

He looked chastened. None of this could have been easy for him, and I began to feel a tiny bit sympathetic, or perhaps my anger was abating. He sensed that moment of weakness and put his hand over mine. I pulled my hand away.

"I am sorry if you feel I deceived you. I hope we can put this behind us. It was an unforgivable thing Nikos did, but it's in the past. You know, if every Greek were to be punished for the sins of their ancestors in our long, turbulent history, there would be no-one left untouched."

I smiled at that comment. I guessed that was true enough.

"I hope that we can continue to see each other before you leave for Scotland. Will that be soon?"

I decided to finally confess the redundancy and how I would stay in Greece long enough to get Angus sorted before I went back to find another job.

Leonidas said, "Well, since we're talking about honesty, I must confess that your father told me today when we met to discuss the burial, about you losing your job."

"Oh, did he now? That old goat!" I said, shaking my head. He smiled, but no more than the little twitch of his lower lip.

"I'm sorry about your bad news and even sorrier that you're still leaving Greece ... just when I have decided to stay," he said with a light shrug.

His comment pleased me and the fact that he felt something for me perhaps. But my mind was made up.

"I believe you would have told me the truth about Nikos in the end. I believe you're an honourable man, Leo, but I'm still leaving, soon. The timing is all wrong. I feel that our friendship is doomed by these historic events."

"Doomed?" he said, turning towards me, looking perplexed. A lock of hair danced over his wrinkled brow. "I don't see it like that. On the contrary, I find it all very favourable. And the timing – amazing!"

"How so?"

"How can I explain this ..." he said, rubbing his chin and muttering in Greek, one of the very few times he seemed stuck with his English. "Don't you see? The fact that you and I ... our destinies have been entwined from the time of the war when Kieran came here. It was set down. Your grandfather and Nikos, tangled in the mess of history in Platanos. Angus and then you, finally coming here at this time ... We were meant to meet. Our destinies have been drawing together even before we were born. Not just in a haphazard way, but very specific. That's a good thing, isn't it? No, it is *katapliktiko,* fantastic!"

He stared at me, his eyes imploring me to see the logic, the beauty in it. And I did. Fate had definitely had a starring role all along. It also occurred to me that, ironically, if Panayiotis had kept Kieran's notebook instead of placing it in the reliquary in 1949, and if he had managed to trace our family and somehow return it, I wouldn't be sitting here at this chapel talking with Leonidas. It was one of the curious twists and turns of fate.

"Okay, I admit the whole thing is amazing, spooky almost, but I thought you didn't believe in fate, Leo? You once told me you were a man whose head ruled his heart. You said, 'I can't say I put much faith in destiny'. Remember?"

He shut his eyes and sighed. "Yes ... I think I did say that once when I spoke of Phaedra. As a man of science, I have had a more pragmatic view of life. I have believed in the law of cause and effect, not chance, or destiny. But since Friday, I have changed my mind."

"Are you serious? You really believe everything you've just said about us, and destiny?"

"Yes, of course. And it just confirmed what I felt anyway. I've liked you since I first met you, even though I didn't want to. There was Phaedra and it was muddled, but I kept wanting to see you. And the day on Kitries beach. I confess − it was not a 'thing of the moment', Bronte. I tried to justify my lack of control. That was wrong. For me it was something very special. When Phaedra came back to Kalamata recently, I knew it was never going to work with her and I already had strong feelings for you, Bronte. I also realised that I could never leave Greece. My destiny is also tangled up with this country, even though some of it is difficult – like Nikos's betrayal."

I flinched this time when he said that name. I thought back to what Polly had said, that it would always cast a dark shadow over us. Leonidas seemed to pick up on my mood, and sighed heavily.

"I know that everything that happened to your poor grandfather is very raw for you still. But I believe you should not carry the past around like a burden. You have to let it go. There are things I don't understand about the past, about Greece, about my family, things that make me furious and ashamed, like Nikos's unforgivable act, but if you let it take a hold of you it will ruin your whole life. These past events that we didn't cause, they are not worthy of robbing us of our present, or future. Don't you agree, Bronte?"

After a heartbeat of silence, I told him, "Yes, I think I do."

I didn't look at him. My eyes began to prickle with tears, not for the first time in these past few days, as if the water table of my miseries had been sitting far too high of late. Leonidas sat quietly, his arms crossed over his chest, staring at the gulf again and the way a sudden easterly wind had brought in a phalanx of silver-tipped waves. Close to the eastern shore, a large fishing boat trailed past on its way to Kalamata and in its glittering wake, a flock of hungry gulls swooped over discarded fish.

With all the rancour spent, it was peaceful sitting side by side, not feeling the need to talk any more. It was enough just to be there, on that hillside. I might have liked that moment to last much longer, but Leonidas finally checked his watch. "I should go. I have to return to Kalamata soon."

"I'll walk down with you."

We stood up and yet neither of us was eager to leave. I touched his arm. "What you said, Leo, about our tangled destiny. It was really beautiful. But ... I need time to really think about it ... about everything."

There was a challenging look in his eyes. "Ah, that's the difference between non-Greeks and Greeks. You must push a thing aside until you're ready to make a decision, while we Greeks make one straight away and act on it. We live in the moment."

"But I *can* be Greek, I assure you," I said.

He laughed, as if the idea was slightly ridiculous. "Prove it then."

I stepped towards him and kissed him. His lips were sun-warmed and sweet. He put his arms around me and kissed me back, but with much more passion, like the day at the Kitries cove: a kiss I had played out in my mind many times since then. But in reality, this was unimaginably better. If this glorious scene was meant to be, as he so eloquently put it, then fate was a saint in my eyes.

We left the church and descended to the village, walking back to Villa Anemos. When we were level with his house, I found I didn't want to say goodbye.

"What do you have to do in Kalamata? Another surgery?"

"No, something else, but it can wait, I think," he said, with a wink. "Come to the house. We will have an afternoon swim. It's warm and sheltered in the garden."

I didn't have my swimming costume with me, of course. But would I really need it?

"And there will be no talk of leaving Greece, okay?" he said, leading me towards the imposing front door of his house.

"Not today perhaps," I said with a smile, looking behind me towards the mountains, where small fluffy clouds were hovering over the highest peaks. Platanos was up there but I couldn't see it. Just like Leonidas, I didn't care. Platanos had played its part. We were done with it.

27

A saint rides on

"You look fantastic, 10 years younger, and nothing like a Greek *papas*," I said when Angus walked into the sitting room, dressed in a well-cut black suit, his ponytail finally shorn, his hair bobbed to just below his chin and soft and shiny.

"Not bad, eh? The make-over was Polly's idea: the suit, the hair, of course. I went along with it. I thought she'd probably ditch me in the end if I went on looking like a clarty old bam." We laughed and I told him that at least he looked more presentable for his appointment the following week at an Athens hospital. He groaned and I knew it was only the fact that Polly had offered to drive us there that took the edge off his anxiety.

For Kieran's interment, Papa Lambros from the village had agreed to perform a small service in the church of the Anastasis in the *plateia,* and then a blessing later in the nearby graveyard. We had been offered a corner plot by the villagers. Plots in the small graveyard were scarce, but Kieran would be honoured as a hero of the Battle of Kalamata. We were assured he would rest there for an 'eternity of eternities'. He would have a headstone finally, instead of a name scrawled on a box in a mountain village. We agreed to have his name carved: Kieran 'Kostas' McKnight and the word *'filellinas'*. 'Friend of Greece'. I think he would have liked that. Marcella had already written to say that she and Shona would come out in the spring to visit the grave and to see how Angus was faring. Or to quote Marcella, "If Odysseus won't go home after 10 years, then home must come to him."

We stood by the front door for a moment before we left. "You look lovely, Bronte," he said, running an eye over my patterned grey dress and black jacket. I felt a sense of calmness I hadn't felt for a long time.

"I can't believe this day has come. It's a miracle really," Angus said.

"I can't either, Dad."

He looked at me, his eyebrows arching in surprise. "You just called me 'Dad'."

"Yes, I believe I did."

"Thank you, Bronte. Despite what you might have thought, I have always *been* your Dad. I have always thought about you."

"I know. We're over all that now. We're moving on."

"I'm so glad you decided to come here. Greece suits you. You look transformed. And maybe it has something to do with Leonidas as well. Am I right?" he said, with a wink.

I laughed. "You're going to embarrass me now."

"Well, he's a great guy. I always said that. Despite what his great uncle – that feckin' traitor – did to Kieran."

"I know, but don't upset yourself." I'd had to tell Angus about Nikos Pantazis before Kieran's burial service because I didn't want him to hear it from anyone else.

"Och, it's all history now, anyway," said Angus, with a shrug.

"Come on," I said, guiding him outside. "Let's go and put Kieran to rest."

We walked arm in arm along the road. The sky was an azure blue, but it was slightly cooler now, with a northerly wind. The Little Summer of Saint Dimitrios, as the Greeks describe an Indian summer in October, had finally ended.

As we walked, our shoes kicked up the dust. Wild purple cyclamen were growing amid the rocks at the edge of the road. A church bell tolled: a deep mournful note. It was like a re-run of my first day when I heard the funeral bell. Now it was tolling for my own grandfather. Angus must have thought the same. He squeezed my arm a little tighter.

"You know something, Bronte. You've been asking me so many times why I ran off to Greece, and I told you I didn't absolutely know, and that's the truth. Yes, it had something to do with Kieran, but not as much as you might have thought. But now that we've found him, I feel vindicated. The past 10 years have meant something after all. And I haven't just found a father either. I've reclaimed a daughter as well. I must be the luckiest man alive. Give me a hug, pet."

And so we did, on the road to the village. A big, powerful hug. Angus's words touched me. I felt that it had taken a foreign land for me to discover that I loved my father more now than at any time in my life. That I loved my life more now that I had lost the things I considered had value, like ambition, career and my small place in the world, and found greater happiness in simple pleasures.

The church was packed and an overflow of people had spread out onto the *plateia*. By now everyone knew what we had been doing in Platanos. They knew about Kieran's fate. They even knew about Leonidas's great uncle. He had said that everyone should know the whole story of what happened in the past and that it was another example of how bad times in Greece could harden the hearts of men and turn ordinary villagers into monsters. I wasn't the only one in the village who admired his sense of honour, his *filotimo*, as the Greeks would say.

There had been much talk and excitement in the village about this special service. Nothing like this had happened for quite a while and some people who had left Platanos years ago for neighbouring villages and towns had made the trek to Marathousa to pay their respects. A young reporter from a local paper had turned up with a photographer to record the event.

In the church I saw all the people I had come to know in the village: Miltiades and his family, and Myrto, who now looked less like a goat farmer and more like a Sydney matron in a dark tweedy suit with a string of pearls at her neck. Elpida was also smartly dressed, her eyes roaming the assembled crowd for some interesting lapse of propriety that she might spool into a piece of gossip later on. Why waste a great occasion?

We sat in the front row with Polly and Leonidas. Dimitris was there too. He had changed the date of his return flight to America. Adrianos Zografos was also present. He had been ecstatic that our contact with Orestes had been the catalyst for this great day. I had no idea what the service was about, only that it was sombre. On a table before the ornamental screen, a new carved box, containing Kieran's remains, was set alongside a photo of him and some flowers. Angus stood on one side of me, and Leonidas on the other. I felt a rush of gratitude for this day of closure that had been 71 years in the making.

While it was a ceremony defined by closure, it was also underwritten by exciting new beginnings. During a particularly devotional piece of the service my hand brushed against Leonidas's and he entwined his fingers delicately through mine.

Papa Lambros swung his censer towards the congregation. A swirl of incense funnelled its way up to the dome of the church, where an imposing fresco of Christ the

Pantocratoras, 'the All Powerful One', kept vigil. From every wall in the church, the Byzantine frescos of saints looked down with stoical benevolence. Then my eyes fell on one in particular: the image of Saint Dimitrios, gallant in his blue cape, riding his russet-coloured horse, spearing his own particular 'dragon'. I had speared quite a few of my own in the past weeks, and I felt his triumph amid my own in the happiest little summer of my life.

Epilogue

On the Monday after the service, Angus was admitted to a hospital in Athens for his heart scan, which showed that two of his coronary arteries were almost completely blocked. It was a miracle, the cardiologist said, that he hadn't yet had a heart attack. It would have been very imminent. But after some intervention to his arteries, he was discharged, with a few more pills added to his collection. Angus has been hard at work on his book about the Battle of Kalamata and is happier than I could have imagined. While I agreed in theory to be a co-writer, I left him to the project and he's making good progress. I wanted time to explore the region with Leonidas, as he promised, and to swim in secret coves before winter set in. I needed to discover how many more interesting cures there might be for jellyfish stings.

I didn't go back to Scotland. After one of my freelance stories on the Greek crisis was published in the Sunday magazine of a London newspaper, it led to more commissions, which meant that for the foreseeable future, I would be busy. Sybil wrote to me from Australia, saying she wondered why she hadn't moved there years earlier. She is now engaged to a wealthy sheep farmer who owns a quarter of New South Wales.

Myrto is now 'bladdy happy' for once. She took Angelos, the new harvesting rookie, under her considerable wing, teaching him how to spot a dud olive. He's taken to the new job with gusto and has even learnt not only how to swear like an Aussie, but also to ride Zeus the donkey, with no arguments.

Marathousa is my home now. I have no need of any other, unless a second, errant Greek saint decides to have a funny turn and take up residence in my handbag, sending my life on a different trajectory. But what would be the likelihood of that?

Sto kalo.

Go to the good.

THE END

Acknowledgements

For information about the Battle of Kalamata and 'Operation Demon', I am indebted to two books: *Tell Them We Were Here,* by the late Edwin Horlington, and *Jack Hinton VC: Man Amongst Men,* by Gabrielle McDonald. Grateful thanks also to distinguished Kalamatan historian and author Nikos I. Zervis for spending two wonderful mornings with me in Kalamata to talk about the Battle of Kalamata and its aftermath, about which he has written in depth in the first of a series of books, *Kalamata: Occupation, Resistance, Liberation* (Volume A) (in Greek). Thanks also to the staff at the Popular Library of Kalamata in the Pnevmatiko Kentro.

Thanks also to many friends in Kalamata and the Mani who inspired me to write this book about a little known era of war history that has had a huge impact on the southern Peloponnese.

Grateful thanks to my husband Jim for his enthusiasm and encouragement of all my projects and also for his excellent editing and formatting of this edition through www.ebooklover.co.uk, and for additional research about the Battle of Kalamata. Thanks also to artist Anthony Hannaford for his outstanding cover.

And finally, remembering Wallace the Jack Russell who passed away in summer 2017 but who had been for years a patient companion through all my long months of writing and featured strongly in my Greek memoirs. I hope his willing heart and maverick personality will continue to flicker through the pages of my books for years to come.

East Sussex, England,
February 2018

The sequel

If you enjoyed this novel, you may wish to read the sequel, *How Greek Is Your Love?* published in March 2020. This new book is again set in the hillside village of Marathousa and features all your favourite characters: Bronte, Angus, Leonidas – and several new ones, including troubled actress/writer Eve Peregrine and the amazing rescue dog, Zeffy. It's a page-turning mystery drama full of intrigue and romance. The book is available from Amazon.

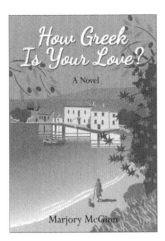

The Peloponnese series

You may also like to read Marjory's trilogy of Greek travel memoirs (The Peloponnese series), starting with *Things Can Only Get Feta,* which charts her four years living in the southern Peloponnese during the economic crisis. The sequels are *Homer's Where The Heart Is* and *A Scorpion In The Lemon Tree*. All three are available in Kindle and paperback from Amazon.

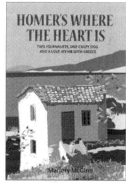

Praise for Marjory McGinn

Things Can Only Get Feta:

"Honestly, you won't be able to put this book down." **Maria Karamitsos, WindyCity Greek, web magazine.**

"A book to relax into, written with wonderment, admiration and wit." **Anne Zouroudi, author of the Greek Detective series.**

"This book might become a future reference source about life in 'unspoilt' Greece." **Stella Pierides, author and poet.**

"I loved the characters, including Wallace, the colour and life, and the enthusiasm that drives the narrative. It was most enjoyable." **Mark Douglas-Home, author of the Sea Detective novels**.

Homer's Where The Heart Is:

"Marjory takes us on an odyssey with mind, heart and great skill." **Pamela Jane Rogers, author of Greekscapes.**

"A fascinating and heart-warming memoir." **Valerie Poore, author of Watery Ways.**

"A book to make your heart sing." **Amazon customer.**

"Marjory is a great storyteller." **Amazon customer.**

A Scorpion In The Lemon Tree:

"This book is rare within the travel genre. It cleverly combines a travel narrative with enlightened observations about Greece." **Peter Kerr, best selling author of Snowball Oranges.**

"Her empathy with Greece and refusal to lapse into sentimentality makes this a witty and poignant book." **Richard Clark, author of the Greek Notebook series.**

"I could read this series forever." **Amazon reviewer.**